THEY KII
THEY

Mohini Hersom, MSc

Self-published in the European Union

20th of January 2022

ISBN 978-1-8383557-2-2

Copyright

Mohini can be contacted by sending an email to spaniel. golden@gmail.com. Please include the words "ABOUT BOOK" in your subject line so that your email does not get lost among newsletters and spam.

Acknowledgements

I used photos from pexels.com to make the book cover, Artists' names Negative space, Atypeek Dun, Cottonbro.

Declaration

"GEEKS" might smirk at the crude finish of this book. Remember: thanks to the new policy created by geeks for geeks, I live in a gulag with no access of anything but women and illiteracy. I am not detained-no further details are provided. I have used epub technology to create this .epub basely solely on what google tells me without conferring with a human being. Generally I suffer from any denial of goods and services the educated would ask for. Doubtlessly, no one would want to plagiarize my book let alone read it. But Aah! Some WOMEN might want to. The two countries I [presently??] [live??]in do not want my legal deposit. I did not know how to otherwise protect my book, and lack the knowhow. This worthless book is the brainchild of MOHINI HERSOM.

Special Information

There could be a racial hygiene policy against me, which is not on grounds of my race. It is my choice that most issues in my life should be public. I am dying in a virtual gulag.

I know how all people will shun me if I say so. I however decided to brave the shunning and want to dedicate myself to telling the truth. People even ignore my offers such as my books and ideas. This shunning typically gets weaker if I go outside the current country of residence and actually goes away if I cross a language barrier.

Documents pertaining to oneself are personal property so one has the right to publish them under Data Protection.

And so I have come up with a smattering of stories. People here seem to think the whole world lies inside the underpants

of a woman, she just has to be a woman and knows nothing, and they have a fetish for "The samaritans" and "paid listeners". I am a person in Ireland who can be deported to India where I will be on the street with nobody and nothing and this is happening to physicist because there is racial hygiene.

They cant allow me employment as I must speak only to women.

Honestly this is hellhole of torture and i will live here or be deported to India. Honestly I do not wish to live under woman support.

Honestly I have made a tryst with my creator that I shall drop dead soon to see women in tragedy especially the kind that run after me to give support. Honestly I am tired of your women and their mental health and psychology. Yes you can force rubbish on me but I have faith that something very bad is going to happen.

Because these pictures of my personal documents in this book/ebook are too small for comfort, I have provided two links where you can download or and view these online. Picture files have to ne edited to improve heir appearance, so I have also provided the original pdfs from where I got those pictures.

If both links don't work, or you want to contact the author of this book, please do so on www.papertigers.me.uk

Link1   https://tinyurl.com/bdhkpdku

Link2   https://tinyurl.com/5c6wuwzy

Dedication

Srinivasan 15/05/1908-
15/09/1986

Padma 12/09/1915
-25/06/1991

This book is dedicated to the loving
memory of my grandparents

Table of Contents

x

Feather 444

PREFACE

"They kill those who they don't like" is a series of anecdotes. The anecdotes contain excerpts from people's life histories, that subtly emphasize the killing concept. The book is intended to revolve around medical abuse or negligence.

However, there are many anecdotes that do not involve medical matters. These could be deemed to be off-topic Speculatively, these non-medical stories might tell you something about the person, which can lead to them being disliked.

Part One is a story spanning the years 2011-2014, about one Regent Exeter who has died. Part Three is about the author herself and overlaps the time period of Regent's story.

Put very simply, Mohini suggests that sometimes people will induce the death of people they don't like, which includes doctors.

The anecdotes are real and the conclusions are speculative as to who might want to hate or kill their fellow humans.

I hope I will have readers, and that they will distinguish between the opinions of the author and reported facts. Of reported facts in general, some are provable while others are not. Reported facts can be accurate or inaccurate.

Whereas opinions are not right or wrong. They are something a person feels. Feelings do not have a physical form.

Like my other humble and reclusive creations, this book was created over time. You can see from the mood of the book that the hope of prosecution has died and complaining would be in poor taste.

The author hopes to attract readers. It was written by a victim or semi-victim and about people she cared about who had passed away.

It is not exactly a murder mystery thriller or whodunit. The skeletal biographies are in chronological order except that I have gone over, say, topic 1 of a certain period (years) followed by topic 2 of the same period. So it is a collection of stories of the same person, of which more than one could have taken place in the same period.

INTRODUCTION

Greetings

Good day ladies and gentlemen. My name is Mohini. I would like to offer my book, "They kill those whom they don't like", to the international public.

I'd like to be readable and to stimulate a wide audience.

The Author of this Book lives like a Tarantula

I express myself through a book. I have been forced to live like a tarantula spider. Just in case you did not know, a tarantula is an animal that hardly moves in its lifetime and feels content to live in a man-made cage because it does absolutely nothing.

God made Mohini, He made her in the night. He made her in a hurry. He forgot to make her a tarantula.

So that's my problem. I hope you are amused and titillated. Please have a nice day, but don't leave just yet.

3

Until the Gas Bills Arrive

One of the advantages of reading this book is that it will save you money on your gas bills. That is relevant in the current Christmas season when the sun is down with the flu, and gas bills are rising.

Humans are unlike animals whose habits are seasonal. Humans indeed "the naked ape", getting gas bills round the year.

This book will save you money on your laughing gas (nitrous oxide N2O) bills and not on cooking gas (Liquefied Petroleum Gas).

If you read this book, you will not need to buy laughing gas or hire any type of crutches/aids that help you to laugh.

Part One

1-0001: The Murder of Regent Exeter

Before writing about my own life, I write about one Regent Exeter who is not a fictitious person. His death resulted from the actions of his doctor. Additional suspicious circumstances were surrounding his death that did not lead to doctors.

I wish to detail everything I know about this real-life story, of which I am a participant.

I knew Regent from August 2011 to March 2014.

My biography of him will be of that period. It is also based on what Regent told me, and what his sister told me after his death.

I met his sister and mother and all the people who were connected with his residence at The Willows in Shifnal.

I also received his medical records, starting with his childhood, 18 months after his death due to my pending complaint to the Parliamentary Ombudsman at that time.

Regent's death was not the end-product of a one-to-one relationship but a many-to-one relationship. Regent benefited the selfish interests of multiple people by dying.

At least they tried to benefit. Otherwise, he may still be alive.

Regent had a testimony about abuses he received in the psychiatric wards (where he was put unnecessarily) which never ended because he did not have a family to pull him out, or to oversee his safety.

I am saying that he was detained unnecessarily. This is at least in part, saying that he was not mentally ill. I know that people will laugh at me for expressing what should be a medical opinion. These happen to be the opinions of a layperson.

Regent Exeter's death certificate

CERTIFIED COPY OF AN ENTRY
Pursuant to the Births and Deaths Registration Act 1953

DEATH		Entry No. 10

Registration district Shropshire	Administrative area
Sub-district Shropshire	County of Shropshire

1. **Date and place of death**
Twenty-sixth March 2014
14 The Willows, High Street, Shifnal

2. **Name and surname** Regent EXETER formerly known as Richard Francis Peterson LINDSAY	3. **Sex** Male
	4. **Maiden surname** **of woman who** **has married**

5. **Date and place of birth**
Ninth October 1959
Tunbridge Wells, Kent

6. **Occupation and usual address**
Lexicographer
14 The Willows, High Street, Shifnal Shropshire

7.(a) **Name and surname of informant** Crystal Frances LINDSAY	(b) **Qualification** Sister

(c) **Usual address**
29 Dinham, Ludlow, Shropshire

8. I certify that the particulars given by me above are true to the best of my knowledge and belief C F Lindsay	Signature of informant

9. **Cause of death**
I (a) Myocardial Infarct
   (b) Coronary Artery Disease

   II Hypertension

Certified by John Penhale Ellery Senior Coroner for Shropshire, Telford and Wrekin after post-mortem without inquest

10. **Date of registration** Sixteenth April 2014	11. **Signature of registrar** C Kiely Deputy Registrar

Certified to be a true copy of an entry in a register in my custody.

K. Thomas { Deputy *Superintendent Registrar   Date – 5 . . 201
                          *Registrar
                          *Strike out whichever does not apply

7

1-0002: An Unpopular View of Psychiatric Lockups

I believe that everyone should be free to express their opinion in a so-called free society.

These days some people are enjoying newly-found freedom while others are buried alive under the debris of the "progress" of a handful. The modern age spells freedom for some and chains for others.

I agree that a doctor's opinion has the legal authority to give medical opinions. But I do not agree that people cannot have an opinion on a subject if they do not have a degree in a subject.

Employees who work in a psychiatric ward are dishonest and corrupt. This is to be expected, as they "work with" persons with subnormal credibility, who may genuinely not have the mental capacity to report coherently, and certainly lack the legal right to make a statement under oath.

If people are not allowed to make a statement under oath, then clearly, their allegations, true or false, would not go very far. This disadvantage is consistent with the law of natural selection.

Obviously, it would be physically possible for persons detained under psychiatry to be exploited continuously and without limit, hidden from the public as time goes on. This is like having a store where there are no checks on shoplifting and no reporting of incidents, where you think there will be anything other than continuous loss. If you think so, you are lying to yourself.

People have their own reasons, which are usually self-serving, for lying to themselves. Any store where all shoplifters are protected against discovery(everyone is supposed to look the other way) and legal penalties must have a substantial and continuous stream of loss unless we can assume that 100% of the shoppers who visit each day are all lily-white angels.

My comment about dishonesty applies to psychiatrists, nurses, and restraint professionals, as well as hospital staff who call themselves solicitors, sometimes, and clinicians at other times.

If out of every ten statements made, at least one is a lie, I call that dishonest. One small lie could make a lifetime of difference, for the better, and for the worse. An individual who reports 10% lies can therefore fall under the umbrella of dishonesty.

If of every ten employees, nine are liars under the above definition, then we could generalize that members of such-and-such a profession are corrupt, or unreliable.

In the above two paragraphs, I have suggested a guideline one can use to see if it is justified that we label a particular profession as a dishonest and corrupt profession.

When I talk about dishonesty, I am talking about lying under oath, and on official documents.

Furthermore, psychiatric department employees are illiterate except for doctors. They tend to be idle people with a Kushi life whose job it is to sit in a warm lounge from 9-5 drinking cups of tea. They merely pick up the phone and say whatever the hell they like to callers over whom they have power.

Psychiatric workers hail from a socially and educationally backward social group of the race or country they come from. Their work is not that of a doctor despite frequently misrepresenting themselves as such. They make idle comments. They talk all the time about "working with" such-and-such people. This is like talking all the time about breathing. It is a sign of personal incompetence.

There is a social taboo against saying someone comes from a backward social group. I perfectly agree this does not make them a good or bad person. However, covering up such facts dampens the understanding of the public. Understanding which is the natural antidote to the psychiatric poisons.

All races and communities would have socially and educationally backward groups. White people argue that there exist no socially or educationally backward groups, just because they don't want to discriminate against anyone. I also know that the poor are commonly seen as socially backward.

But being deprived is not the same as depravity. Backwardness has more dimensions than a lack of the advantages that money buys.

The type of "work" done by mental health staff is uncomfortable for most people and favors the recruitment of developmentally backward individuals.

Anyone uncomfortable with seeing blood and bones agonized screams of persons restrained against their will; molestation of comatose people, and irresponsible passing of judgment, the pot calling the kettle black.

If these things worry you, as they appear to do most people, you are not suited to work in mental health.

It turns out that people with a special bent of mind work in places like that, and it turns out the scenario favors individuals whose upbringing was traditionally considered lowly.

Women are not guilt-free, nor are they more decent than men. They act as "secondaries" to all the brutality; they abet what goes on.

The men will restrain someone and the "sweet" woman may give an injection or pop a cookie in the victim's mouth, or utter some cute "nurturing phrases" which are if you delve beneath the surface, superficial and counter-productive.

Mental workers are paid disproportionately for their input and competence level. After all, bribery of dastardly individuals is the only way to have staff who perform a dirty, but "important" service. This service is to rid society of unwanted people and more importantly, to rid society of "unwanted information", so the public may stop understanding human nature as well as they used to do. This "unwanted information" is lost with time as it is directed at these staff members, instead of sprouting and spreading naturally, all over the place. And mental workers are dastardly people different from the mainstream who function as an anti-splash toilet for information dumping. They don't giggle or have a sense of humor. They are too low to have inhibitions. Talking to them is like talking to a clot of clay. As a result what you tell them never spreads. Thinking outside of modern indoctrination, this might not be a good thing

When a particular type of problem "X" is always addressed to mental health services, it is never addressed to a member of the public.

With time knowledge of the fact that someone could have such a problem, "X" is deleted from the minds of the public. The public loses their ability as time passes of understanding people, as years roll by with the mental health system in place.

They now see a person with the problem "X" as someone without that problem, as they don't know about the problem.

This will mostly result in the public seeing that person as taller than what they really are. But they will see them under the blanket definition "suffers from mental health problems".

Whether this looks good on the person or not, there is an unending drive to remove the stigma against mental patients. If this drive is successful, people will respect that individual who "suffers from mental health problems" like they would respect someone who has got a cold and fever.

Their "problem X" remains a secret forever.

This is supposed to bring advantage to the "mental person" who has "X" except no one will know.

In that case, the employees of the mental system serve to boost the public images of certain people who would otherwise not be respected by the general public, based on their deeds. Their lying under oath results in detaining the person longer or making them seem more "disabled" than they are.

Assuming this type of " virtual personality boost" is good for a person who has "Problem X" (which it may not be), there are two sides to each story where one small lie wins a huge war.

You see, it may be human nature to fake it, but there are persons on the opposite side of the fence who would be better off if the concealment of persons who have "Problem X" were to be exposed.

It is understandable, for example, that some people would like to present fake qualifications at a job interview, but the interviewer would rather he or she found out.

You see, mental health is a money-making business, served by people who don't appear to have anything better to do.

I think they do not have enough work to do. If they were honest, most of them would get laid off and the lockup facilities downsized.

But they try to keep folks detained as long as possible, to keep those dreaded psychiatric lockup facilities running.

Psychiatric detainment is a virtual body bag. You shouldn't be surprised if you end up in a real body bag if you are locked up in places like that. They have a high death rate even when they deny being death-machines, where they drug you out of your consciousness, to maximize your potential to act and seem like a fool.

No? Did your Doctor say No, there is no "death manufacturing" in psychiatric facilities? Well, then trust him, and check into one if your doctor tells you to. I am sure they will take good care of you.

All mental health professionals, whether educated or illiterate, are harbingers of death whose "health procedures" would sometimes serve as a distraction technique from underlying issues that may not be medical.

If you have a cardiac event because of the injections medical staff gives you, they may just not resuscitate you if you are in a psychiatric ward. In a non-psychiatric ward, you would have a much better chance of survival if you get cardiac arrest from an injection.

If you die, they will not only get away with it, but life will continue to be milk and honey for the ward staff and injecting staff. They are like the bastard waves of an unforgiving ocean that causes death and goes on lapping. A psych ward is a special place with an altered perspective of right and wrong. Human society is guilty because they let it be like that.

A psychiatric ward is an unsafe place of high death probability where a person is subject to involuntary medicines.

I have said plenty of dismal things about a subject most people would not like to hear. These are my opinions, but if you want the truth, try to do your diligence, assuming you have access to first-hand verification.

Most people who have been in psychiatric lockups lack the mental capacity to know if the actions of the doctor were morally right or wrong, like an infant that cannot judge if a parent's spanking was appropriate. This is also known as the inferior ego, or one person's conscience being SUBJECT to another.

Most people in captivity commit "spiritual suicide", or start to obey and respect their captors without resentment.

Also, we realize any people under lockup may grumble from time to time. So why should we take them seriously? After all, they are deemed by "experts" to be mentally incompetent.

Who are the "experts"? Aren't free, proud, and wealthy people also mentally incompetent?

The UK authorities say in the media that psychiatric lockups are good places. They probably believe what they say, as they have had no first-hand experience.

Among laypeople in the UK, most women feel that psychiatric lockups are "sugar spice and everything nice". That is, counting only those who did not have first-hand experience.

Women (other than any type of casualties) live a charmed life knowing nothing, but with supreme self-confidence.

They are a bit like the historical figure Marie Antoinette, who said "If they don't get bread, give them cakes."

She was the queen of France at the time of the French revolution. She was the wife of Louis the XVIth, who did not understand that the subjects of the French empire were starving.

She was guillotined (put to death) by the angry people along with her husband. But history shows that, like many royal family members, she herself was a victim of circumstances.

Her father was King of Austria, and he had forced her
to marry the French king at 14. She was afraid of her
husband and literally a prisoner in his house. She had
received no education and knew nothing.

Is that a good thing for UK women who are so ignorant,
to be so opinionated? It was not a good thing for Marie
Antoinette, who got guillotined for that innocent but
ignorant comment.

Although we don't want to guillotine the standard British
female, she always annoys those on the other side of the
fence, through her positive outlook on punitive procedures
carried out on members of the same sex or race.

The standard British female is a classic example of a
secondary ego, which is subject to the political views of
the state. These heavily protect her only mission in life:
to have sex and children. So she does not worry about
anything, which is normal for a human female, who does
not really concern herself with world affairs, only with
family.

Now post-internet people have redefined reality, and no
longer believe that the difference between a man and
a woman is that the woman is not concerned with the
external world.

However, you can see the sprouting of a culture riddled

with leaflets agencies and organizations that mirror every human need, and there are literally 1000s of women advisers who work in those agencies and organizations.

These women advisers do not have the ability to give advice and are coached by learning leaflets by rote-leaflets printed by the state whose words and ideas they are instructed to repeat. This habit serves as a cover for low ability.

When you have 100 employees working as advisers let is say 80 females and 20 males have been employed. The advice given by those 100 people is mostly an illiteracy crutch, but most advice-seekers do not understand that. Not understanding that they are illiterate and unintelligent boosts the self-esteem of the illiterate public.

In addition to giving illiterates some of the advantages of educated people through agencies they can use, they are protected from understanding that they are illiterate. They are made to feel it is normal to receive help for each and every issue in life.

Feeling no one is better than you adds quality to your life. This quality is of the kind enjoyed by kings, which is given to you artificially by society. Like the old man that chases girls but cannot remember why, a society filled with help agencies forgets over time the concept of an ignoramus. Your illiteracy and infirmity needs are provided before you can blink, or anyone can say "cheese".

A third advantage of the system is of course the advice-seekers are getting as a figure of speech, every crack filled. The fact there is a basic difference on average between a man and a woman. Women are less able to think or act independently compared to men. This difference has been with humans since the Stone Age. They have masked it in "developed" countries by introducing the mental health system, agencies, and organizations.

If we assume most of the 80 female "advisory employees lack the the mental capacity to give the advice they give, without the government-provided leaflets as a crutch. And that most of the 20 males do not lack it. All 100 employees are required to obey identical rules. All are required to repeat off the leaflets pretty much without variation, as a condition for employment. This results in masking of the difference between a man and a woman.

A man will lose his job if he fails to mask his nature as per rules. Failing to obey those rules means a man will disrupt that cleansed environment of equality. He is obliged to behave exactly like a woman to keep that idealized environment going. This policy of the government ensures that with time, the public will forget that men are more intelligent that women. This way of escaping from the truth globally gives women a better quality of life as they are not lesser than men. It gives men a better quality of life as there is "scientific" proof their mates are equal, and will eventually become the treasure pot at the end of the rainbow.

Herds of advisory automatons who cannot think have been created by the state(s) for "woman boosting". There is lifelong spoon-feeding of persons in charge, although these persons are really boosted menials. They do not exist on higher levels of the government.

"Diversity policy" in the UK says the service-seeker has no right of preference. You have to hook yourself up to whichever advisor they assign you. If you develop any sense, you won't bother to complain. The "support" of agencies is devoid of the human aspect. If this policy was scrapped, often service-seekers would ask for men as they are better at giving advice and more responsible. But when men are complaint with diversity policy as described above, they come across as having a sociopathic personality.

The boosted woman is not a child pampered by Daddy or her husband. She is an adult child who is a housewife to the state which has awarded her several "man-made lollipops" and "man-made credentials" that are not based on merit. It is based on the merit that the state feels you ought to have.

1-0003: The Murder of Regent Exeter Continued

The reason I mentioned the historical figure Marie Antoinette in the previous section, is that people, in general, don't understand subjects I am discussing. These subjects are directly relevant to the abuse of my good friend Regent (who lacked help from relatives when he was inside) which culminated in his death.

I also claim Regent was one of the sanest people around, so without further repetition I leave it to the reader to assess my controversial comments for credibility.

Regent had oratory skills. He could perform as a comedian. He made crowds laugh on the streets. Everyone liked him, He spouted his poetry extempore. In his personal life, he was a fat laughing ball of fun with a heart like driven snow.

Both the drugs that killed Regent - Depakote (sodium valproate) and Flu-penthixol are illegal and banned in various countries as they had the highest death rate.

Regent belongs to a minority that did not commit spiritual suicide under prolonged captivity, which would have made him incapable of raising a finger (mentally) against his captors.

He simply did not lose a clear understanding of the human rights abuses being done to him.

People who have a clear sense of right and wrong regarding harming others can probably not (under stress from a threat to one's survival), be deceived into trusting their captor as respectable.

Regent's doctor just waited on God to kill Regent once the debilitating effect of drugs had brought on heart failure.

Whereas he was fat like an elephant, his breathing was soft as a baby's. Not enough breath to support his bulk. All this was done to a slim and healthy guy before the forced administration of the above-mentioned two controversial drugs.

Regent's doctor made a secret of his diagnosis of high blood pressure, which was guaranteed to kill in due course of time if not treated.

A couple of months before his death, Regent alleged his doctor was giving him something to make all his symptoms worse.

The doctor of course denies the allegation. We will never know what happened. Regent lived (and died) at 14, The

Willows, in Shifnal, Shropshire.

His sister Miss C, said she found different tablets by his bed where he was found dead by police. These could have been the tablets that were allegedly given to make him worse. She didn't want them investigated through. She and her partner also did not want an inquest, which should always be there when there are suspicious circumstances.

Miss C said she felt guilty about not calling an ambulance on that fatal morning when he confided in her at 5am that he could not breathe, but she had rolled back and gone to sleep.

Regent and Miss C had just fought for their mother's will. Their mother Anne, getting over 85 , had Alzheimer's and was not competent when her will was written on her behalf by Miss C and her uncle, Anne's brother.

Regent, who was a middle-aged male, told me (before he died) that the previous occupant of his flat was (also) a middle-aged male.

And Regent said that before that guy, there had been another middle-aged male in the flat. Both the former occupants had lived 1-2 years in that flat, #14, The Willows, and died suddenly of a heart attack.

When Regent told me this, he had just moved into the flat which was vacant due to its occupant's death, in August 2011. A similar thing happened to Regent himself when he died there in March 2014.

They had all taken psychiatric medication over the long term. They all died between the ages of 50 and 60. Shifnal is a pretty small place and had one (at the most two) medical surgeries, and all of them met their end in their flat while under the care of Doctor B and Doctor S.

During our time together, Regent would occasionally talk about his death.

He must have suspected that he would die. No one could know for sure or predict the time of one's death exactly.

Regent would say his ghastly cough was due to smoking, and that it was sure to kill him. I saw no evidence of smoking.

I found out Doctors B and S just allowed that cough to fester. Anyone could tell it was serious. Doctors B and S did not enter the cough into his medical records.

Regent had one of those contraindicated symptoms, called "Elongated QT waves" in the ECG(Electro-cardiograph), which would lead to death. He took a class of drugs called neuroleptics which caused "Elongated QT waves" and he was given these non-stop throughout his adult life.

Everybody who takes neuroleptics continuously from their 20s will die between 50 and 60 or at least get "Elongated QT waves" [which I am sure doctors knew better than anyone else in Regent's case]

The medical records showed that Dr. B wrote to a cardiologist about Regent's "Elongated QT waves" in January 2014. The cardiologist asked him in a reply to stop the Flu-penthixol and that these would almost certainly get better.

Dr. B also told him he was going to give Regent medicine for high blood pressure. But he did not do so, right up to the time of his death in March 2014. Medical records showed Regent was prescribed Amlodipine a day or two before his passing.

When I met him in January 2014, he greeted me when I got off the train and hugged me. He had become even fatter.

He had developed itchy purple spots all over, but it was brushed aside by his Doctor B. Those purple spots were the last stages of dying from long-term use of Flu-penthixol.

My last two visits to him were in January 2014 and March 2014, the latter being a week before his death.

In the new year of 2014, Regent spoke of all his symptoms getting worse. He kept remarking that Doctor B was giving him "new stuff" which he said was designed to get him worse.

He told this story of how Doctor B wrote, instead of his monthly prescription for Flu-penthixol, a strange code, a string of alphanumeric characters which Regent was to take to the village pharmacist.

Regent had asked Doctor B what he was prescribing. Dr. B had said the meaning of the code was top secret, and that no human could understand it but himself and the village pharmacist.

Regent had taken Flu-penthixol for years and knew what his daily tablets looked like. Regent said the pharmacist to whom Regent took the strange prescription gave him something looking very different from what he was used to.

Sometimes tablets can be of different colors and shapes because they are of a different brand. We will never know what actually happened.

There is no evidence Doctor B was administering something to shorten his life. Pharmacists may sometimes make up mixtures and preparations that are not marketed by mixing them on-site. They can make up special concoctions for clinical trials or special needs.

The "altered preparation" was a capsule. However, it would have been child's play for a pharmacist to open a capsule and pour out the powder and fill it with a different powder.

I suppose we do not expect a doctor to have things like that done, to shorten our lives.

In 2012 and 2014, I tried to change Regent's doctor.

Both times my wishes were overruled by Regent himself, but I feel guilty that I was not forceful enough.

The only excuse is that as I am not a doctor, I did not have a clue his problem was serious enough to lead to death.

In 2014, with Regent's consent, I had also phoned a lawyer in Shropshire about whether one could take legal action regarding Regent's psychiatric medication.

The law firm told me they had been approached about the same matter before, but suing about overdosing with psychiatric medication was not possible in the UK, although in theory, it is possible. "That sort of thing just cannot happen in the UK.", they said.

I did not know about Regent's heart trouble and long QT waves until after his death. Long before meeting Regent I had heard that in the US many people sued their doctor over having developed elongated QT waves (a side-effect of certain psychiatric medications) and were able to successfully get a payout.

I did not know about heart failure, nor that cough is one of the symptoms. These days there are a lot of treatments to improve people's lives and make them live longer. I mean, heart failure is not a death sentence anymore unless, as in his case, the doctor wanted to let him die.

At the time of his death, Regent weighed an unhealthy 18-22 stone.

I was told by Regent's social worker Kevin that all Willows residents had a coughing and gagging problem because the psychiatric medication made their saliva more solid which irritated their throats constantly.

Regent had already approached a solicitor to take action against his sister, Miss C, who was going to put his share of his mother's will in a trust because she felt he was mentally incompetent. He had the law on his side, and would win. he had said.

Regent could not fight against the psychiatrists during the first part of his life - his youth. He lacked family members who were able and willing to help him, once he was holed up in the psychiatrists' gulags.

I myself feel unwanted in human society. I know very well how most people will consider me to be "pure garbage" just for saying I am treated like garbage. But people do not believe such an allegation can be true. They feel it is all my mental illness.

1-0004: MY PERSONAL EXPERIENCE OF DEPAKOTE (SODIUM VALPROATE) INJECTIONS IN THE UNITED STATES AS IMMIGRATION DETAINEE

You see, I had been dosed with Depakote and Zyprexa (Olanzapine) in the US after going on a hunger strike asking to be released from immigration detention.

At this time, I had also complained extensively about detention staff. They sent me to a special place to be medicated. They claimed they were about to lose their jobs because of me, and they could not let that happen.

In that special institution, I was sent off and on from 2001 to 2003, and I was there during 9/11.

This special institution located in the state of South Carolina has subsequently become listed on one of the USA stock exchanges like I understand that sometimes, brothels and funeral homes do.

In this special place where I often traveled in the elevator with dead bodies alongside, they gave injections as punishment to make me go for smokes with "the females" who were the "baddest" girls in America.

Under US law, they do not have to follow a legal procedure for the involuntary committal of immigration detainees. Only US citizens are protected from detention without a charge under their human rights law.

Therefore, forced drugging of aliens is allowed without the rigor of two doctors seeing you certifying you as mentally insane or gravely disabled, in order to satisfy requirements for involuntary committal. A much lower standard is required for forced drugging and detainment of aliens. This means they can just grab you and lock you up or medicate you. They are not obliged to release medical records to non-citizens.

Luckily, this would only happen infrequently.

I guess the weight gain caused by Depakote would vary from person to person and would also depend on dose and duration. The doctors kept fussing over my weight gain, not disclosing it was a side effect of Depakote.

They'd say in Texas, "You are now 45 and unless you put on weight, it would be bad for your self-esteem".

There was a permanent shift in my BMI (body mass index). I have not lost those extra pounds in 20 years.

I did not become very fat but had been thinner before Depakote. Albeit not life-changing like Regent's weight gain, mine too was irreversible.

The detention staff asked the medical officers why the injections were making me so ill and tired. The medical officers had replied that the injections were doing exactly what they were meant to do. They said they wanted me to keep quiet.

They said if I refused to take those injections, I would be shipped back to that special institution XXX where I met and traveled alone in lifts along with accompanied corpses.

Quoting the Monopoly board game, their psychologist had said, Go to XXX. Go directly to XXX. Do not pass go. Do not collect 200."

At that time I was trying to get deported from the US so that I could get married to my Canadian boyfriend. Their psychologist had said they would not let me get married if I did not take those injections.

My intake of psychiatric drugs ended when I was DEPORTED. After deportation, I had a tremor in one arm and a facial tic. The tremor disappeared in a week following my deportation to India, while the facial tic took 5-6 months to resolve.

Upon landing in the home country, I was seen by a
psychiatrist who said I qualified as marginally suffering
from tardive dyskinesia. He said my symptoms were
not strong enough to write it as a diagnosis. Tardive
dyskinesia is a permanent disablement of the nervous
system that some people have after they have been on
psychiatric drugs for a substantial duration.

1-0005: THE BIOGRAPHY OF REGENT EXETER

Regent Exeter was born Richard Lindsay on October 9, 1959, in Tunbridge Wells to a wealthy English family. He was the oldest of three children.

He attended the posh Westminster school for boys. As a five-year-old, he had been sexually assaulted regularly in nursery class by his teacher, one Father Brown, along with the other male infants.

Regent had lost his father at the age of 11-14. His mother was often mentally unable to cope and was admitted to a psychiatric hospital for depression.

In his early teens, Regent felt harassed by a gay schoolmaster, one John Field, at the same school.

Shortly before he died in 2014, Regent had shown me an anecdotal book belonging to Westminster school, where the late headmaster John Ray had admitted that the teenager Regent had been subjected to homosexual advances by Mr. Field.

Regent had then been suspended from school for his truancy, which had resulted from Field's harassment.

His stories of homosexual harassment had not been taken seriously by the Headmaster at the time they happened. Ray felt that Regent needed to be checked up by a psychiatrist for making such ridiculous allegations against a respectable teacher at a respectable school.

Ray ruled that the boy could only return to school if the psychiatrists were convinced that he was cured.

At this stage in his life, the young teenager Regent had never seen a psychiatrist before nor started to receive any mental treatments. However, when the psychiatrists took control of the life of a helpless young man with no family support, they stopped the clock on his evaluation or care.

[At the time of his death, at the age of 54, the psychiatrists had not completed their study and evaluation.]

This meant Regent could not go back to Westminster school. He, however, did some college at Cambridge, where he studied humanities subjects and foreign languages. He could speak Latin.

Regent helped compile the Oxford English dictionary, where he is mentioned in small print under his birth name, Richard Lindsay.

Regent was 11-14 when his father died, and when he

was being harassed with a sexual slant by a teacher, John Field, at Westminster school.

As the oldest and only surviving male in his family, Regent wished to protect his two sisters and his weak and widowed mother.

He felt heartbroken when he perceived what he felt was a new romantic relationship that seemed to be starting between his mother and Mr. Field.

Regent's mother Anne herself believed that she was in a relationship with Mr. Field. During this time, Field gave Anne the wrong money advice to sell her house and move into a smaller house. If Anne had not sold their ancestral home, it would have been worth two million pounds a short while later, said Regent.

Field also gave Anne wrong advice to buy a house in Ludlow, after which there had been some talk of Mr. Field moving in with Regent's mother.

Young Regent was shattered as he felt his baby sisters (who were under 10) were also liking and listening to Mr. Field.

It ended up, though, that Mr. Field was gay, and did not deliver, as far as the relationship went, leaving Regent's mother disappointed. Field just left the scene at this point, never to return.

Regent said he wandered from home a few years later, broken-hearted, and visited various places, one of them being Fiji, where he worked illegally and slept in strange places due to a lack of money in his late teens.

Regent felt he may have been deported from Fiji (to the UK) but is not sure if that happened. He felt too ashamed of being deported to admit it to himself. He says the Fijian authorities locked him in an airport lounge overnight and put him on a plane to the UK the next day.

So, at 19-20 years of age Regent was back from his foreign travels in London, homeless, and broken-hearted, seeing nothing good in his future. He did not want to go home to his mother.

"I decided to ring the doorbell of a mental hospital, and ask if they could offer me free accommodation," said Regent, amid peels of laughter.

Regent said the hospital staff told him they could accommodate him gratis, but he would have to make a small sacrifice for them. Regent had agreed.

The sacrifice was to take "one small injection in his arm."

Regent says he had initially been admitted voluntarily, into the mental hospital, where he had sought free accommodation. It had taken him over three months to recover from the aftermath of that sacrificial injection. He had been released from their custody after six months, a drugged wreck, a shadow of this former self.

The psychiatric treatment that was to engulf his whole life began the moment he had rung the doorbell of a mental hospital and asked for free accommodation.

Regent then studied for some years at Cambridge Polytechnic, which is now known as Anglia Ruskin University.

Regent was seen off and on by a psychiatrist, while at university.

During the time we spent together, Regent told me of his life at Cambridge Polytechnic. The young university student frequently visited and wept over the graves of mental patients buried in Cambridgeshire.

He frequently visited a place in Fulbourn, Cambridge, where such graves were known to be abundant or closely spaced, under the soil, in large patches of land containing no monuments.

[He must not have realized at that time, that he himself was to die as a side-effect of neuroleptic medication].

Regent wanted to pay a visit to sites where persons had died after being trapped lifelong in the medieval mental prisons of the UK. The prisons themselves may have been abolished, but there were bodies deep under the soil, a historically documented fact.

Regent said he could literally feel the sorrow coming from under the soil as he walked around these sites. Tormented souls who were chained for life after losing their liberties.

These souls never found peace after they died; they were haunting graveyards, he said. Hidden away from human society, some of these poor souls could not even speak, said Regent.

When someone related to Queen Elizabeth in the British Royal family gave birth to a pair of mentally-retarded children, they were ashamed and concealed the birth of the daughters, said Regent.

These women were locked into a mental institution for life and upon dying (of old age) were buried in secret, he said. Princesses who were placed in an unmarked grave, he said, just so the Royal family could hide their shame.

After his studies, he lived with his mother for several years in Ludlow.

Regent liked to play Nazi music which I had never heard before. It sounded so joyous, and certainly not evil. And Regent would cry for the folks that died in the Second World War.

1-0006: FAMOUS WOMEN UNDER THE SURGEON'S KNIFE FOR INTELLECTUAL ADVANCEMENT

We talked about Rosemary Kennedy, the sister of the assassinated US president J.F.Kennedy, who was given a frontal lobotomy. It was performed by the official Father of Lobotomy, Walter Freeman.

Walter Freeman did this to hundreds of people for "depression" and left them as "basket cases" in other words, wheelchair-bound cripples.

He discovered the lobotomy procedure, which involved inserting a knitting needle into the eye sockets at the top of the nose.

The "doctor" would he chatting with the victim, and slowly insert the needle deeper as people held her down to stop her screaming with pain. When the victim could no longer speak, the damage was done and the operation was over.

Walter Freeman and another man (a doctor) used something like an apple-corer into the brain to take out small "corings" from the brain to "relieve stress."

They renamed the lobotomy, which means cutting a lobe in the brain as "leucotomy" where "leuco" means white and they were taking out little bits of white matter from the brain with a brain-corer to de-stress agitated people.

Someone tried to assassinate Freeman, but he did this procedure to hundreds of people, leaving them severely disabled for life.

President Kennedy's father ordered his daughter Rosemary, a college student in her twenties alleged to have learning difficulties, to be lobotomized as a treatment for nymphomania.

President Kennedy was one of 9 siblings and there are stories the future president asked for the lobotomy as well.

Anyhow, after the lobotomy, she could never walk or speak again. She was confined to a wheelchair and needed round-the-clock nursing. She died at a ripe old age.

1-0007: The Biography of Regent Exeter Continued

We shared many many stories.

Following his study at Cambridge Polytechnic, Regent was sectioned off and on. This often involved his anger and frustration as a young man living alone with his mother -in Ludlow. He would explode into a temper and his mother would call the psychiatric authorities to "fix" him.

Regent's two sisters were Mrs. A and Miss C, who was the youngest child. I do not know why, but Regent and C were all not on speaking terms with A, who had got married and gone away a long time ago.

Based on the story shared by C after Regent's death, I think his confinement in his mother's home was not Regent's fault, any more than that of his mother Anne.

But Anne herself knew nothing. She had been going in and out of the mental hospital with depression even before her husband's death; she was a person who needed help and was not in a position to give it.

Miss C's attitude was a very stereotyped view held by British females. She scorned her brother's frustration and anger at having to live at his mother's house.

She was much more capable of coping than a man would be, with staying in inactive confinement through her youthful years.

1-0008: The mental health system takes women from zero to hero

In the UK, a woman is a delicately-protected rose who never raises her voice. She would gladly take Prozac to maintain her feminine poise when things go wrong. She feels that being passive and unperturbed is a requirement for all humans to be respected. She sees feminine passivity as a moral virtue. She is contemptuous of those who have less of it.

No tragedy is too great for a UK female to bounce back from, through the use of the all-time SCIENTIFIC GODHEAD, the mental health service.

1-0009: Biography Continues

She described her brother's anger and frustration as disgusting. She did not see him sympathetically when they were young adults.

When Regent was sectioned off and on, he had only one living relative, his younger sister Miss C, who could support him.

He did not get any support from her. He languished in those mental prisons for months and years at a time. No kith and kin to fight for his release, or to raise a stink about an over-medication issue.

Regent felt even worse when Miss C started taking psychotherapy from somebody older than their (deceased) father and was being raped by him.

Miss C realized years later she was seeking a father figure and that it was improper of the old therapist to exploit her vulnerability and stop her from getting her life's goal, to become a wife and mother.

But her complaints of rape fell on deaf ears as the medical community laughed away her allegations.

Regent, who was under the care of psychiatrists, was

sectioned intermittently. The lockup periods were excessively long, as he had no family to visit him or fight for his release.

1-0010: "EAT YOUR SLOBS AND MOVE YOUR CARCASS"

Regent recalled how people were holed together like sardines in dirty facilities and drugged into zombies. He remembered how one male staff member had called him a "unit".

I suppose the detained people were seen by staff as a coalesced pool, with each person of the pool being a unit of the aggregate.

Whatever the hell "unit" meant, it was not nice.

Regent would also be shouted at by a male staff member at one location "Eat your slobs and move your carcass"

Regent said a man and woman from India were psychiatrists in one of the many locations where he was detained.

Regent said that on one occasion, he had decided to be playful. He had bear-hugged the male psychiatrist, (whose name was Qatapa), from behind, and pinched his bottom, shouting, "You are the mad one".

Qatapa probably deserved this assault.

But human beings are not angels, nor are psychiatrists above-average in kindness or moral character. If you annoy a shrink or talk back, he or she will typically give you a diagnosis of severe mental disorder. Your dose may be doubled. You won't be released from detention if you get up to tricks like that.

But you can see how isolated the young man was, his body in custody, his mind trapped in a cloud of medication, living a life without freedom, love, friendship, or communication.

Regent said he also asked the Indian woman psychiatrist who was to evaluate his progress if she was still getting her monthly periods. The lady shrink who was nearing 60 years of age, had shouted, "Mind your own business! he said".

A lovely sane and gorgeous person was detained wronged, exploited and chemically murdered.

1-0011: A Particularly high Level of Injustice

This story was told to me by Regent the year he died, and by Miss C after his death.

On one occasion, Regent got frustrated in a long-term crowded ward. He got completely naked one morning. A male guard stopped Regent as he was leaving a hallway. So the nude Regent slapped his face.

It was one small painless slap. The guard raised the alarm, and Regent was brought to the ground with pepper and mace and handcuffed.

Regent was removed from sectioning so that they could conduct criminal proceedings.

Miss C may have attended his criminal court, but it appears she did not defend him or try to appoint legal counsel for him.

Very few men undergo criminal proceedings for slapping another man in the face. It is too petty an offense to even be recorded.

Anyway, those criminal proceedings were conducted

inside the mental hospital where he was still being detained.

Does the reader agree with me that it was unfair to take Regent off his "sectioned" status to conduct criminal proceedings?

If the section was done for genuine illness, then under the law he is exempt from criminal proceedings.

By taking him off the section they are claiming his illness became unreal as soon as he slapped someone. He is already detained under the mental health act and as a mental patient, he has the legal right to enjoy freedom from criminal proceedings.

If they did take him off the section, he had a right to walk out of that place, and seek legal assistance.

Anyway, for one little slap, the criminal court inside the mental hospital gave an unusually severe verdict: two years in prison!

Whoever in the history of the United Kingdom has ever got a two-year custodial sentence for slapping a heavily muscled guy once in the face.

Regent was then put back on section and forced to serve

his two-year custodial sentence in a mental hospital in Northampton.

That was the only time his detention was two years when he was never let out. He also did not see relatives (mainly Miss C) as she dumped him to suffer and stew.

This is one of the highest forms of injustice.

I heard that one of the reasons why Africa is called the Dark Continent is the absence of historical records of erstwhile generations.

These days, though, I think every continent is a Dark Continent, in terms of there being no historical records of offenses committed by women and offenses committed by mental health staff.

1-0012: MADE FAT THROUGH HARMFUL CHEMICALS

My gorgeous, wonderful friend was forcibly overdosed with Depakote(sodium valproate) in a psychiatric lockup in 2008.

Despite giving him agonizing belly pains, Depakote continued to be forced by the psychiatrists, causing him to go from being a genetically slim and "hyper" person to someone weighing 18-22 stone.

Made fat through harmful chemicals, yet cute and charming, the change was irreversible.

1-0013: Fat People can't become Thin Easily

Fat people can't easily become thin. Once a person bloats to 18-22 stone, various vital organs start to fail as a side-effect, or there is direct damage to them by psychotropic drugs that are designed to alter your mood by making changes to your heart and nervous system.

After taking those drugs, whether or not you had a genuine mental problem to start with, you are severely disabled physically. Being fat is a social problem too. A lot of supportive medical treatment is needed to maintain you once you have become an elephant from Depakote or similar drugs.

1-0014 TRIBAL WOMEN COMMAND HELICOPTER FLEET TO DRIVE REGENT AMONG GRAVES

Has the reader ever come across a doctor standing at a police station late into the night, petitioning for some man to be hunted down by a squadron with a fleet of helicopters for "health reasons"?

I doubt such a life-threatening "health emergency" would genuinely arise.

That type of "kindness" not shown by doctors is also not found in men.

It is generously practiced by women who have all the time in the world.

With the supply of "women's kindness" exceeding demand by a factor of ten, natural laws of justice would have women devalued to dirt unless there was an artificial, or manmade maintenance system in place to keep women floating in the sky.

We are talking about women like those that worked in the below-documented Pesthilenseroke Society. I refer to them as illiterate tribals.

Which description of them is just bringing up the truth, which is just and fair, if you don't want people to forget where they came from, and who they actually are under their silk and velvet skins

.

They were making a claim that Regent needed to be sectioned as a medical emergency to save his life.

Lifesaving would be a typical story that would be told by anyone who successfully takes extreme measures (such as police collaboration) to act upon, or against an unwilling party without facing censure or criminal prosecution.

Anyway hocus-pocus "medical" cases like that are always respected by a trusting public, so the feeble-minded, but hedonistic pursuers enjoy power and thrills. There are so many articles, photos, and videos on the internet praising female genitalia. I suppose all healthy and red-blooded men would argue a woman is a thing of delight, whose actions can only be praised.

Lastly, if the British are proud of how they have women giving orders to a battalion of army men, here is a beautiful example.

Tribal mental health women commanded the respect of

lifesaving police and helicopter men, to chase Regent by
helicopter using an infra-red camera, to section.

Regent ran into a graveyard, with the aircraft circling
above him in the sky. He dived into dense shrubbery and
felt sure he would be caught, but the infra-red cameras
could not see him. His body heat was masked by the heat
from the plants.

Although Regent won this battle, he (later) lost his life
and a result of these repeated abuses. His death was
induced by chemical and not psychological means.

1-0015: How our Paths Crossed

I am an Indian citizen born in 1958. I stayed in the UK from 2004-2018. During this time interval, the Home Office did not give me a legal right to work. I hope you agree that is a rather long time for anybody to not work.

Had I been an illegal immigrant, during those 14 years, it would be understandable that I would not have a legal right to work. Such a person would either be unemployed or they could work illegally.

By "illegal immigrant" I mean someone who does not have papers to remain in that country, and therefore is hiding from the authorities.

But that was not the case with me. I was applying to stay in the UK.

This application lasted right through 2018 and was pending when I left the UK. That explains my entire UK immigration history condensed into one sentence.

In case there is anybody who does not understand, your country of citizenship is the same as what is on your passport. People with a passport from aN EU country can enter and work automatically in the UK.

If you have a Non-EU passport (such as an Indian passport in my case) then you cannot work without the Border Agency's authorization. They will need to stamp work permission on your passport unless they have already given you indefinite leave to remain.

What happens if you work without an authorization?

I think if you are caught working illegally, the UKBA (United Kingdom Border Agency) will give you an indulgent smile if you are somebody they like.

But if you are not somebody they like, they could give you the maximum penalty for working illegally (which is deportation). Persons have been deported from the UK for working illegally based on unproven rumors.

So, then I was unemployed long-term in the UK. I did not work illegally.

Temperamentally, I am not an idle person. I try all sorts of things. I am a hermit without any social networking. My isolation imposes a limit on what I can achieve.

I was expelled by the Institute of Physics [www.iop.org] London in 2006-2007 for bringing them into disrepute.

At first, I assumed that my expulsion was not serious. I

thought of it as like being expelled from a pub. You could drink elsewhere.

I got a rude surprise, though, in 2011 when I located my old classmates from the Physics class at the University of Manchester of 1983.

However, in 2011, I traced three of my old classmates from my UMIST Physics class of 1983. Their behavior gave me a rude surprise. I learned that I was hated by the larger Physics community.! This hatred had not been present at the place and time of my graduation, which was Manchester and 1983.

I had lived in the UK for 7 years (2004-2011) at the time I met Regent. My experiences with psychiatry are described in full detail in my paperback, "The first part of my life", ISBN: 9781838355715.

The above-mentioned book begins at my birth and ends in the year 1986.

In the UK itself, I had suffered psychiatric abuse before finding out about Regent and meeting him.

But my psychiatric abuse in the UK was not the conventional type. Police and the UK Border Agency were after me, trying to get me sectioned.

As it was not the doctors who wanted me sectioned, sectioning did not take place, and all the medication threats from police or Pesthilenseroke remained a threat.

Meanwhile, a lot of fictitious rumors were created about me on the UKBA legal records. I have never had access to these records. I have been exposed indirectly to a tiny bit of them. There were details in those records that I knew were fabrications. Hence my concern.

The persons making those allegations in the UKBA records were unnamed.

I know that people are not supposed to give psych treatment if they are not doctors.

But in the UK people can do anything they feel, when it comes to psychiatry, which is used for the pursuit of happiness by them that are empowered to do so, especially females.

At least the UK police said they could section anyone if they liked, without even a nurse being present. They did not do it, but the whole thing was (years of) prolonged torture.

Their stalking was supposed to have sprung because of my father making a malicious referral to psychiatry, beginning with a bogus missing person report to a Hindu police constable working in his area. PC Karnail Virdee.

Back in January 2011, I had almost died of an overdose following a police incident connected to my parents. That was 7-8 months before meeting Regent.

At this time, I was trying to learn some Photoshop and messaged an online teacher of the same on Facebook, who was Regent's acquaintance.

Regent asked on Facebook messenger how I knew this man, and we started talking.

Regent said, "today at the age of 50 + I have had the biggest achievement of my life. I have learned to spell my name backwards."

I suppose some folks would have assumed that they were speaking to some kind of mental retard. I, however knew right away I was talking to an intelligent and lovely person who was making a joke.

He had changed his name a few years earlier to Regent Exeter because R-e-g-e-n-t when spelled backwards letter by letter, and E-x-e-t-e-r spelled forwards letter by letter, rhymed with "c-l-e-v-e-r" spelled forwards letter by letter.

"Because I want to be clever", he said.

Regent had said on Facebook chat, "I am a mental patient, and do not work."

I could see the soul behind the meek exterior, the high mental development that had taken place. I could feel the purity of the soul behind the man-made facade awarded to him by human society.

I was shocked to learn how badly he was being abused by psychiatrists. So much so, I took a train to meet him. I have heard that laughter is the best form of sanity, and he had plenty of it.

I took a bus on a rural route to Shifnal. He asked me to come to a bridge by the bus station. He picked me up from there and walked me home. He had a flat in a locked and secure multi-storey building that housed only males, and everyone there had been released at some point from a mental hospital.

1-0016: Visiting Regent for the First Time

I met Regent in August 2011.

The front door was not locked to residents wanting to exit. Visitors had to be let in by an attendant round-the-clock, and the flats were cleaned; everything was managed for inmates.

Regent was kind and hospitable. He offered me food and drink as soon as I arrived, and put me at ease.

He asked me, "What do you think of the art on my walls?" His walls were covered with his created posters in English and German, colorful patches cut and pasted on card paper. They did not make full sense to me.

He added, "If Doctor "X" sees these posters, he will want me locked up, and increase my medication."

Regent "had" several psychiatrists, including one called Simon Smith of Ludlow. I don't recall the name he mentioned that day.

I said no one had a right to medicate anyone or label them as mentally disordered for creating works of art.

Regent told me he would get into trouble for keeping me as he was not allowed, overnight guests.

"Such restrictions are bullshit at your age", I said. He agreed that I could stay a couple of days and keep a low profile. He feared being locked up under psychiatry or given extra medication for having a woman stay overnight in his flat.

The men in neighboring flats of the locked multi-storey building at The Willows would not tell the attendant that Regent had an overnight visitor. There was an attendant, a female version of a porter, who slept overnight in a unit provided for her on the ground floor. She did not keep awake all night but maintained vigilance at the entrance during the day.

Regent said a flat#14, The Willows had fallen vacant. It was not in the locked building. The occupant had passed away. The flat opened onto the Willows driveway and there was no vigilance to prevent visitors from coming. He would ask reception if he could move into that flat.

The next day I realized why those works of art were there, even though they looked a bit strange at first. Regent was a hermit expressing his creativity without any feedback from human society.

I am, to some extent, a hermit myself. Hermits do their

own thing, and no two hermits are created equal.

The next time I visited Regent, he was comfortably settled in No 14, The Willows. It was a double bedroom flat for a single occupant.

From the day I first met him, Regent had been coughing very badly. This cough remained untreated and undiagnosed right to the end.

1-0017: A HEAVY-DUTY LEGAL MATTER

I lived in the UK from 2004 to 2018, when I left voluntarily, while an immigration appeal was pending.

From 2006 to 2018, I was on "immigration appeals" with no legal right to take on paid or unpaid employment, and from 2010 I officially carried IS96.

I wanted to move in with Regent in 2012 and offer him companionship. But unlike most women who wanted male companionship, this was a heavy-duty legal matter, requiring the consent of other government departments, and cartloads of women.

I even changed my "reporting center" from East/West London to Solihull, the closest point to Regent's residence.

They decided Regent had no proof I was not earning and paying him thousands of dollars (even though I was not working). So if I moved in with him, he would lose all his disability benefits, they said. Regent was receiving a generous disability allowance and had been granted a two-bedroom council flat to live in.

I did not want to take a chance, nor did Regent about

losing his entire disability allowance. I mean, we gave up the idea or would have needed legal advice.

1-0018: Coughing himself to Death

I asked how come the GP hadn't given him care for his horrible cough.

If I could have only changed his GP –(I think it's my fault that I did not insist) -but Regent eventually did not want to change his GP. I also went with him to one of the GPs, Doctor S, in 2011 so he could ask about his cough in my presence.

The village Doctor S was very mean to Regent and I was myself scared of them, whereas I do not scare easily.
I also took Regent for a spirometry test privately, in Manchester, who referred him to a lung specialist, and I made him see that lung specialist.

Regent was happy to be on the train to the lung specialist, and phoned me from the train to Manchester and started making beautiful chattering sounds like a monkey. He was messing around, and I loved it. He felt loved. Nobody had given him enough love in his life to send him to a specialist.

That sweet chattering of his was accidentally taped, and when he died I wanted to cherish those lovely sounds he made. Unfortunately, the taping, which had been accidental, had got accidentally deleted.

I did not do well with Regent, as I ought to have gone
with him to the lung specialist who did not do very much.

Doctor B must have realized that Regent was getting
outside attention.

After that, for a few months, Doctor B gave Regent
a brand new inhaler which greatly improved his lung
condition.

Regent was lovely in 2013 and did a lot in his new,
improved state of health. He took me to his local
Jobcentre in a different village, and we snacked at a Fish
and Chips.

Right at the Jobcentre, they fixed him up for a college
course in Accountancy so he could work afterward. I was
also telling him to write down his poetry, not to just spout
it and forget all about it."It's a gift" I told him, which
others don't have. It belongs in published books where
you show the world your talent.

Soon Regent found a publisher, Robert Agar-Hutton. and
wrote a book on his favorite subject, "Phonetics" and
called it "Pushmepullyous"

Regent was trying Weight Watchers and said he met ladies there who were as fat as himself, who were also a failure at losing weight. I said he was lovely, and he must not stress too much about fatness.

He was trying various social groups and you know how people are not kind or friendly as they used to be. He was regularly getting visits from a Jehovah's Witnesses couple. One of the times I was visiting Regent in Shifnal, they visited. I did not want to meet them, so Regent said to stay in the room and not come out.

I decided to come out and say Hello. I said I was not feeling well without realizing Regent was far more seriously ill than I.

The man of the couple said to me, "Never grow old. I have become old and don't feel well." I could feel his bitterness.

1-0019: Doctor is Reducing Quantity of your Life to improve Quality

Regent had another visitor when I was staying with him. "Hello, V", Regent said one morning after a woman entered without knocking and sat down on a chair in the living room.

I realized she had been rude to enter without knocking. But Regent introduced her to me, politely saying 'This is V, a psychiatric social worker.

Ms. V, who belonged to another ethnic group, said she was just dropping in to say hello.

Regent and Ms. V chatted briefly and Regent mentioned his funeral. Nobody seemed upset, and Regent himself was cool and collected.

Ms. V replied. "The doctor has decided to reduce the quantity of your life, to enhance its quality".

I was going to say something very rude, Indian style. I bit my tongue to remain silent, as I felt Regent would want me to be nice to her.

1-0020: Miss V: Adult with Mental Capacity of Child

I thought about the female brain and the plethora of "INTIMACY JOBS" given to them in the UK to suit their PROSTITUTIONAL NATURE.

Modern society has created jobs for persons whose consciousness is naturally limited to sex.

Jobs of pretentious purpose that are designed to make the "worker" come out as a high achiever in a man-made paradise stuffed with illusions. Jobs where they are paid mainly to receive with little to give.

Miss V is an example of a "sugar plum". She is sugar spice and everything nice. Someone whose conscience never grew.

Someone who will piggyback on another person's conscience.

Someone who has been provided with leaflets containing words of "kindness" and how to make conversation in various situations, whose "job" it is to simply learn and repeat stuff from those leaflets.

Examples of "intimacy work" or "paid comforter" are the kinds of things mental health workers do.

Women also work as substitutes for painkillers. They stay in the room with a person howling with pain.

Women "WORK WITH" riding in police cars to "JUST BE THERE" when somebody gets a home visit from the police when they are going to do something unpleasant. For example, people would feel good to have a woman in the room when they are being arrested.

I felt Ms. V had self-confidence like a cat that comes and sits on your lap, which (to me) does not look nice on a human being. I like it on a real cat and don't mind it on a small child.

I see Miss V as a 5-year-old child, who happens to be present in the room when her mother and father are plotting to kill someone. The blessed child understands everything her parents talk about, except that killing is wrong, and socially unacceptable. So she claps her hands and runs off, ringing every doorbell, spreading the good news about the plans of her blessed parents.

1-0021: What happened after Unwelcome Visitor V Left

Regent often made me sad while we were together by saying it was every Englishman's dream to be buried in a churchyard.

He took me to Shifnal's St. Andrews church and asked me to marry him. I had a lot of unresolved issues. I said. After the service, Regent walked around the church with me and there were lots of graves and oak trees that looked centuries old.

He then took me to the whole area covered with flowers and flower pots, to a secluded area with seating that went 360 degrees around and was extremely beautiful and floral.

We sat there for a while, and I was choking back my tears because of a strange feeling I could not explain. "It is so peaceful here," said Regent, "I wish I could stay here forever."

When we went home, Regent made carrot sausages by roasting carrots. They were delicious.

Regent said, "You can marry me and you will soon be a widow, and I will leave you lots of money."

"I won't let you die," I screamed foolishly. I felt I could stop his dying. How idiotic-well-people live in denial. I said, "I won't marry you if you plan to die, besides I will not speak to you if you say awful things like that."

He took me to the RAF(Royal Air Force) Museum near Shifnal and two comedians' shows including that of Ken Dodd. Regent liked literature and so we went to Stratford-upon-Avon to a museum and Shakespeare festival.

That is, I used to visit Regent for the weekend or for a few days at a time. I was on UK immigration appeals throughout the period. My status in the UK was described by an unflattering document called "IS 96" bearing my black and white low-quality mugshot. It said, "You can be detained at any time."

1-0022: Police Chase Drama in my Life

I made many train journeys, between March and July of 2013, but I doubt that any of them would have been to Regent's home. He was on Skype with me one night when I was alone at Mr. A's home, and the police were trying to trick me into opening the front door without realizing they were police.

Regent was very supportive of the screaming and banging of the unidentified female caller. I found out a few days later via a different route who the bangers from time to time were.

Subsequently, I turned up at the local police station to ask what the police wanted of me. But they said dishonestly that the police did not want to speak to me throughout the UK.

There was no problem, they claimed, and asked me to go away. They also refused to give me written proof of police station attendance, which I had been advised to ask for by a solicitor. The police again turned up at my place on Easter Sunday night within 10 minutes after Mr. A had stepped out.

Mr. A and I had by then conducted a study that showed us

that on days and times when Mr. A was expected to be at home, (weekends or evenings) police would ring the bell within 10-20 minutes of his stepping out. There appeared to be some sort of surveillance so the police would come to know I was alone and it was time to jump into their cars (from wherever) and come.

By not giving me proof of attendance at the police station, the police were keeping open their option of an absconding charge, which had become false as soon as I attended the police station.

The police preferred I open the door when Mr. A was away, as they wanted me to be unprotected when they arrived.

The police preferred I open the door without realizing it was the police, so I would be unprepared.

I kept repeatedly phoning various non-emergency police with 101 and eventually, one PC admitted the police were indeed after me and gave the name and number of the case officer, WPC Carla Hammond.

That was close to 19 April 2013 one of the days of the London Book Fair. I called the police officer and went out by train to see her.

1-0023: LONDON SELFISHNESS FAIR FOR BOOKS

The London Book Fair is in April each year. The one of 2013 was the last one I attended. I did not attend the one in April 2014 as I was mourning Regent, who had just found a publisher for his first book, when the end came.

It is not a place worth going to anyway.

Most exhibitors are men, and each stall has women to "jump" on people to try and advertise the men's wares. Very off-putting and makes sure other authors and interested persons have no opportunities, except to be "jumped on" by women. I think it should be re-named as London Selfishness Fair.

1-0024: 2013: A Gray Overcast Sky

A very unusual thing happened to me which people would likely say is untrue. I was falsely sentenced in July 2013.

I think I took Regent for Spirometry in 2013 to Manchester. Later I asked him to go by himself to a lung specialist there. I cannot remember when I did these things.

After the sentencing, I was electronically tagged until November 2013. At the end of October 2013, I was served a notice deporting me for the public good and detained for over two weeks at Yarl's Wood IRC.

These notices are not the same as a different notice which they give you for physical deportation. Later lawyers said the criminal conviction was too petty to be the reason for deportation for the public good, and that no reason had been given for my deportation.

1-0025: THE PESTHILENSEROKE SOCIETY

Now there was a Pesthilenseroke* Society. I did not engage with them, but my sister and parents, who lived several miles away from me and each other, did engage with them. Now you are not supposed to write a report or assess someone based on what someone told you.

Mental assessments are not allowed if you have not met the person you are assessing. Also, you are obliged to tell the truth at all times.

Because people who write a mental assessment meet their client in private, only God is a witness, sometimes to whether they are telling the truth in their assessment.

For example, if you met them, and did not tell them you wanted to harm someone, they are not supposed to report that you said it, and not include such fabrication in creating your assessment. In some cultures, illiterate women won't be in charge of making mental assessments.

My sister and parents had engaged with Pesthilenseroke, and my sister, and minimally my father and brother-in-law, who forged his wife's signature were plaintiffs in the conviction.

I am aware that most convictions are made of the guilty.

I am aware that almost no one will believe I was falsely convicted as most people trust the legal system for accuracy and worship the mental health system for their salvation.

Furthermore, many citizens detest my describing mental health workers as illiterate women. They won't be friends once I've said that. They'll treat me like a nutcase once I've said that.

However, I have already explained that these women frequently describe themselves as "clinicians" and this behavior (in my opinion) makes them "filth".

I have also explained about this habit they have of lying under oath. This habit is known to lawyers but is tolerated by the legal system which has made mental health workers not punishable under the law.

This criminal immunity is not officially in print for the public to see and understand. Some people will object when they learn mental health workers are not punished. This is one of the many laws of the UK that is always in practice, never in print.

Understandably, people would need a bribe to perform a

"dirty job"..

This same Pesthilenseroke Society kept banging and
kicking the door. This society (comprising of socially
and educationally backward people) is supposed to have
testified that I am linked to a cat-burglar family and that I
have connections with the Russian Mafia.

However, I was detained overnight at Basingstoke police
station in April 2013 and called, among others Regent,
who sobbed, saying BASTARD WOMAN.

He was referring to the plaintiff, who lied under oath
about me and whose husband forged her signature on
what was supposed to be her statement. I had explained to
Regent that it looked like my sister, through her personal
protection officer, WPC Hammond was petitioning for me
to be deported on the spot.

They called a home office staff member to come over.

Deportation is a legal procedure, and if based on a crime,
that person would need to be charged, and then convicted,
before they can be deported for a crime.

You do not have a criminal record after being charged,
before you are convicted, and cannot be lifted off the
ground and flown out.

As such from the smallest to the most serious crime (shall we say that is murder) being charged won't always result in a conviction, and that decision won't be made on the same day.

As such some crimes would be too petty to be considered for deportation while others may involve deportation automatically if they are serious enough.

My sister the primary plaintiff of the case, and her protection officer were trying to get me on the plane right away, and the visiting home office lady was polite and apologetic, saying she did not know if I was guilty and had come because she had been called.

My sister made up irrational and fraudulent allegations based on which I received a criminal conviction three months later.

Mrs. Wortley removed my signature and date from a letter I had written three years earlier, by scanning my letter and cutting out unwanted parts, namely my signature and date, and printing the resultant digital file.

While there was nothing criminal in the letter, which asked her and my parents to stop causing me grief, she presented false evidence I was writing anonymous letters to her, and she "traced" me.

The allegation was that I wanted to harm her children who at the time these allegations were created were well-built and strapping adults. The plaintiff never came to court, nor was anyone at the Magistrates allowed to get a glimpse of her children.

Viju made a parallel civil case in a different city containing disjointed allegations, reconstructing my life story where she openly wrote I was an idiot since birth, while she was brilliant. There she requested a ban from my entry into three different counties of England or part thereof, as her children traveled in buses in those areas once a year or more frequently. She feared I would kidnap them in the bus, she said.

The court was practicing topsy-turvy justice on purpose. I am sorry for making such a remark, which is my foolish opinion. Many readers, if I had them at all, would not believe my remark or find it annoying.

At the same time, I feel, the Magistrates Court would have thrown out the plaintiff's case, of course conducted in absentia (she never appeared) if they had seen Miss Wortley and Master Wortley were twice my size, and it would not have been possible for me to kidnap them, as a fellow passenger in a bus.

Although the name of my conviction was "harassment without violence", it had many features, according to lawyers at the time, of a murder case.

1-0026: Living in Britain without British Reflexes

Late one evening, I was waiting at Shifnal Railway Station to return to London. I was supposed to change trains at Birmingham..

The entrance and lamps of the small station were near each other while I waited on a bench in semi-darkness. A pair of young men came along and said they were going to Birmingham to get drunk.

I said casually, "Don't drink too much". The man replied, "Bitch, if you think you can stop me drinking I have a sharp knife in my pocket and will slit your throat." He put his hand in his pocket, and I thought he was taking out his weapon.

So I stood up and walked towards this man. I did not experience feelings of terror, nor did I scream. People cannot control or fake their reflex actions.

By walking towards the guy, I was also walking towards his companion, the electric lamps, and the only entrance/exit of the station.

Actually, I knew I could not prevent the stabbing, but was reducing its chances by being in a more conspicuous place. As well as the time of arrival of the train was nearing and there would be others on the platform.

His companion told him to behave. I was standing beside the two men now. The offending man got a sweet from his pocket and threw it on the railway track, saying, "Here! I have no weapon!"

The train came, and some people (including myself), got on one carriage, while the two lads got on a neighboring carriage. The train moved, and I was afraid they would walk through to my carriage.

I told the ticket inspector what had happened. He would not have believed me, except this was the second time he was hearing that complaint. The police made me get off the train at Wolverhampton where they arrested the man.

I had to spend the night sitting in a police station adjacent to Birmingham New Street railway station where a police officer needed more details about the incident. He was surprised I did not feel intense terror. I realized my reflexes were not British. I explained, "I am not from here". The PC said I had done the right thing, to walk towards the pair when threatened by one of them with stabbing.

The man spent a night in a cell in Wolverhampton, without a criminal charge on the premise that he had been drinking. If it had not been his second offense nobody would have believed me, because I do not feel "British women's terror" and am calm and collected as would be acceptable to the law if found in a man.

If I had had "normal British reactions", the man would have probably spent a year in jail and been tainted for life.

If I had had "normal British reactions", I would have been shaking in terror for hours and possibly days. I would have been put in with a female officer employed to handle "female terror" and to provide wholesome, safe "intimacy" in a male-free environment. I would be in a "women's" safe house in which is highly respected.

I think it is not nice that the gender inferiority (or whatever you want to call it) of a woman can be used to sentence a man who is a stranger to her.

You can only be punished for your actions. Others' reactions are outside one's control esp when those others are strangers or have anomalous or unpredictable reactions..

A person with an inability to do something is protected (by the law) in a manner they can live equally well without that ability, in the UK. This is achieved through an artificial man-made environment filled with virtual prosthetic devices such as the mental health system, and concocted psychological gimmicks. This 'equally happy living" means ideally that neither you nor the rest of the world understands that you have that inability. The next best to divine perfection.

Women can live as if they have all sorts of abilities they do not, and never will.

This means women with "normal reactions" (who will feel intense terror) will always get the revenge they want when they complain about someone to the police. A female officer is provided to support female terror.

This does not mean a man should be locked up any longer if they did the same offense to "normal women" than if he did it to me. Just because you are weak of mind, people who clash with you cannot take extra punishment to make your escape developing awareness of your infirmity.

As my sister, the plaintiff of a trumped-up criminal conviction I have mentioned is likely to have similar reflexes to me, she must have been faking terror that I would harm her children.

Female terror is a racial or regional characteristic of the UK. A UK man once told me it is almost certain if a man orders a woman, she will obey. This is why there is a law to treat her like a delicate rose. A legal paradise for the feeble-minded, a "death-hole" for certain others.

This is not true of Indians. "SHELL-LESS SLUG" females are rare in India. They would probably be seen as mental cases.

A crime victim simply would not feel that amount of terror as to qualify by UK standards as needed to jail or hang someone.

1-0027: MODERN PEOPLE KEEP CERTAIN COMPASSIONATE SECRETS

Finally, I do not follow that convention whereby one has infinite compassion towards prostitutes so as to keep their activities a million-dollar secret as soon as I learn about it.

New arrivals to the country need to be forewarned about the special effects of that country, not just herded in like invaluable garbage, and fed. This method only brings the lowest rung of overseas society here. This may be what the authorities want because incompetents from overseas provide hours, and years of fun to women advising and supervising them.

Such a warning is not possible, as these special effects are supposed to operate in a way that no human is supposed to know they exist.

This is not possible where they have created a virtual reality in which some women are using virtual prosthetic devices awarded by the law and state, that no one might learn about their moral and intellectual deficiencies, compared to men. Nobody understands this-maybe a small minority do, but keep this a compassionate secret from all humanity.

You see, if the virtual prosthetic devices I speak about

do exist, and if using these makes certain unattractive features found in women less obvious, then concealment is going to be 100% successful if nobody knows about these virtual devices (gimmicks) and those who know ALWAYS KEEP MUM about them.

In my case, I need to be with people who will have a good laugh and who do not want to live in sub-cultures where I will be lynched by women for criticizing or joking about a prostitute. As long as I know they are not around, I want to be free to say what I like. I want the 3rd World War to arrive to account for men trying to pimp my flesh all the time to Samaritans and social workers. Bloodshed has to happen, even if it's just my death

1-0028: MENTAL HEALTH WORKER'S LOWER TORSO SELLS SEX, WHILE HER UPPER TORSO SELLS COMPASSION

Anyhow, I don't think Regent would mind my narrations if he were alive. He would be in peals of laughter if he was around.

You see, a prostitute would not get any business unless she tells men at some point she is available.

You see, the "female porter" that stayed in vigil at the locked unit of The Willows had her own tiny ground floor apartment. A lady was paid 35 pounds just to sleep overnight, as there were seldom incidents.

A female porter W was staying overnight. She was aged around 60, had a daughter O, aged around 30. They spoke a different European language. W told Regent she and her daughter lived together and made as much money as they could. A married man was W's regular; he drove around once a month and paid 300 pounds for sex. W said she was open to sex with anyone if she was paid well.

Regent was smart and took the daughter O instead. She initially promised to marry him and have his babies. But she ran off, as she preferred to date women.

Another woman on the internet, who was located in Africa promised to marry him and have his babies. Regent was getting a generous disability allowance and she tricked him into sending her 2000 pounds. He said she had given him the slip after getting the money, which she told him was used to build an additional room in her house.

The local village prostitute also threatened Regent. Everyone was surprised when she got married. But her husband and many other guys were standing outside Regent's flat when she came in with a bottle of booze and started to embrace him. She pretended to have financial difficulties and said she would do anything for him. Regent saw the men lying in wait outside his house and asked her to get out.

He got fooled too, by someone who made him send payment to an unknown address, or the police would catch him for watching porn. He also had a website with a crooked web host who asked for extra cash to be sent in the post to make changes to the site and domain name.

There was a mental health woman who would come around and take the Willows men to the swimming pool. Regent and the other competent men at The Willows hated her as she pressured them to get into the water in a bathing suit and did not give sex. The woman told them she was married, and had an astronomical IQ.

Why would a "nurse" take you for a swim when you are physically able to go there yourself? Regent said that David, one Willows resident was clinging to her for dear life because she was the only female he had. You see the type of weight gain from neuroleptic drugs is not reversible and makes you very disabled.

Nobody who is on them makes old bones.

However whether gain happens or not may depend on the individual as well as what drug(s) they are taking, the dose, and duration. I myself had a smaller weight gain resulting from Depakote injections in INS detention, which was irreversible.

As such you will always have other side-effects such as your head being in a cloud all the time. Some of the Willows residents, who were able and willing were allowed to attend a university. It was unlikely they would work, though.

Some people become incontinent as a side effect of taking psychiatric medication. Regent would say their only human right was to wear their plastic pants and stay at home.

One man Mark in the locked unit was only 21, wearing an extra-long trench coat. The trench coat made his girth slightly inconspicuous. I don't want to keep using the phrase "elephant" but Mark was a lot fatter than Regent because of psychiatric medication.

I got Regent the linoleum flooring and bathroom mirror of the design he wanted. He was scrupulously clean. I fixed his router and got him a picture science book I found at a sale. Regent said he really enjoyed it.

Often I told Regent I wish I could get out of the UK when to would respond, "I also want to get out of the UK. Why don't we die in each other's arms?"

1-0029: When is my Final Year, and Yours?

2014 was Regent's final year.

But the new inhaler was withdrawn by Doctor B, as it did not agree with Regent after some time.

His condition started to deteriorate. He no longer felt well enough to commute to college.

In January 2014, I visited him again. On that occasion, Regent alleged that his doctor was giving him a new medicine, which was making him much worse..

Regent greeted me when I got off the train and I hugged and kissed his beautiful self. Once in his flat, he said he had discontinued visits from Jehovah's Witnesses.

He said the man of the couple had died and the woman was dropping in with friends from the church. Regent had asked them not to visit again.

He took me to a free meal (for an umpteenth time) at a tapas bar with a restauranteur who owed him money. We sat on high chairs and Regent collapsed with a profuse nosebleed on the floor.

I took him home and he said he sometimes had a nosebleed and would be okay. It was his drinking, he said. We did not know the nosebleed was due to high blood pressure, and that his BP was life-threatening.

A few days after visiting him in Shifnal, Shropshire, in January 2014, I was back in London and trying to catch a taxi late one night in Watford. At that time, I chatted to Regent on my mobile phone in the cold bleakness.

Regent said Doctor B wrote a strange mixture of alphanumeric characters instead of the usual monthly prescription for Flu-penthixol.

When Regent asked him to explain what it was, the doctor answered that he (Regent) didn't need to know. It was through an understanding between himself (Doctor B) and the pharmacist.

Regent was on this unknown preparation since the start of the year 2014 and told me about it when I visited in January 2014, and in March 2014.

He said the capsule provided by the pharmacist in response to Doctor B's strange alphanumeric code looked nothing like the Flu-penthixol he had been used to for over a decade.

Moreover, Regent said he felt the unknown preparation was making him feel much worse.

Regent was concerned about the behavior of his GP. Doctor B. He told me Doctor B said he had diabetes and wants to give him medicine for it. He had high blood pressure and wanted to give him medicine for it.

Regent asked me if he should take Doctor B seriously, and should take all those pills.

I said yes, he should pay heed to the doctor's advice.

Regent said he was not convinced about the correctness of Doctor B's bad news, but did not explain why.

A week or so later, Regent spoke again on the mobile phone about Doctor B, to whom he had made yet another visit, in addition to the routine monthly visits that had taken place for years, to just get a note to take to the pharmacist to get a 30-days' supply of Flu-penthixol.

This time, Regent said, Doctor B had changed his mind, and he told Regent he did not think there was any diabetes. He said he would need to do some more tests before confirming diabetes.

Regent was relieved, but I wasn't.

1-0030: How a Patient can find out a Doctor is Lying

Laypeople understand some facts coming from doctors' lips and not others. A doctor, when lying to patients, cannot possibly assess the intelligence/general knowledge each patient may or may not have.

Very few patients could know if a doctor lied in the medical record. They'd have to be clairvoyant, (rather than be a doctor), to know that that had happened to them. I do hope and pray that that type of lying happens infrequently, and hope it does not happen to me.

Whereas one could, as a layperson sometimes know a doctor is lying if one feels quite ill over a long period, and the doctor repeatedly reassures one that one is in the pink of health.

Whereas I met Regent on Facebook and then face-to-face in August 2011, I had taken an overdose following a police incident in January 2011, which was followed by the strange behavior of the A and E doctors. More details of this are in Part Three.

A month after my overdose, I had had a satellite cardiac event and spent the night in a different hospital where I chatted to a male fellow patient, whose GP had ordered him to trust the doctor at all times and to stay away from "dangerous Google" which could lie, mislead and "stress out" patients.

The doctor had forbidden the trusting and unintelligent patient from doing any independent reading on the

internet to find out more about his medical condition.

1-0031: Doctor B. is screwing your Life

I knew diabetes is a common illness and there are simple, and well-known tests to verify if someone has it. My father is a diabetic for example. I know a doctor is not supposed to provide confused answers, nor to go back and forth on the subject of whether someone has diabetes.

At this point, I became sure that Doctor B was screwing around with Regent's life; that Dr. B was trying to cover a potentially serious condition.

I said, "Well you are intelligent enough to understand your medical condition. If Doctor B cannot explain to you in a way that you understand, it's his fault, not yours. You need a second opinion."

"Doctor B is playing games with your life," I said.

I asked if I could help change his Doctor with the NHS(National Health Service). This is easy to do and requires no complaining about the existing doctor. I later felt I should have pressured Regent to change his doctor, while I took him only once to Telford to see a GP, who, I noticed at once, had a much better attitude.

Regent opposed any change. He said " I will just stick

with Doctor B. He is a nice man."

1-0032: The Last Time I saw Regent

I visited Regent again in March 2014, which would be the last time I was going to see him.

He was waiting when I got off the train and seemed even bigger than in January 2014. His black coat was flowing around him like a Jewish rabbi, his long, uncut hair blowing in the breeze.

The decor of his flat had changed dramatically since my January 2014 visit. The living room was filled with tables whose surfaces were filled with hundreds of glassware. There was little moving space. I made him cross as soon as I arrived by knocking a glass vase over and smashing it as I followed him into the kitchen.

His home looked unfit for habitation, but it looked like it was a derelict place where nobody lived.

Like a garden that was overgrown with weeds, but the weeds were in his home; they were the glassware.

I said the place was a bit cluttered. Regent visited the charity shop in Shifnal regularly, and being a remote village, antiques and items of monetary value would end up there, selling for a pound or two.

Regent bought toys and board games; he played alone. When he had played enough, he would re-donate them to the charity shop... He showed me with delight a complex mechanical toy he had just found in the charity shop, which he had great fun sharing with his baby sisters in his childhood.

Regent wanted to share fond memories. He played a tape from his childhood when his father was alive and the voices of the three siblings as infants came through.

Regent said he had withdrawn the legal case against his sister. He also wanted to forgive the psychiatrists for what they did. He cursed his new medicine once again and said his body was deteriorating fast.

He said he had confided in Kevin, the social worker, that he needed a new microwave but was not feeling well. Kevin had said not to worry as he would do all the paperwork for the microwave to be brought home and installed.

I had had a strange episode(an illness) like never before in bed a week or so before visiting Shifnal in March 2014.

I had attended A and E without a diagnosis resulting. Even in Regent's home, I could feel the ground rocking -but it was all in my head. Regent said affectionately, not to worry, if you have a stroke, I will take you to hospital.

I felt cheered up by the mechanical toy, the tapes, after the initial dismal feeling the glassware gave me. Regent also had an old handwritten book - like those old books that used to exist before printing existed-very neatly bound, or I can't exactly remember. In this book, his late headmaster Mr. Ray had admitted John Field had indeed made homosexual advances towards the young teenager Richard Lindsay, which he had not believed at the time. It was all kinds of anecdotes about that school.

Regent had thought it would be a good idea to bring a complaint about the Catholic father who had molested every male infant including Regent aged 5 in their kindergarten. Regent had been told there should be more than one complainant, to formalize the complaint. Regent said he located a pilot who had been his classmate in that kindergarten. But the latter said his life was going straight and did not feel the need to complain about an old story.

I think my visit in March 2014, which was the last time I saw Regent, was a short one. I arrived on a Thursday or Friday and left Monday morning, which was the 17th of March 2014.

I had multiple stresses to cope with. As already detailed, I was on Notice IS-96. This involved a monthly reporting obligation to Eaton House in West London. While I could not leave London close to reporting dates, UKBA, having made a decision that I was not a flight risk, had orally permitted me to leave Mr. A's home for 2-3 days at a time.

You'll understand that my IS-96 had my low-resolution mugshot and Mr.A's address on it. My IS-96 said I had to reside at Mr. A's address all the time, and if I wanted to move, I had to request permission in writing. UKBA said owing to my record of compliance they trusted me to travel out of London for 2-3 days at a time, without telling them; otherwise, they would insist I stay there all the time. Yes, it was a very weak form of custody by the UKBA although Mr. A was keeping me very kindly. I HAVE LIVED FOR YEARS CONSIDERING MYSELF TO BE A "DEATH PERSON" AND WHEN ANY MAN SAYS HELLO, I TAKE IT AS A BONUS. AFTER ALL, I AM CURSED TO LIVE IN A WOMAN-GULAG AND BE SMOTHERED TO DEATH BY POOLS OF PURE WOMEN.

Mr. A was cross that I visited Regent; once he made me sleep outdoors in winter after I returned from visiting him. I did go to Heathrow Airport in that situation. I am not British and have a mild response to some things British see as terrible and feel some things that British think are acceptable are terrible. I would not mention anything I consider to be bad about my friends here.

As I explained a British female is an "extreme female" who will feel extreme terror from men and go into safe houses with female terror officers. The more terror the women shake with in front of the female terror officer, the longer a man's sentence. Other women of Europe cannot feel as much terror as British females, I was advised.

While I grew up with a strong concept that lying about someone's mind is a crime against humanity, I still fancy that value, which as you know is the opposite of UK values. Mental patients are welcome to stay in the UK. Lawyers wanted to fabricate "Mencap" for me to prevent my deportation. So in the UK fabricating mental disorders is not morally wrong. It is commendable behavior.

However, I can understand that for a person who is aware she is living under a fabricated mental disorder, she may prefer it to a public disclosure that she does sex work. It's socially acceptable to be labeled a mental health sufferer. Groups of women are constantly campaigning to remove the stigma from mental patients. Women are often able to live a contented life under mental health "charges", both real and imaginary.

Anyhow with all these stresses, I planned a short visit, which ended up being my last one. Regent took me out onto the High Street, and there was a fire in a building. He joked and made the firemen laugh. Regent went for the two burnt cats- but all the humans had been brought to safety. He knew the mayor of Shifnal and ran into him on the High Street. He introduced me to the Mayor. On one night he took me to the co-op store and pub with his buddies. A man in a wheelchair came joined us and wanted to talk all about his deformities. I felt under pressure, as I had come to spend precious time with Regent

The following night, I sat with Regent on the sofa and I clutched his hand saying spontaneously, "It feels very special to be with you. A great honor. I am so happy I had this wonderful experience.

Regent wanted to sit up all night and watch a soft-porn comedy. I agreed. On his tablet was this video coming up of spanking sessions, where a schoolmaster would spank the bottoms of naughty female pupils. The women actors were around 40 and acting as schoolgirls. Holding his hand, I realized Regent had dozed off, with the video still blaring. I too fell asleep.

I awoke at some point in the night and found the video had ended and Regent was not beside me. I called out his name but got no answer. But I could hear the unmistakable drone of his breathing, which had gotten louder than ever before.

1-0033: GRAND TICKING WHALE

I started searching for him when I heard that loud drone-like metallic breathing.

I used to call him a "grand ticking whale" affectionately, while he called me "cheeky monkey".

There were ticks you could hear in his regular breathing; the sound often split into two or three strands with a component that sounded metallic, like a guitar.

I knew it was not appropriate for someone to breathe like that. I did not realize it was life-threatening all the while I knew Regent.

In his sleep, he would gag once in a while when his face would go bluish, and soon everything was back to normal.

Regent was soaking in his bathtub and had fallen asleep in it. I woke him up, and he said he liked to dunk in a bath of hot water because his body could not maintain temperature. "I want to stay in a warm water bath 24 hours a day because that feels good", said Regent.

I said, "Well you are not a fish, but a land animal. You need urgently to see a specialist. It has to happen as Doctor B. is not going to help you."

"You must come to London and we are seeing a specialist," I said.

Regent agreed to ask his sister, Miss C, for permission to stay with her at her London flat. Regent said he had lots of loose cash in his mess.

He agreed he would bring whatever cash he could find and I would pay the rest. Money was not important, but Regent's life.

I did not know what kind of specialist Regent should see but was planning to start with a heart specialist.

1-0034: WHY DID THEY LIE ON MY MEDICAL RECORD MARCH 17,2014

The following morning was Monday 17th March 2014, and I was scheduled to return to London. Regent begged me to stay. He took me into the shopping center, which was like a catacomb, and got me breakfast at one of the internal cafes.

Despite having seen Regent, the "Grand ticking whale", abandon my side to immerse himself in a tub of hot water to keep his body from going cold, I did not have a clue that he might be dying.

Maybe I was living in denial. However, I lacked sufficient medical facts to suspect that this was a sign that death was nigh.

To date, nobody has told me whether this is a sign that death is nigh. It probably is.

Hell, I did not know. Had I known, no one could have moved me from his side. Not that at that stage I could have saved his life, although I may have delayed his death. Maybe the doctors could have delayed his death by another two years. Not me. But if they were not willing to try out much-needed procedures, only God would be a witness of the doctors' secret.

I am not the type that would overstay somewhere from feeling and skip an appointment or other activity. I caught that train back after we hugged and kissed.

As my train got closer to London, I did not feel well. I decided to go straight to A and E, rather than home, at the end of my journey.

At the A and E, I waited some hours then told a doctor I could not wait and felt very poorly. The doctor agreed to see me; however; when he or she was questioning me, I fainted without realizing it.

I became aware of a commotion around me and they were talking about a woman they wanted to be moved to a ward quickly, and after a couple of minutes realized they were talking about me.

They asked me to get into a wheelchair, which I did not mind anymore. It was a long ride and my left side became so weak I felt I could go to sleep forever and there would be no pain or suffering. I felt okay about sleeping forever.

However, I phoned Regent on my mobile, from the moving wheelchair and asked him to pray for me, as my left side was weak. I guess I would not have asked him that, had I had a clue that he was going to die.

Once they had got me into my bed, I read a notice in front which said I was at high risk of a heart attack or stroke. But they gave me toast and tea and my left side started to get better.

They removed the board and denied I was at risk of a heart attack or stroke. They even denied that they had put up such a board. It was less than 10 minutes since they had removed the board. I fancy that if I had been unable to read what was written on that board, the doctors would have retained the board by my bedside, and possibly even given me treatments that they felt might help.

Telling a patient they do not have an illness when they do can result in withholding much-needed treatment. In some cases, the patient can die. However, the focus in my case is not to make me die, (which may happen as a side-effect of their actions), but to make me feel at all times that I am perfectly healthy. This is part of a long-standing pattern I have noticed.

In my opinion, if a doctor was motivated to kill me or another hospitalized patient, it would be criminal, and extremely rare to carry it out. A passive way to achieve an intended death, (as was carried out in the case of Regent Exeter) is to just neglect them. Lie to them they are normal until they are dying. If the doctor is lucky then maybe the patient would die too soon to ask the doctor any questions about his or her condition.

I suppose this type of passive killing may be hard to prove. Therefore, illegality is not relevant. Medical malpractice lawsuits are also not relevant, as they would be outside the reach of most people, I think.

I repeat: Active or passive killing of myself would not be a motive of the medical profession. That is just my personal opinion. I could be mistaken. Their motive, I feel, is to make me believe I am in the pink of health at all times, even when I feel very ill.

But the medics don't understand that in some cases they have not fooled me. A doctor cannot assess the literacy or intelligence of patients, and their lies are detected from time to time, on the spot.

A couple of days later they were giving me no painkillers in the hospital and I had a lot of one-sided facial pain. I decided to get myself discharged against their wishes to eat painkillers.

Later they had fake medical records of me that I had come to the hospital because I sprained my ankle. Nobody would be admitted to a hospital ward -or would they- because they sprained their ankle. But that's what they put on record.

1-0035: Nice Plans

Regent and I had planned that he would visit London in April 2014, and we would see specialists there. We would try to see them on the NHS, otherwise Regent would bring whatever money he had, and if he did not have enough, I would pay the rest.

He planned to stay with his sister in London, and he had written a book and wanted to attend the London Book Fair. We had arranged everything.

1-0036: WE LOVED BIRD AND MONKEY CALLS

There was a room in the British library where we were going to go and listen to the calls of thousands of birds and animals. Regent, who called me "cheeky monkey" liked to make chattering noises like a monkey.

1-0037: I did the Right Things, but not at the Right Speed

The only mistake was that I did not know how urgent the matter was. I did not worry sufficiently about the unknown preparation that was making Regent worse, even though I knew it was wrong.

I must have left the hospital around the 19th or 20th of March 2014 after being admitted on the 17th. At that point, my plans to take Regent to the London book fair had to be canceled. "I just do not feel I can walk around a building," said Regent. We decided we would do nothing other than medical visits as soon as he came to London in the first week of April.

Regent had shouted, "I am in! I am in!". He was a human being and a good one. He wanted to live, love and laugh.

1-0038: But He did not make it into April

Foolishly, I thought my darling friend was going to recover in London and we would go to those places he loved.

Regent died unexpectedly on the 26th of March 2014.

After a brief hospital stay after my last visit to Regent's home in Shifnal, I was doing the "immigration thing" as always. I was using the phone a lot and I had an appointment with the lawyer. I was just about to leave home and my mobile phone rang. It was the 26th of March.

I heard some weird sound; it sounded like a woman gasping, but I wasn't sure.

I had had so many phone and online pranks played on me that I thought this was just another prank from an anonymous caller. Unperturbed, I attended the lawyer's office. .

1-0039: Three Unusual Happenings on a Single Day

The next day was the 27th of March when something very unusual happened. I had been living with Mr. A since sometime in 2006 or 2007. For the first time, I locked myself out of his house. I had no place to go.

I went to the nearby pub called Leftelsex Arms. I bought myself a meal because I had nothing to do but wait until Mr. A came back from work at 5:30.pm.

The pub lady served me two meals instead of one. This was the second unusual thing that happened. She said it was an accident but not to worry -to eat them both.

As I ate, my mobile phone rang. It was Regent's sister speaking more coherently now -she said Regent had died. I was sobbing. The pub lady didn't say a word but looked the other way. It was 5:30 pm, and I went home. Mr. A came home and let me in, and I told him what had happened.

I was going to go to Miss C's place in Waterloo where she stays with her partner Mr. F from time to time, and a "gaga" mother, Anne, who doesn't understand anything.

When trying to check-in at the London underground

barriers to go to Waterloo, I realized I didn't have any money on my Oyster card. But the man working on the ticket barrier said I could travel without a ticket. He opened the barrier with his magnetic card and waved me through. This was the third unusual thing that happened to me, and I arrived at Miss C's.

1-0040: Plunged into the Darkness

The other thing I did in March after the bad news on the 27th was to visit Shifnal. I did not tell anyone and arrived after midnight. I did the 10-minute walk to Regent's house. I wanted to enter and felt terrified of seeing his body. I decided I had to face it.

Whenever I slept or closed my eyes, I could see a knife with drops of blood falling from it. I wondered why I was having such dreams; would I discover clues around his body?

I knew he had had difficulty breathing, had laid down, and died. I did not realize police would remove the body. But they had changed the lock as part of their procedure. I shone the light on one of Regent's toys- a green plastic grasshopper lying just outside the locked door. It was upside-down, looking like a real grasshopper that had just died.

I did not need accommodation. The railway station was the only place to spend the night. It was past 1 am. The station was locked, and outside there was a bench in the moonlight, where I sat down, and contemplated dozing off.

I have traveled with a shoulder bag and wonder what would happen to that bag if I went off to sleep on the bench, in the cold. Soon I realized more was at risk than my bag at that isolated spot. A lone male loitered towards the railway station and started to pester me.

He told me if I had some fun with him he would give me hotel money. I replied I was here following the death of a friend, but he just went on and on talking about giving him some fun and he would pay me very well. I started feeling scared as he put his arm around and a cop car drove past. I shouted for help to it.

The cop just drove away, but luckily, the man seemed to sober up. He said to me he was waiting for a taxi. I said I, too, was waiting for my taxi. His taxi came and he left.

There was a toilet outside the railway station near the bench which I opened with a radar key bought on eBay for 2 bucks. I knew it was illegal to sleep in there but unsafe on the bench. It was toasty warm inside and I snatched a few hours of sleep before someone entered in the dead of night.

It was the cleaner on his early morning rounds. He chased me out and helped me get a taxi. I was dropped off at one of those rest places on the highway which are open round-the-clock for weary travelers to fill petrol and break their journey.

I did have sufficient money for coffee and taxis, just not for a hotel stay. I took a taxi back into Shifnal late in the morning.

David and Jonathan, Regent's friends saw me standing by the road and there is only one main road in Shifnal. David had not realized Regent had died. Jonathan asked me to stay the night on his couch. There was a complicated way to enter without the female porter knowing.

If she found out, she would scream hell and murder and put me on the street at 2 am, and the men who let me in would be severely punished probably through psychiatry, and increased dosage. She would make a case she had to screen guests before entering premises where "vulnerable" people lived.

Jonathan said the night after Regent's death his lamp seemed brighter and it felt like Regent's ghost was telling him he was okay now, and not to grieve anymore.

The next morning I went back onto High Street and tried asking how it happened, but they weren't speaking. I learned later police do not release records of a deceased person to family and close friends.

The town witnesses, however, were generous with information. On 25th March I had a strange anonymous email sent to my Yahoo mail. At 10 pm that night Regent had paid a visit to the same pub we had been to before we said our goodbyes for the last time. He left his cap there. At 5 am on 26th March he phoned his sister about having difficulty breathing and asked for help.

She said she and her brother had been in a fight and she did not realize it was urgent and had gone back to sleep. At 7 am I was chatting to Regent just about frustrations and never once did he let on that he was in peril or feeling very bad. Eyewitnesses then saw him go for a walk and back home, walking extremely slowly.

He left his mobile and wallet on the kitchen counter and walked to the bed. He had not gotten up from the bed, and police said death had come very fast, in 5-10 minutes. However, they confirmed that Regent had not suffered a "myocardial infarct".

Regent's front door was bolted from inside. Jonathan had knocked on Regent's door for a casual chat and found that he was not answering. Jonathan had informed the female porter in his locked building that Regent was inside the house, but was not answering.

She took her own sweet time to call non-emergency police, who eventually broke Regent's door at 10-11 am to find Regent, who looked as if he was sleeping peacefully in his bed, but had died.

The charity shop ladies said Regent had been to Princess Royal Hospital in Telford and then to a lawyer to write his will. He had gone into the charity shop wildly waving an A4-sized brown paper envelope jubilantly at 4 pm on 25th March. Regent told the charity shop ladies he had just written his will and seemed thrilled about it. Naturally, they had not expected that he would die the next morning.

The charity shop ladies said Doctor B must have told him he was about to die, days before the end came, based on the kinds of remarks Regent was making about Doctor B.

Regent had bought some vases earlier, and before he died, he had re-donated them to the charity shop. The charity shop ladies said they loved him to pieces, and each one bought off one of those vases to take home in memory of him.

That night the female porter saw me trying to enter the locked building. I could not stay at Jonathan's. Luckily it was possible to get a train to London. Before April began Miss C's partner, Mr. F asked me to stay with them for some time to keep company with Miss C.

On April 2, before getting a train to Ludlow from London, I received a call from a young lady who called herself Jasmine and wanted me to invest in Gummy Bear movies. I link her to the Gummy Bear emails series, which I feel may have been referring to Regent.

However, while my niece is also called Jasmine (Wortley) I was sure due to her regional twang that she could not possibly have been my niece, who is an Anglo-Indian. My niece was interested in acting and film production.

In Ludlow, we drove to Shifnal and had the door opened by police as pre-arranged. She found pills near his bed she put in her bag while we found the will and his next psychiatric appointment, which was soon, and his cardiac result was to arrive on 27th March. We also saw the village lawyer who wrote Regent's will.

Miss C and Mr. F did not behave well, as Mr. F became hostile when I talked of foul play. Mr. F was aggressive about not wanting an inquest I was in tears and tried to leave. He wanted the whole thing to be over as quickly as possible.

Mr. F wanted Mrs. A, the surviving sister of Miss C placed in lifelong psychiatric care. Regent, Miss C, and their common mother Anne had not been on speaking terms with Mrs. A until Regent's death. I realized that Miss C and Mrs. A were inheriting Anne's estate and that Miss C would have it all if Mrs. A could be placed in lifelong psychiatric care, which Mr. F would partake of, as her husband.

Mrs. A lived by herself in a council flat and had a lifelong love-hate relationship with her husband. Miss C said Mrs. A's husband's name was "Court". He also lived separately in a council flat. They could not live together or apart. Miss C had been with her partner Mr. F, who hails from South America, for 15-20 years, and they lived apart from mutual consent.

Miss C remained in her mother's Ludlow house taking care of her mother, while Mr. F worked and paid the rent on a posh London. Regent had said Miss C stayed in that house with her mother, so she could inherit the house, while Mr. F gave her the advantage of having a posh place to go in London. In return, he got a posh place to live in. I don't think Miss C was having a business relationship with her partner-it was a personal one- however, they lived apart by mutual consent.

They said it was madness, I could not go at this time of night, which I insisted must happen. Miss C and Mr. F telephoned Ludlow police and lied that I had threatened suicide and that they were family who wanted to prevent me from leaving.

Miss C even snatched my mobile and phoned Mr. A in London, from whom I had lived apart intermittently, and tried to convince him I was presently insane.

When Ludlow police arrived, luckily they ruled I was free to leave and drove me to the railway station. It was a late evening with no method of buying a travel ticket. The ticket offices had closed. I boarded a train without a ticket, knowing that it was the last service until morning.

The ticket inspector came by. I was sure there was going to be trouble, but asked loudly, when he was still far away, "Would you like to see my ticket please?" To my utter disbelief, he waved me by. This train was the last service, and Wolverhampton was the last stop.

A taxi driver advised me the local police station would be appropriate for me to stay the night. I had cash to pay for the taxi, but not a hotel.

They were very kind at Wolverhampton police station and allowed me to sleep on a bench in the waiting room. At about 4 in the morning, I was able to take a taxi back to the rail station. It had just opened and was freezing. I thought I was alone but saw in the distance a staff member carrying coffees in a tray. She was walking towards me. She gave me a coffee. It was so nice of her.

1-0041: By Coincidence, I walked into a Hospice near one Regent's Canal in London

I was given legal advice that the only thing for his family was to contact Regent's other surviving sister, Mrs. A, and inform her of her rights to inherit (half of) their mother's property along with Miss C.

Regent had told me all of them were not on speaking terms with Mrs. A.

Miss C and her partner Mr. F had said Mrs. A was a mental case and recluse who did not welcome visitors, not even themselves.

I was able to find Mrs. A's last name, using 192.com. Men always have the same last name. Unmarried women keep their maiden name, and married women go either under their maiden name or under their married name.

If you are unable to trace a female because you don't know her married name, this can be often found on Google without hassles. Public address databases, such as 192.com hold historic information in a jumbled-up mess, which makes them useful for finding last names and other information you don't have. Googling the full name of a relative or housemate can lead to finding an unknown last name when you know a person's first name.

Withheld phone numbers may actually be public on a different register, or a tenant may be using a homeowner's number which he or she is keeping as being under their own number but keeping it unlisted.

Using her first and last name, I looked on the London online electoral register and got a list of persons under the same first and last name. I was able to strike off most of them as mismatches, based on their ages and description of people living with them. I found one record that was almost certain to be the person I was looking for.

Using a Google map I walked a considerable distance around the mazes in Hackney. I found the address in question, but no one answered the doorbell, nor did the house have a nameplate. I left a note under that door for Mrs. A, not knowing if it was the right place.

On my return journey home, I found myself on the main road leading to Bethnal Green Underground Station but believed I had lost my way. In front of me was a canal intersecting my road, and the road became a bridge over that canal.

It was called REGENT'S CANAL. With misty eyes, I got to the lower level and watched the barges crawl under the bridge. This man-made waterway had a 1-foot wide concrete pavement on each side, under the arch of the bridge. Some people walked on the water's edge under the bridge. I decided it was dark down there and could be slippery as well, so I gave up the idea of walking along the canal under the bridge and climbed to the street level.

The only place where I could ask my way was St Joseph's Hospice on the left side of the road, before the bridge. I would not normally go into a hospice but was thinking of Regent, and the fact I had come to a hospice just next to a Regent's canal in London town.

Inside the main building, I entered a large hall. There was staff seated at tables near the entrance. Some were extremely fat and others had seemingly misshapen heads. I decided that all the receptionists must be terminally ill; nonetheless, they told me how to get to Bethnal Green underground terminal.

The notable thing was at the hospice, there were lots of tables filled with vases and other glassware that had a look of abandonment. There was an unmistakable resemblance to the décor in Regent's house when I was with him for the last time. All that clutter of glassware looked like weeds growing in an empty field where nobody would go. There was a feeling of derelict ruins and lifeless wilderness.

1-0042: Summary of the Medical Side

Doctor B must have told Regent he was about to die, on or shortly before March 25th, 2014. Regent disclosed something to charity shop ladies on 25th March which made them sure of this.

So, the death was not a surprise to the doctor. It's just that family and friends didn't know and the patient himself didn't know. That Regent was expected to die was the GP's well-kept secret.

The long-standing arrangement had been for Regent to attend Doctor B's surgery once in 30 days. During those meetings, Doctor B. would write a prescription for Regent's long-term, "maintenance" dose of Flu-penthixol. He would also go over him with a stethoscope and write down his blood pressure as doctors normally do.

18 months after Regent's death, I managed to get Regent's medical records because they were ordered to release them by the Office of the Parliamentary Ombudsman. The records office in Shrewsbury took six months to release them after a request was made. Those blood pressure readings were in the medical records, a thick file.

These records revealed that throughout 2013, (that is,

on 12 different occasions), Regent's blood pressure was noted once a month when Dr. B had found it to be above the danger level.

As you could guess by now, Doctor B did not give Regent any medicine,

Any doctor knows better than laypeople that blood pressure is a killer. Doctor B knew better than everyone else that he was shortening the man's life by not giving him blood pressure medication. By keeping the BP diagnosis secret, Doctor B prevented Regent from seeking treatment for the same from a different doctor.

This situation is the same as for anyone else who has a life-threatening condition, which their doctor keeps secret, waiting for God to remove the patient from the planet in His own time.

Medical records also showed that Regent was invited to take part in a 24-hour blood pressure monitoring in October 2013. The invitation to take this test was a deceptively-worded letter.

The letter claimed if Regent didn't turn up and collect the equipment, the time slot would be given to someone else.

The letter was designed for the patient not to understand

that he had a serious or life-threatening condition.

His blood pressure was very high in the 24-hour blood test as well.

But the doctor never informed him and didn't give him any medication for his soaring systolic, 200-220+.

1-0043: Non-medical Forensic Evidence of Death Hope Plot

About the two email series

Two series of emails plagued me for six months following Regent's death. I can call them the "Gummy Bear" series, and the "graveyard series". I recieved a total of around 200 emails in the series out together. They lasted out for around 6 months, the last one (belonging to the graveyard series) in September 2014, when the sender advised I get a life insurance policy and commit suicide. Both series appeared to target the death of Regent, making all kinds of bizarre jokes about the same

The sender had enough skill and sense of course, to conceal his(their)IP address and physical location completely.

In both email series, the sender(s) owned up to the sender name Jasmine

The Gummy bear emails started BEFORE Regent's death, and lasted for less time than the graveyard emails which started shortly AFTER his death. The graveyard ones were from one Jasmine alias "ICI". They petered out by the end of September 2014. as "ICI" on these emails (a sample is displayed) was connected to an encrypted, or gibberish email, a website for a company with that name was not present. I do not know if it is an existing company.

I put all these emails, as they kept coming through the months of 2014, into a customized folder of my Yahoo mail. I also made pdf prints which I saved to disk. **The very first email arrived on the evening of 25th March, which was the eve of his death.**

I had already saved that offending PRE-DEATH email of 25.3.2014 to disc. It is the first email of the gummy bear series, and I have displayed it here, in this book.

Description of the Gummy Bear email series

The Gummy Bear emails were about a movie called "Gummy Bear". These emails urged me to put money into the movie. I feel that "Gummy Bear" could refer to Regent himself, based on his physical appearance. The emails read, "8 billion people watched and loved Gummy Bear; 8 billion people can't be wrong."

It was obviously a fictitious item of information. I do not think the world's population is at 8 billion today, in 2021, and would have been a lot less in 2014. And it is not possible that every human being in the world watched that movie.

Can I track who sent the gummy bear emails because

they (apparently) came from a domain called spicefactoryfilms.com? See my "gummy bear" slides below to view this information

Domains on the internet can be looked up for free on who. is. That will give you the name and address of its owner. But the truth is more complicated.

Domains with the suffix ".uk" are British, and they are under Nominet, who don't allow domain owners to hide their name and address. However, you just have to pay for a domain, and don't have to show ID. Poeple could easily give a fake name or address to Nominet. The address (location) of the owner could be fake, or the name of a company, or the address of their website host or registrar. No one but the police who can subpeona a website/ domain owner's details can trace a website/domain owner.

The domain used, spicefactoryfilms.com in the gummy bear email series is a dotcom (American) domain and it is legal for a website/domain owner to conceal their identity completely for a fee, or for free. Only a police investigation would be able to track them. Almost everyone, but not everyone can be tracked by police.

What happens if who.is says that a domain you type into its search box does not belong to anyone? It will say this is available, and you can buy it. This means either the domain was never owned by anyone, or someone owned it, and stopped paying their annual subscription for the domain. If you do a paid search on who.is, you can tell if a domain (for example spicefactoryfilms) was registered to someone in Tonbridge Wells at any point in history, ever since the internet started.

Clues I found in the Gummy bears emails of which 1 email is displayed below

The web domain quoted here, spicefactoryfilms.com was addressed to an owner in Tonbridge Wells. By coincidence? that is where Regent was born. There were the numbers 14 and 70, and coming up from a deeper analysis of the longer version of the emails, and the address where Regent had died was 14 The Willows.

A deeper analysis of the Gummy Bear emails also led to an acting school. By the way, my real niece Jasmine of Hampshire had gone through a stage when she was interested in drama and acting.

Who could have sent those emails? My clues

 In September 2014 someone (not myself) had (obviously) entered my Yahoo mail and deleted ONLY the email that I received before Regent died. This is very suspicious indeed. The sender(s) must have known hacking, in a way that he might potentially hold of someone's email password, AND he/they regreted sending me THAT ONE PRE-DEATH

EMAIL mocking the death. The remainder of the 200 (or 199) emails (approximately) that were in one of the two above-mentioned series were also mocking Regent Exeter's death, but they were all POST-DEATH.

I assume that the sender(s) of the emails were not sure (as nobody can be) that the police would not investigate this matter. I assume the sender(s) of the emails felt the fact he/they knew of the death BEFORE it happened, was far more incriminating than the simple fact they were gloating over his death.

In the analysis above, I am making a strong assumption (1)the sender(s) was/were not a medical professional, nor (2) were they a personal friend or acquaintance of Regent Exeter, who did not have friends with IT skills and that type of mischief.(3) I feel the sender(s) is/are either a lone, tech-savvy male who singlehandedly engineered this mischief, or a group of evil/hateful adults including one or more tech-savvy persons

It is now proven Regent's doctor(s) deliberately shortened Regent's life, there is also mere speculation Doctor B administered an unknown substance (prepared through secret instructions to the pharmacist) speeding up of the man's deterioration starting in the new year 2014, or carried out a high-risk clinical trial or scientific experiment.

Why would a doctor share that type of information with a

non-medical person(s) that one of his patients would die soon, when they are not friends or family of the victim? It would be a confidential secret among one or more doctors, unless they chose to advise the patient of the bad news.

I further assume, (or estimate), that (4) the sender(s) might have needed at least two weeks time to prepare these two series of emails, which means the sender(s) knew (only source was Regents doctor(s)) two weeks or more prior to Regent's death he was about to die. Which suggests the doctors were sharing information on Regent's deterioration with one adult or a group of adults who would be glad if he died. Which is unbelievable and suggests persons in the non-medical community had a vested interest in his death, or at least rejoiced when it came

That offending PRE-DEATH email of 25.3.2014 was deleted by someone in September 2014 leaving the rest of the emails intact. (5)I am assuming the email was deleted by the person(s) who sent the gummy bear series of graveyard series of emails, or someone who is their ally and friend. He/they may have hoped I won't notice the deletion. I did notice the deletion, and the approximate date of deletion, which wad September 2014.

Finding about Jasmine my niece in internet searches

My mother had said my real niece Jasmine Wortley born

in 1997 was interested in drama and romance, while her younger brother wanted to become a pirate when he turned 18.

Internet searches,that were not conclusive, suggested that Miss Jasmine Wortley had an internet companion, also aged around 15 years, who lived in the Indian village of Dundahera.

This was where my father had worked as Chairman of Indian Drugs and Pharmaceuticals and kept me a virtual prisoner in his home for 9 long years 1986 to 1995.

And whereas my father keeping me virtual prisoner is historic (many years ago), I carried out these internet searches in 2011-2013, and any information I found out about the real Jasmine was fresh

This 15-year old Indian teenager in Dundahera, whose name was Trisha or Trishna was making childish films, and her parents, obviously loaded with money, were allowing their young daughter to buy film shooting equipment.

My father would not have any connection with Dundahera (location) except that he had worked there, and if this teenager was known to my niece, it was through my father because Trish's father must have been an IDPL employee to live in a weird place like Dundahera.

My father must have introduced his granddaughter (my niece) through the internet to a girl in India of her age who aspired to become a film producer and had already gone into amateurish production. The Indian teen visited Singapore and had stuck photos of English boys on her blogs, and it was clear she was crazy about the idea of having an English boyfriend. She may have hoped my niece would introduce her to local English boys, which would be a motive for the friendship.

Anonymous caller used my niece's name to advise on the Gummy Bear emails she said she sent. The graveyard and gummy bear series of emails both carry in print a sender name Jasmine

I also got a call from someone on a withheld number who called themselves "Jasmine" on April 2, 2014, asking me to invest in film production, I noted it was the voice of a young female.

Based on age, it could have been my niece. However, my niece is an Anglo-Indian, and the caller was a native speaker of English with a strong regional twang. My blood relative could never sound like that.

Description of the graveyard series

The sender who constructed those Gummy Bear emails had spent a lot of time, effort and ingenuity had gone into their authorship. The same must be said about the graveyard series of emails.

The keyword of the graveyard series was ICI an acronym that allegedly stood for a company that sold graves in Hampshire. I cannot remember now whether I did check this out and whether such a company did exist.

This email series said, "You can't prevent death, but you can become rich from it.". The company was selling unused graves to people who would hold them for a few years and sell them at double the price to people in need of a grave when the grave prices were much higher.

The tone and message changed gradually in the graveyard emails, which went from urging me to buy unoccupied graves to pretended sympathy emails where the sender pretended I was dying of cancer and constantly sent support and coffee invitations from Macmillan's.

The emails claimed repeatedly that I can enjoy life even when I was dying of cancer.

Towards the end of the series of these emails, the sender was musing about the afterlife and one of the last ones asked me, "Hersom! Why do not you buy an expensive life insurance policy and then commit suicide!"

The sender of these emails was obviously poking fun at the fact I had faced the death of a dear friend. But the thing about ICI was that it was also the name of the company Imperial Chemical Industries, where my father worked 29 years and finally in the UK branches, and was dismissed from ICI.

ICI, a chemical company making pesticides and paints shut down in 2007 and gave rise to child companies AstraZeneca and?/or Akzo Nobel.

My trip to Ludlow to Regent's sister's place, and medical findings

Later that same day (April 2, 2014), I traveled to Ludlow. Miss C and Mr.F picked me up at the railway station.

Mr.F had been told by the police who discovered his body that Regent had not had a heart attack and that the cause of death was undetermined.

So, in January 2014, the medical record states Doctor B took Regent's ECG. There was a letter from Doctor B to a cardiologist at Princess Royal hospital in nearby Telford, saying Regent had elongated QT waves.

This is a type of condition showing up in the ECG which leads to death. Long-term consumption of psychiatric medication often leads to this.

In this correspondence to the cardiologist, Doctor B also stated that he intended to give Regent blood pressure medicine. This happened in early January 2014.

Their cardiologist had written back to Doctor B, asking him to stop the psychiatric medication, and he said the condition would almost certainly get better. "If you need to give Mr. Exeter psychiatric medication that you should use a different preparation", the letter said.

As January 2014 came and went, Doctor B failed to give Regent blood pressure medicine, and continued to keep it a secret from him.

I discovered much later that doctors often do not tell a patient they have a serious, or life-threatening condition. It is very scary.

Regent fell off a high stool at a tapas bar where he had taken me for a meal, hit his head on the ground, and suffered a nosebleed. But he said he had recovered, and we went back home. He said it happened sometimes. He had just been drinking, and felt unwell, he said.

Neither Regent nor I knew the fact that high blood pressure is a silent killer, and that nosebleeds are a common side-effect. Regent kept blaming his awful cough on his smoking. It was obvious that he was not smoking. He had smoked years ago. Who hasn't?

Regent and I did not have a clue the cough could be from a heart-lung condition, or heart failure, often found in people as fat as he was, and as a direct consequence of his long-term intake of Flu-penthixol.

I told him though the problem was a real ailment needing a doctor, and not because of smoking. Regent would obsessively blame his smoking, saying "this cough is sure to kill me". Like it did in due course of time.

I started to get sick a couple of years after Regent died, with heart problems and high bkood pressure

You see, I became ill at the end of 2015, which chronic cough, and tiredness, and this was heart failure, which doctors have been denying to this date. This problem, and my spiraling blood pressure which was similar to Regent's, have been controlled by Bisoprolol given in Ireland shortly after my arrival. I continue to be semi-invalid needing further diagnoses and care.

However, I now have the knowledge I needed to have in 2011-2013, to extend Regent's life and increase its quality as well. I would have got him to doctors the first day I met him, had I had any comprehension of the problem and the late Regent Exeter would have only been too happy to avail of such help.

I think at the time I took an overdose, in January 2011, I had "SVT" on my ECG and my QT waves were elongated up to 470ms, while Regent's QT waves were showing as 440ms two weeks before he died, and Google says above 500ms causes death.

I suppose my QT waves were not good the night after my overdose and had I not had a friend save my life from the doctors that night, I may not have seen the sun in the morning. This may have been a full-blown heart attack except they made it a secret and even wrote I pretended to overdose.

They suggested in the medical record of my overdose date that I was pretending to overdose and that I suffered from depression. This magical word means anything I say can be trashed. That's how the public is. But the Medical Records Office acted independently of doctors and released my medical record of the overdose day, including an ECG taken during the event, whose details would support the possibility I did overdose.

Maybe I suffered permanent cardiac injury as a result of that episode. In that case, failure to admit I had a heart attack or whatever, and thus failing to record this fact, and failing to provide post-cardiac support, may have been malpractice and may have risked my life close to the event.

I have not understood exactly what depression means but feel women and depression go together like horse and carriage. When a woman is announced as suffering from depression, I think everyone feels happy.

But I should not think of myself, as I have suffered little psychiatric abuse compared to Regent, an alpha male of the species, and want to remember that he was one of the men imprisoned in a female-dominated category.

I just recall what has happened to me in the years after Regent's passing, I realize if I had had such understanding at that time, we could have together increased the quantity and quality of his life, mind you heart failure had already set in.

My elongated QT waves were longer than Regent's, but maybe mine died down but his stayed elongated over a long period, leading to death.

Regent got worse and worse, as all his medical problems were kept secret by Dr. B until his passing.

How the hell did these emails happen?

Since both series come from a Jasmine, and both

series joke about the death of my friend, and since an anonymous caller said she was Jasmine, and wanted me to invest money in the Gummy Bear movie, I must assume the senders of both series of emails are the same party, person or group of persons

The Gummy bear series indicated a knowledge of Regent's physical appearance, his address(where he died) and place of birth, as well as the fact my niece liked drama

The graveyard series indicated a knowledge of my father's place of work which is ancient. My parents left the UK in 1983. He left ICI under dismissal and fighting in 1983-84. ICI was shut down in 2007, and hardly anyone would know about it.

My parents lived in India since and did not come to stay in England until I arrived as a newlywed in December 2004, following me around like death around the globe. They and my sister made phone calls to my husband, and flashed their money around creating a prison for me which was now supported by the British system

This time, my father was 70 and long-retired. They bought a freehold house in the UK in 2006 and pretended to me they were still living in India permenently and only visiting the UK until 2010, when I had discovered their secret.

As if anyone would know where the geriatric person next door worked if they lived in multiple countries, and the company was shut down long ago! Maybe an Indian person, also elderly would have information like that about my father. Now my father does have some cronies like that, but they don't fit the bill. They would not send emails mocking someone's passing

My parents live in West Reading and my sister lives 6-12 miles from them and is close to the Atomic Weapons Establishment. My parents are old Indians. Regent was someone I met on Facebook, who lived in remote Shropshire.

Regent had nothing to do with my family. So it is not physically possible there could be any person who knew my family and also knew Regent.

I cannot think of a human being that would have insider knowledge of my family as well as insider knowledge of one of Doctor B's patients, the late Regent Exeter

Trumped-up criminal conviction

Since I am the subject of a trumped-up(I claim) criminal conviction in 2013, where the liars were my blood relatives, I cannot put them past all kinds of dishonesty and misconduct. See 1-0025 The Pesthilenseroke Society for details. Furthermore, the stalking of myself by the them is detailed in 1-0025, 3-0012, 3-0022, 3-0027, 3-0029

Therefore, if the sender of these "Gummy Bear" and "Graveyard" emails had details of my family, the first people I would investigate as culprits would be members of my own family.

But unlike my family, I have scruples against making up unfounded accusations to the police.

No other member of my family except my mother had any scruples in this matter of lying to the police.

They are unafraid of criminal activities.

I, on the other hand, need to be truthful. To me, victory is to win by telling the truth.

To me, a happy relationship is one I tell the truth and get accepted on that basis. I would never find happiness in a relationship if I was accepted while pretending to be who I am not.

My mother 86, is computer illiterate like most women of her generation. To my knowledge, my father does know some hacking and IT tricks, but the content of the two emails series -the nature of spite in them-involved youthfulness (I felt) and a different kind of hatred than was typical of my father.

I know my father, and these emails were certainly not authored by my father. I am confident my sister and brother-in-law Viju and Steve Wortley do not have the IT skills to do it-I would bet my money on that. The children Jasmine and Robin are too young for that level of wickedness.

I believe the young are pure of heart. Corruption sets in much later in life.

Both email series referred to Regent's death, and I infer were sent by the same person or persons.

I would say to make all these elaborate plans to poke fun over Regent's death, like buying/using specific domains would have taken at least two weeks of preparation.

That is, in my estimation, they took two weeks or more to plan these creative acts of hatred.

Thus I infer that the culprit(s) knew that Regent would soon die two weeks before they send the email on 25 March. On 25 March the culprit(s) also had the privileged knowledge that the time of death was drawing close.

If you accept that considerable IT skills went into these creative acts, poking fun of Regent's death, we must remember that skill and spite are not always companions.

So if you want to do an act of spite, but lack the skill you will need to pay someone with skill to help you engineer such crafty moves. Essentially that skilled person is unlikely to have the spite. If you poke fun at someone's death, skilled people with scruples won't assist you in exchange for payment.

In my opinion, the culprit possessed a combination of skill and spite, that they are no child. I also do not expect a medical doctor to have IT skills or spend time on an activity so different from the type of work they do.

This means an adult(s) who is not a medical professional, and possesses a combination of skill and spite engineered those emails, possessing personal information about Regent Exeter and historical and in-depth knowledge of my family members, who I consider, except for my mother, to be plaintiffs of my criminal conviction.

If you agree (you may not) with no reasoning thus far then one or more adults with no medical background knew that Regent would die soon two weeks before he died, who were hostile to Regent and me.

I met Regent about 7 days before his death and I can say

confidently he did not know for sure it was coming. He said he was getting worse but talked about wanting to build a house and go on a world tour. He was not suicidal and not sure his death was imminent.

So the non-medical culprit(s) had this knowledge which Regent and people close to him lacked, and I would have thought such privileged information would rest solely with medical professionals.

What all happened the day before he died

Moreover Regent went to the charity shop after a hectic day, 25 March 2014. On that day, he visited his GP and visited Princess Royal Hospital unaided, and using public transport, and walked to the village lawyer, paid 100 pounds, and wrote his will. He then walked into the charity shop jubilantly waving a brown A-4 sized envelope and told the ladies it was his will.

I infer that Regent had received fresh information, which he had definitely lacked 7 days earlier when I was there with him, that death was coming very fast.

Regent was on a running race against death to write his will and was jubilant that he had won that race.

I am not sure whether I have fully and properly explained

my reasoning here. If I have done, I know people may agree or disagree. Based on facts stated exactly as they are here, can I come to the conclusions stated here?

I told him I hated how I was treated in the UK, which is like a woman-gulag, and that I would like to leave the UK.

Regent often said "I too want to leave the UK and go somewhere pleasant. Why don't we just die in each other's arms?"

I mean, Regent did not act like he knew his death was imminent. He had always said his cough was so uncomfortable he was sure it would kill him.

Let me call this person (or party) who sent emails making fun of Regent's death and then creating my virtual death scene was a single human being. Let's call him "Mr. X" I do not know who he is plus the police do not want to open that Pandora's box.

Let's say, "Mr. X" either knows his identity is safely secret.

Or "Mr. X" is unsure of his privacy. He worries that people might find out who he is.

In either case, the March 25th email had information that Regent was going to die several hours before his death. All this makes Regents death look like it was a HOMICIDE.

Miss C and I: outcome of complaint process: The end

I had saved the March 25th email to disk shortly after it arrived. So when someone got into my email and deleted it, I still had a copy.

"Mr. X" spent a lot of time and effort (to put it briefly) to create (buy) two domains. The owner's name is of course suppressed because it is an American dot-com domain where one is allowed to buy privacy.

I got a right from the Ombudsman to have a one-to-one meeting with Doctor B. I traveled from London to Telford to a fairly remote location. Miss C requested a similar one and received it. I asked for permission to tape my meeting and she was given the same automatically.

Miss C had not originally understood there had been foul play. After she caught on, she said she wanted to complain independently. She felt people would refuse her if she showed any connection to me who was a hated individual. That was clear.

But then I'd want her to have such an advantage. But in the end, I think she ended up getting nowhere, just like me.

She copied me and asked for the same to be given to her. Doctor B gave me an appointment in a different city Telford (not his usual clinic in Shifnal) to interview him.

It was far away from the city center, and he had evacuated the surgery for the day to use for our interview having just me, him and his secretary, and the lady that looked after the reception.

The office of the Ombudsman wrote back that they have rejected my complaint against the doctor and would put me in prison if I showed any person the correspondence exchanged between me and themselves, except for the final refusal decision.

MPs office

I also tried the office of Regent's MP Mark Pritchard for Telford and Wrekin districts, alleging that there were irregularities involved in the death of a kind and gentle man in Shifnal. They replied, "We are only obliged to care for our constituents, and a dead man is no longer a constituent."

He quickly realized his mistake, and added: "We are very interested, so please call in if there are any developments."

Lawyer sad over Regent as his crony, and there is no way to go forward with such a matter in the UK as per the best sources

And I showed this file of emails to a lawyer in an Eastcote building with Mr. A. He was also from a London Elitist school and was sad that someone he could have played football with from a neighboring school had died.

The lawyer was several years older than Regent. He said that normally people paid a thousand pounds to just sit in his presence. But he was seeing me for free as his peer had died. He promised to provide me with the best solution possible in the UK to such a problem.

He phoned many people he knew and then said the only thing that could be done is to write a letter to the Superintendent of Police in this county, Uxbridge, and if they are interested, they will contact you.

If the police decide not to investigate something, there are no remedies in the UK. Some people had already told me there are a lot of problems in the UK which have no legal remedy.

When Regent was alive, a law office told me it was not accepted practice for law firms to dispute medical malpractice (to that date) if the malpractice was psychiatric

During his lifetime I phoned a lawyer about whether we could have a lawsuit about Regents medical damage and obesity under the psychiatric drug Depakote (alias sodium valproate!!).

This in early 2014, was when Regent had found a lawyer to fight with his sister about his mother's will. They said other people had made inquiries about suing for medical damage due to psychiatric drugs and we won't take the case as we do not think such a complaint can be made in the UK.

The connection between my (trumped-up I claim) criminal conviction and the gummy bear and graveyard emails series

The other detail I wish to provide is about the trumped-up criminal conviction. There were a lot of documents including extraneous and irrelevant ones presented to me as the allegation list while I was held overnight at Basingstoke police station.

I was shown what looked (based on thickness) like 700 pages of A4 size they alleged came from Pesthilenseroke which is surprising as I never engaged with them. What could they possibly write about me? It was also a fraud if they had written anything about me without meeting me.

My family the plaintiffs met Pesthilenseroke but the latter is not supposed to write an assessment of me without meeting me, which is seen conventionally as fraud. I felt the mental health workers were illiterate and lacked the mental capacity to write letters and reports. I felt Pesthilenseroke must have had literate staff to write letters and fight the battles of the mental health workers.

Still, this would have meant I would later comment or complain about fraudulent assessments by Pesthilenseroke, the lawyers disappeared this file without me opening it.

Other documents shown to me were – one that had been printed off the Basingstoke police station computer printer-another that had been printed on my father's computer. That is based on the watermarks (or small marks along the margin identifying the printer).

This shows that something printed on my father's computer was used to help incriminate me. Did my father help my sister to print out things to incriminate me? Why not, if I am guilty?

It turned out the exhibits were emails I sent to the late

Regent Exeter. Any communication between me and Regent Exeter does not constitute harassment of the plaintiff Mrs. Viju Wortley.

If private one-to-one emails between me and Regent Exeter were printed off my father's computer, they must have been printed by my father and were not a submission of Viju Wortley, who has no hacking skills, and who did not have access to my private communications.

Emails I sent to Regent would not be harassment of my father, and harassment of my father who lives in a separate household 6-12 miles away would not be harassment of Viju Wortley.

Later, my father claimed he did not hack my Gmail, but that I had put these private communications on the web for everybody to see. Nothing could be farther from the truth.

My father had formerly proved he had the ability to force my mobile phone to call him back when I only pushed the button to listen to his voice mail. He fiddled the yahoo clock and was able to send me high-profile emails that always stayed on top of other emails unless deleted.

So why is it impossible he could not hack my Gmail and look around my personal communications?

I am an adult woman, so it is illegal and unethical of my father to check out who I am emailing and what I am saying.

The emails I sent privately to Regent had a story from my own life that is historic, or took place long ago, and it was a story Regent would like. It looks like my father was able to read them, which was not possible under my father somehow found out my password for my gmail email. Below is why my father might now want this story to get out, why he would prefer this story to die with me, why my family would like to keep me in constant pain so the facts die with me. Keeping me as crazy, depriving of a partner so I can be bombarded day and night by Pesthilenseroke, deporting me, keeping me unemployed(life sentence) are distraction techniques to win time till my end, which may or may not be death, comes would keep my testimony away, or no one would believe it.

In these hacked emails I was sharing with Regent Exeter a real-life story of how my parents came to America to abort my studies and life. How they visited Tucson Arizona in 1986 without my knowledge, flying all the way from India, approaching the Tucson Hindu temple for assistance with their goal.

I was getting silent calls as well as threatening calls from the Tucson Hindu Temple, in the wee hours of the morning. The callers were women with South Indian accents saying my mother wanted me to give up my

164

studies and go back to India.

A young Tamilian man Ramanath Gopalan and his wife Meena were presidents of Tucson Hindu Temple. This man was a budding psychiatrist – a resident in psychiatry at The University of Arizona.

This man said to me after kidnapping me that my father had been standing outside Kino Hospital at 6 pm asking him to lock me up for life.

I disbelieved totally and said so. However, a decade later learned this was true.

In 1984 and 1985 my parents visited Tucson and attempted to get psychiatrists to chase after me. They had contacted me on those occasions.

There had been a trip to the US in 1986, kept secret from me, when my mother may not have accompanied my father. I came to know this a decade later, after being in my parents' home from 1986-1995 a virtual prisoner.

I had managed to go to Canada in 1995, after my grandmother passed away, and left me money to leave India. From Canada, I had accessed Gopalan's court records, including his incident with me, which had ended my studies as a graduate student in Physics, and my stay in the UK.

The latter record I had obtained in 1995/6 from Pima County Superior Court in Tuscon, AZ, stated that my father attended that court, along with Gopalan, and requested the court to sanction my involuntary committal.

These court records said my father had said he had come to the US on his business. This was a lie and my father had not disclosed to Pima County Superior Court he was coming to the US to sabotage my studies.

Regarding this story that my father did not have any business in the US, one woman asked how I would know my father was not doing business at the time.

The woman asking that question is someone with GENDER INFERIORITY. She is someone who would leave everything to the menfolk, and live a domesticated life with no interest in what her father does.

It is entirely physically possible that a son or daughter who happens to know their Dad pretty well, to know(or not to know) for sure that the Dad does (or does not) have any business in the US.

The woman asking hostile questions cannot be sure I would not know this fact. She assumes I am exactly like her, ruling out the possibility I might have higher intelligence.

As such women these days are angered by my story these days. Women have not changed or grown in intelligence in the last few decades, but their humility, decency, and kindness have plummeted.

Most others who have been victimized as I have been are men. Women have a lower average mental ability than men to put up a moral resistance.

That is why there are so many agencies and organizations today -to compensate for the mental deficit that distinguishes a man and woman. These support systems-agencies and organizations-have caused people to no longer understand that women lack moral fiber and need others to lean on.

A typical female equivalent of my suffering would be stories filled with and limited to body functions.

She does not go as far as a university or foreign country when her parents are keen on doing her in. These days, such things as going to new places have been made infinitely easy for women, which is why they go.

So under my circumstances, only males (mainly) would

have got where I got. Females under my circumstances would have followed the parents to India, and not gone to the US on their own. If (like was done to me) they were not allowed to get married, they might have become "mentally ill".

This is not per se a genuine mental illness but her God-given weak nature of lacking courage and aggression, and being unable to cope, which has been labeled as "illness" and handled by doctors.

An extreme case of gender inferiority is when a woman prevented from marrying runs away from home and becomes a prostitute.

Women are doing many things today they would not be able to do if every fear factor had not been removed, and allowance made for gender inferiority in an invisible way.

Accordingly, a woman official who says I should be deported unless I receive counseling is a normal female with a normal mental deficit, who would not be an official if she did not have those modern crutches.

SHE needs counseling for every little thing. She wants me punished for not obeying her parents as she has a normal female moral deficit where sexual reproduction is the be-all-and-end-all of life.

She cannot face the thought the baby she produced turned against her to the extent she will punish me (an adult stranger from overseas) for not obeying my parents.

When they started allowing women to work, there was no special "golf handicap" for the female mental deficit, and women like her did not work.

Now, this deficit factor had been rendered mostly invisible, she cannot see that she has a female mental deficit, nor does she see that this would vary from person to person.

Men become violent with me these days if I don't like how a woman is treating me. There is no court of appeal in 2022 when a woman wants me in counseling or will otherwise deport me.

Men will lie that this did not originate in a woman. She is also allowed to have the last word.

My father allegedly told them he had come to the US on business but he never had business in the US. His only business was to fly across the globe to wreck my life studies and legal and social status.

In the US sectioning, known as an involuntary committal, was done through a judge. The psychiatrist would petition for someone to be brought in against their will for 2-3 days under psychiatric observation. If they did not want to come a warrant was set up for their arrest.

The judge would have to approve the application based on the doctors' report plus the patient or accused had the right to defend themselves in court that they were not gravely disabled.

If the judge felt the person was not gravely disabled mentally, and that the psychiatrist was making up the whole thing, he would refuse to allow the warrant. If after 2-3 days of observation under lockup, the patient was found to be gravely disabled the fresh evidence would be taken to the to consider granting involuntary committal.

Gopalan lied to the judge I was gravely disabled. He asked three other psychiatrists(all white Americans including a female) to also lie under oath they had seen me and found me gravely disabled when I was working a summer job as a grader at The University of Arizona.

They assured the judge I was mentally incompetent and would not understand. They urged that I should not be informed about the hearing I would otherwise have a right to attend.

When the judge realized that 4 psychiatrists were saying I should not be advised of the right to attend my hearing and defend myself, he decided to waive that rule, trusting that they were telling the truth I could not understand the proceedings.

Gopalan was able to get a warrant for my arrest, and local police did not know my address, but I was easy to catch in the Physics department where I was a graduate student In Physics.

I was taken at midnight by police in the Physics department while chatting with 20 people.

I was driven to Kino hospital by an evil-faced social worker who snapped to me in the steel-caged back seat, "You will stay here a long time".

I waited several hours in a cramped space with others from the city who had been brought in through the same procedure. They explained to me the name of my petitioner was Gopalan, and I was to wait till offices opened and he would do my intake.

The door of the hospital was locked, but it was possible to wander inside. I accessed a telephone directory and desk phone in a side-room unnoticed and telephoned the Head of the Physics Department Dr. Scadron.

The latter was not angry that I had called him at 3 am, due

to the circumstances.

He was very shocked and did not think what had just happened was appropriate. He said, however, that if this was just a prank and not the truth, I was going to be severely punished.

That should show you how times have changed since 1986. Today, there are no living people, other than medical professionals, who would say or even think, the actions of a psychiatrist sounded absurd. Naturally, this is also something your GP won't do very often. Laypeople (non-medical professionals) are (or act like) they are someone without the mental faculties to analyze potential absurdities carried out by a registered doctor.

Of course, this means all your friendships and relationships with modern people will come to a tragic end, as soon as you realize they won't support you in a complaint about a doctor. This is about personal relationships and not about medical complaints.

You may know somebody for 20 years. All of a sudden, you need support against the alleged mistreatment by a medical professional or psychiatrist.

And your long-term friend, who had supported you through thick and thin, says if the doctor tells you that you are crazy, just trust him or her.

Modern people, such as social workers, like to say I won't admit to myself I have mental health problems that cause me not to get along with women.

You are talking about me, a cat among dogs, imprisoned virtually in a crowd of people from illiterate parts of the world as well as local ones, including prostitutes, where women would get along with women.

I feel that my right to prefer persons of a particular sex or race for personal contact is not understood in Ireland, where "Equality and Diversity" is popular philosophy, as in the UK.

The social workers would need to define what a mental health problem (a very diffuse term) means, before asking me to admit I have it, or even ascribing that label to me.

I think the social workers do not possess enough intelligence to comprehend such matters as analysis.

I also think ascribing that label to me automatically vindicates many mediocre folks, including women, particularly social workers, of being what was once called a "dud".

I think social and mental workers, and the mediocre woman population mainly rely on their urges and instincts to tell them how to act and rely on peer support to come out as never engaging in any type of misconduct.

I had a life up to 1986 because I did not have to live under the mental health cloud. Except for members of selected professions, people like the Physics Department head used their judgment to decide about the validity of mental health "accusations" against someone they knew at a workplace.

In a sense, people live without dignity in 2021, which is the year we are in right now.

But modern people have an important advantage over old-timers like me, and modern women have a king-sized advantage compared to men.

A person with that attribute feels no anger shame or loss of self-esteem when labeled with terms of the modern mental health vocabulary. "Retard" has been eradicated and replaced by "someone with learning disabilities".

In modern times, a woman who objects to being told she suffers from mental health problems" is a greater gender-bender than a Lesbian, Submissive, Masochist, or post-operative male transsexual.

I think the reader would understand that Domination-

Submission and BDSM are respected and renowned branches of porn preferences today, whereas in most cases, the women are still the majority of the submissives and masochists.

Modern woman's relationships do not break up if her near ones do not support her allegations of abuse by medics or insulting misdiagnosis.

She is incapable of (correctly or incorrectly) detecting doctor misdiagnoses, just like a pig is never going to play the piano always provided to it.

This is just a discussion of how the human race has received a new, and anesthetic makeover from the man-made mental health system, since those good old days when humans did not wear a mask and did not enjoy 100% immunity against remorse and inferiority.

Gopalan showed up at 8 am. He told me that while I had been waiting inside for daybreak, my father had been standing outside the building at 6 am asking him(Gopalan) to lock me up for life.

He then proceeded to tell me that he was going to move me into an isolated cage in a Phoenix hospital where no one would visit me but himself.

No one will respond to your screams and I will be the only person to see you and visit your cage," said Gopalan.

He said he would drug my brains out, and I would lose my case against involuntary committal as I couldn't testify.

Each committal was for 6 months, and I would have lower and lower brain functioning as time went by, so there would be no question of whether I was mentally disabled. "Soon the fight against your defenses will become dead easy", and I will keep you for life", said Gopalan.

Right then I who aged 28, realized that this 36-year-old Tamil-speaking man wanted to render me incompetent through chemical slingshots, and exploit me in a cage as a sex slave.

The university appointed a solicitor for me and due to being detained, I was entitled to free legal aid.

The only good that came out of having a solicitor, (which I suppose was a lifesaver), was that he ruled that nobody could lay a finger on me.

This is because I had been detained for a 2-3 day assessment, and only after this and only if the judge, reading the medical verdicts, decided to grant 6 months of involuntary committal. That's when they could force drugs.

The place was reeking with doctors having sex with patients.

There was one single American girl of similar age who told me she had lost her case against committal thanks to lies told by Gopalan about her. So she had been put in for 6 months and Gopalan was trying to have sex with her.

I refused to go into a room with Gopalan without a female escort. He publicly attacked mentally incompetent "zombie" women.

Unfortunately, they publicly responded to his sexual advances. Only severely retarded and comatose women had sex with Gopalan.

Doctors, nurses, and other staff, as well as inmates, were constantly viewing these public exchanges of "affection", yet no complaint had gone through, which had taken effect so as to have the doctors disciplined.

Gopalan kept getting extensions of time detaining me for observation to do additional tests on me unto three weeks.

He submitted hundreds of false witness testimonies by

hospital staff, but the court rejected the application as lacking evidence I was gravely disabled and they were ordered to release me.

In 1987, Gopalan was found guilty of having sex with a terminally-ill patient. They had a court date to conduct criminal proceedings.

However, the terminally-ill woman who was under the care of Gopalan's cronies conveniently popped off before the court hearing date. In America, you won't go to jail if your victim dies before a court date, and evidence is now based on hearsay.

Only God would be the witness who can tell if she naturally popped off before the hearing or they helped her along the way.

You may only need to blow on a terminally-ill patient to hurry them to the grave.

With so much to lose if some body-bag candidate kept lingering on and so little to lose from her induced death, it is anyone's guess what might have happened.

The following documents have been included as slides at the end of this section, 1-0043. They are the newpaper cutting (reproduced) about Dr. Gopalan,

and his disciplinary report from the medical panels of AZ and MD states of USA. This is followed by 1 example from the gummy bear series, that happens to be the one sent before Regents death, which the culprit fearfully entered my yahoo mail(I believe) 6 months later, and deleted. After this is a sample email from the graveyard series, marking the end of chapter 1-0043

Summarizing the whole situation, which helps the slides that follow to be appreciated

These -newscutting and disciplinary report- are details of one Dr Ramanath Gopalan with whom my father conspired to lock me up for life thus abort8ng my self-funded Physics studies at The University of Arizona 1983-1986

I am Mohini, and l lived in the UK from 2004-2018. I stayed under immigration proceedings all the while. Moreover the Home Office chose to ban me working or taking unpaid work as well as stopped me having a boyfriend or husband on UK soil for those 14 years. My bans in the UK came to an end through my voluntary departure from the UK

I had a friendship with one Regent Exeter born in a wealthy English family, who was abused overdrugged and detained unnecessarily all his life by psychiatrists after becoming orphaned.

I knew Regent from 2011-2014 when he died under suspicious circumstances, His GP kept his high blood pressure >12 months a secret waiting for God to come and take him in His own time, without medical intervention.

Shortly before his death, Regent alleged his doctor, Mr. B wrote a strange set of characters and numbers in place of the regular prescription of Flu-penthixol, a drug which is banned in the USA and India for causing lots of deaths.

Doctor B had told Regent he did not need to know what the secret code meant as this was a secret between himself (Doctor B) and the pharmacist.

Regent had also said this new preparation (dispensed using that secret code) was making all his symptoms worse, shortly before passing away.

There was also Miss V a psychiatric social worker who walked into Regent's flat without knocking when I was there. She said Doctor B had decided to shorten Regent's life to improve it's quality. That happened in 2011 or 2012.

While Regent's death came in 2014, we see from the above details that Regent's doctor wanted to shorten Regent's life and did so.

However I used to visit him off and on, traveling from London to his place in Shifnal.

During this period I was convicted at Basingstoke Magistrates of a crime I did not commit, the harassment of my sister Mrs Viju Wortley, who is the wife of an Atomic Weapons Establishment scientist.

This criminal conviction was called "harassment without violence" and in many ways resembled a murder trial. I was sentenced with this, in July 2013 and awarded a leg tag for 4 months.

At the end of this term, I was taken to Yarlswood IRC and given a notice deporting me for the public good.

Several false allegations were presented by the plaintiff who never made an appearance, and the Pesthilenseroke are alleged to have lied about me .

There was a statement written in Steve Wortley's handwriting signed by him and statement written in Viju Wortley's handwriting and signed by Steve Wortley who made his handwriting fat and rounded to resemble that of his wife, and signed as Viju Wortley

Worse still my father had submitted to Basingstoke police as part of Viju Wortley's complaint file some emails I sent

181

to Regent Exeter in 2011.

These were emails I exchanged privately with a friend, and so were not a harassment of my father, as they were not sent to him.

As my father lives miles away from Viju Wortley harassing him would not constitute harassment of Viju Wortley

So all sorts of irrelevant details were presented and used by police.

If Basingstoke police were honest, if they wanted to punish wrongdoers and not innocent people, they would have arrested my father for hacking my private email to a friend.

Well my father never respected the law nor considered it wrong to lie under oath. He also never respected my privacy and wanted to snoop around my gmail to see who I write to

The emails hacked by my father of me to Regent were things my darling (deceased) friend would enjoy.

It was the story of this USA Tamil psychiatrist in Arizona where I was a graduate student in Physics, and he was a resident in psychiatry there.

This man was found guilty raping a terminally-ill female shortly after I was forced to give up my studies as a result of his fraudulent detainment of me.

My father had phoned various people in Arizona from him home India, and had also made plane visits to Arizona to abort my studies and force me back to his home in India to stay a prisoner.

One institution that always helped my dad to set up a manhunt for me in North America, which the local police would consider unlawful, was the nearest Hindu temple to my physical location.

Upon looking in the Tucson Hindu temple for helpers, my father had come across the budding Tamil psychiatrist, who was the temple's president at the time.

Because they story albeit true says my father did unethical things, my father would not want anyone to know.

Now Regent, who died in 2014, was alive at the time of my criminal conviction and "public good notice".

When he died in 2014, I got two kinds of emails mocking his passing. I named them the Gummy Bear Series and graveyard series. I have given details of these in this book, but reasoned why the sender is not a medical professional

Both series were from a sender who called themselves Jasmine, (namesake of my niece) and I was also called by an anonymous young lady calling herself Jasmine who owned up as sender of the emails. The emails also displayed a graveyard company bearing the same name as where my father used to work, ICI, (Imperial Chemical Industries).

These series of emails indicate the existence of non-medical persons, who knew my family and had a vested interest. in Regent's death.

MAYBE Basingstoke police believe that people who criticize psychiatrists should be exterminated systematically, and secretly because psychiatry is women's salvation.

Both Regent and I criticize psychiatry and we have had our lives made chronically uncomfortable by the system.

That's why the Basingstoke police entertained a complaint of that nature.

I conclude by declaring that I suffer from no mental condition that would make me believe that people will believe or like what I say. I do not demand the same.

I knew Regent from 2011-2014 when he died under suspicious circumstances, His GP kept his high blood pressure >12 months a secret waiting for God to come and take him in His own time, without medical intervention.

Shortly before his death, Regent alleged his doctor, Mr. B wrote a strange set of characters and numbers in place of the regular prescription of Flu-penthixol, a drug which is banned in the USA and India for causing lots of deaths.

Doctor B had told Regent he did not need to know what the secret code meant as this was a secret between himself (Doctor B) and the pharmacist.

Regent had also said this new preparation (dispensed using that secret code) was making all his symptoms worse, shortly before passing away.

There was also Miss V a psychiatric social worker who walked into Regent's flat without knocking when I was there. She said Doctor B had decided to shorten Regent's life to improve it's quality. That happened in 2011 or 2012.

While Regent's death came in 2014, we see from the above details that Regent's doctor wanted to shorten

Regent's life and did so.

However I used to visit him off and on, traveling from London to his place in Shifnal.

During this period I was convicted at Basingstoke Magistrates of a crime I did not commit, the harassment of my sister Mrs Viju Wortley, who is the wife of an Atomic Weapons Establishment scientist.

This criminal conviction was called "harassment without violence" and in many ways resembled a murder trial. I was sentenced with this, in July 2013 and awarded a leg tag for 4 months.

At the end of this term, I was taken to Yarlswood IRC and given a notice deporting me for the public good.

Several false allegations were presented by the plaintiff who never made an appearance, and the Pesthilenseroke are alleged to have lied about me.

There was a statement written in Steve Wortley's handwriting signed by him and statement written in Viju Wortley's handwriting and signed by Steve Wortley who made his handwriting fat and rounded to resemble that of his wife, and signed as Viju Wortley.

Worse still my father had submitted to Basingstoke police as part of Viju Wortley's complaint file some emails I sent to Regent Exeter in 2011.

These were emails I exchanged privately with a friend, and so were not a harassment of my father, as they were not sent to him.

As my father lives miles away from Viju Wortley harassing him would not constitute harassment of Viju Wortley.

So all sorts of irrelevant details were presented and used by police.

If Basingstoke police were honest, if they wanted to punish wrongdoers and not innocent people, they would have arrested my father for hacking my private email to a friend.

Well my father never respected the law nor considered it wrong to lie under oath. He also never respected my privacy and wanted to snoop around my gmail to see who I write to

The emails hacked by my father of me to Regent were things my darling (deceased) friend would enjoy.

It was the story of this USA Tamil psychiatrist in Arizona where I was a graduate student in Physics, and he was a resident in psychiatry there.

This man was found guilty raping a terminally-ill female shortly after I was forced to give up my studies as a result of his fraudulent detainment of me.

My father had phoned various people in Arizona from him home India, and had also made plane visits to Arizona to abort my studies and force me back to his home in India to stay a prisoner.

One institution that always helped my dad to set up a manhunt for me in North America, which the local police would consider unlawful, was the nearest Hindu temple to my physical location.

Upon looking in the Tucson Hindu temple for helpers, my father had come across the budding Tamil psychiatrist, who was the temple's president at the time.

Because they story albeit true says my father did unethical things, my father would not want anyone to know.

Now Regent, who died in 2014, was alive at the time of my criminal conviction and "public good notice".

When he died in 2014, I got two kinds of emails mocking his passing. I named them the Gummy Bear Series and graveyard series. I have given details of these in this book, but reasoned why the sender is not a medical professional

Both series were from a sender who called themselves Jasmine, (namesake of my niece) and I was also called by an anonymous young lady calling herself Jasmine who owned up as sender of the emails. The emails also displayed a graveyard company bearing the same name as where my father used to work, ICI, (Imperial Chemical Industries).

These series of emails indicate the existence of non-medical persons, who knew my family and had a vested interest. in Regent's death.

MAYBE Basingstoke police believe that people who criticize psychiatrists should be exterminated systematically, and secretly because psychiatry is women's salvation.

Both Regent and I criticize psychiatry and we have had our lives made chronically uncomfortable by the system.

That's why the Basingstoke police entertained a complaint of that nature.

I conclude by declaring that I suffer from no mental condition that would make me believe that people will believe or like what I say. I do not demand the same.

"Gummy Bear Emails" and "Graveyard Emails".

I shall try my best to make these scanned pdf documents from my computer-readable.

It is important to me that photos I display on my e-book will be visible to potential readers. I have not used epub readers and am presently doing my book using Adobe Digital Editions on my laptop to view the epub. There aren't magnification facilities in my software, which I assume one would need, in order to view documents published on epub pages. I understand that accessibility is important.

Hopefully epub reader tablets will magnify as much as needed for those who want to view the exhibits, which I hope are not too blurred for readers to figure out what was happening. I made a pdf binder from these two series of emails in chronological order at the time I received them, which was March-September 2014.

This is to indicate to potential readers that stories narrated in this regard may have really happened.

Important or salient parts in an exhibit are circled or marked in red ink as well as I have tried to display those marked portions magnified, as a separate exhibit, after the email in question, to maximize the possibility of the evidence pertinent to my story being visible.

Note about the gummy bear and graveyard sample emails below

is a 6-page email I printed to pdf in 2014. This was the first email of the gummy bear series. I believe the expression "gummy bear" was a joke about the physical appearance of Regent Exeter, indicating that he had died, and was now none more than a legend or movie watched by people; he was historical. The following morning after this email was sent to me, Regent died, which was unexpected by people close to him.

I learned from what people told me in Shifnal after his death (Ch. 1-0043) that Regent himself knew from medical professionals his death was imminent 1-3 days prior to death. Regent himself did not know this a week before his death (when I was with him) that it was coming. A doctor is the best person to know death is nigh, but not the exact moment, or (usually) date it will happen.

Doctor B did not kill Regent. Doctor B knew better than anyone connected to Regent, that the man had high blood pressure. Investigating the matter was not easy. I wrote a complaint to the Parliamentary Ombudsman, and after a long wait, 18 months after his death, the medical records were released to me by the Shrewsbury office.

These medical records showed that since January of 2013 or earlier, a very high blood pressure was recorded by Doctor B once a month for Regent Exeter. This means that Regent, who died on 26.3.2014 had life-threatening blood pressure levels for at least 15 months before he died

Doctor B was a doctor, so he knew better than Regent and better than anyone close to him, that the man's blood pressure if left untreated, would kill him in due course of time.

In fact, Doctor B did not give Regent a clue he had blood pressure and it was above danger level. Blood pressure has no symptoms of its own, and you may just feel unwell when you have it.

In fact Doctor B monitored and recorded these blood pressure readings monthly and records were released from the beginning of 2013. There was a letter in the records dated October 2013, written by Doctor B to Regent, to have a 24-hour blood pressure check. The letter was deceptively worded so that a person who knew nothing about this, would not understand he had a life-threatening condition.

As the blood pressure was kept secret, Regent had no way

of suspecting he needed treatment for it. The 24 hour test also revealed the same had results with a systolic touching 220 like the monthly charts. Before and after this 24 hour test, Doctor B did not give Regent any tablets for high blood pressure. Therefore the purpose of conducting the 24 hour test was not to give care; only to monitor who close the grave the patient had gone.

6-18 months before his death, I was standing in his hallway, on one of my visits to him, and a psychiatric social worker, Miss V entered w/o knocking and sat down. She told Regent the doctor had decided to shorten his life to improve its quality. I have expressed my opinion that doctors shared their plan that Regent should die with Miss V, who is, (because of her role) in the medical community despite being illiterate.

I have explained Miss V blurted the truth, even though she sticks by the medical profession, (the hands that feed her)she had difficulty understanding what is morally right and wrong, owing to a subnormal intelligence. I have also claimed social and psychiatric outreach workers, being mostly female, all have a subnormal IQ

In 1-0001, and 1-0003 I have provided motives why someone might want Regent to die. Doctor B might have felt someone on such prolonged psychiatric medication was better off dead, or knew that should he recover, would influence crowds about the evils of psychiatry, as he was fully there, and his conscience did not die in the years of psychiatric detention and virtual lockup that made up his life.

In January 2014 and March 2014, a week before he died, I visited him, and both times Regent claimed Doctor B was giving a strange preparation,(one without a name) provided by "secret code" written by the physician to the village pharmacist, in place of his usual daily Flupenthixol

Both times Regent said he felt sure the new preparation was making all his symptoms worse. He said he had no idea what he was taking. It reminds me of the American story of "Mike the Durable"

That sounds like Doctor B realizing Regent was taking too long to die, gave him some small thing to speed up the deterioration. But we will never know if this happened. The doctor denied it saying not to trust a mad person, which does not tell is if it happened or not. In a talk I accidentally attended at the Institute of Physics in mid-2014, they said most clinical trials in the UK were carried out without a patients' knowledge. Was this a risky clinical trial on a person whose life did not have value in the doctor's eyes?

Regent was visiting Doctor B once a month for years, as his lethal sounding cough and abnormal breathing remained untreated by Doctor B and Doctor S of the tiny doctor surgery of Shifnal village. I myself had accompanied Regent to Doctor S when I had met Regent for the first time, about the awful cough. At that time Doctor S had expressed a strong contempt for us, this contempt was connected to psychiatry

Coming back to the nitty-gritty of foul play, if there was only a doctor involved our so-called crime has only one dimension. This type of doctor action probably happens from time to time, in the UK, and also everywhere else. It would probably be called medical negligence or medical malpractice, probably serious enough to have a doctor struck off. In actual practise, it may be the policy of the state not to take action against the doctor in such cases. Britain is female-dominated and perhaps they block out of existense all matters that are very different in character from sugar, spice and everything nice, so the place is devoid of any information incompatible with sweet, sticky chocolate-candy

I believe it is probably the policy of the state to allow such wrongful deaths to go undocumented, and taking action against miscreants would not keep in undocumented

Anyway we see this case has a non-medical dimension. We assume the sender of these emails is not a medical professional. This means when nobody is supposed to know (but Doctor B and Associates that Regent's death was nigh, on the eve of his death, a non-medical person knew about the anticipated death, and sent email joking about it. I also speculate the non-medical sender also knew he was to die the next morning or in a few hours, but that is wild speculation

The sender was vicious, and took time and ingenuity to create these emails. It appears that 1-3 days prior to his death doctors whispered in Regent's ears he was soon to die, and these doctors might have very well whispered the same bad news to the vicious, non-medical sender of the emails, and it was good news for him (or them)

July 10, 1987,NY India Abroad.-by Lynn Hudson

New York-The Arizona Board of Medical Examiners has
censured and placed on probation a Tuscon
psychiatrist Dr. Ramanath Gopalan, after his earlier
admission of having sex with a terminally-ill patient. A
spokesman for the board Douglas Cerf said the actions
came from a hearing in Phoenix on June 26th. He
said that Gopalan had admitted in a hearing in
Phoenix on April 9th to two incidents of oral sex with a
32-year-old woman patient in 1986, while he was
treating her for depression related to severe cirrhosis
of the liver. Arizona state law prohibits doctors from
having sexual intimacies with a patient in the course
of direct treatment.

Admits Wrongdoing

Cerf said that in admitting to the acts in the hearing,
Gopalan had told the board, "I admit it was wrong."

The patient, whom the board would not identify, died
in December.

Gopalan was ordered at the April meeting to undergo
psychiatric testing, and evidence from those tests was
presented at the hearing in Tucson.

Cerf said a degree of censure, a formal disciplinary
action had been issued against Gopalan, 36, and that
he had been placed on probation for five years.

197

The censure was based on finding of fact, and on conclusions of law. It was circulated to all states in the country.

Cerf sold that he did not expect a criminal prosecution to be brought because the patient was now deceased and any evidence in such a case would be based on hearsay.

The board had the power to revoke Gopalan's medical license if it had seen fit, but censure and probation actions did not prohibit him from practising during the period of probation.

The board learnt of the sexual incidents, Cerf said, after the patient discussed them with a doctor at the hospital.

Cites father's illness

Cerf sold that at the April hearing, Gopalan offered as mitigating circumstance the fact that his father had died of cirrhosis before the incidents and that this had affected his behavior.

Gopalan was a 1976 graduate of the Topiwale National Medical College of Bombay, Cerf said, and had taken psychiatric training at the University of Arizona beginning in 1980.

He was licensed as a psychiatrist by the state of Arizona, Cerf said. In Tuscon, Gopalan is associated with the Arizona Behavioral Medical Associates.

Neither Gopalan, nor his attorney, Charles Buri, could be reached for comment.
End of story....

Page 1 of 5 Gopalan disciplinary report from USA state medical boards

Federation of
STATE
MEDICAL   **Physician Profile**
BOARDS

Home

Report Date: 03/26/2008

In response to your recent inquiry concerning the individual referenced
below, the following summary of reported information is provided.

NAME:
             Ram Gopalan, MD
ALTERNATE NAME(S):
             Ramanath Gopalan

The Federation Physician Data Center provides names previously used by
reporting entities. This information is provided to consumers to assist in
identification.

BOARD ACTIONS/DISCIPLINE/SANCTIONS

Reporting State Board	ARIZONA
Date Of Order	06/26/1987
Action(s)	MEDICAL LICENSE PLACED ON PROBATION Term: 5 Year(s) CENSURED
Basis for Action(s)	Unprofessional Conduct Sexual Misconduct

Reporting State Board	ARIZONA
Date Of Order	06/22/1991
Action(s)	PROBATION TERMINATED
Basis for Action(s)	Not Applicable

Reporting State Board	MARYLAND
Date Of Order	08/20/1993
Action(s)	APPLICATION FOR MEDICAL LICENSURE DENIED
Basis for Action(s)	Unprofessional Conduct Due to Action Taken by Another Board/Agency

A report containing no reportable actions is just as valuable as receiving a
report with disciplinary actions, because it indicates that the individual you
searched against the national database has not been disciplined by a state
medical board or regulatory entity. Of the physicians disciplined in 2006,
86% have held licenses in 2 to 35 different state jurisdictions.

200

Page 2 of 5

DocInfo - Service provided by the Federation of State Medical Boards   Page 2 of 5

Entities reporting to the Federation include U.S. state medical boards and its territories, and U.S. Department of Health and Human Services (Medicaid/Medicare). In addition, reports are received from numerous international jurisdictions including Canada, England, New Zealand, and Australia.

Disciplinary actions taken by licensing and regulatory entities can vary widely in scope and nature. Actions may range from warnings or letters of concern to the revocation of the privilege to practice medicine. Actions may be either disciplinary or administrative in nature. In deciding to seek treatment from an individual who has reportable actions, the patient should closely evaluate the nature and consequence of the action and decide if the action could potentially impact the quality of care received.

LICENSE HISTORY

State Board	Date Issued	License Number
ARIZONA	08/16/1985	15598
VIRGINIA	04/30/1993	0101-049249
VIRGINIA	04/30/1993	0101049249

The licensure history is provided as a resource to disclose states of past and present licensure previously reported to the Federation Physician Data Center. The License History is not to be used as licensure verification and may not be representative of the current licensure status. For the most current information contact the above listed boards. Contact information can be found at www.fsmb.org.

MEDICAL SCHOOL

Topiwala National Medical College, University Of Mumbai
Country: India

It takes many years of education and training to become a physician. Typically, after completing a four-year undergraduate or pre-medical program at an accredited college or university, a student may enter medical school. Once admitted to medical school, it generally takes four years to earn a Doctor of Medicine (M.D.) degree or Doctor of Osteopathic Medicine (D.O.) degree. Typically, a medical student spends the first two years in classroom and laboratory instruction, which is often referred to as the pre-clinical studies, and the final two years working under supervision of experienced physicians in clinics and hospitals, known as the clinical studies, where students observe and take part in the care of actual patients. Rotations on clinical services such as internal medicine, obstetrics and gynecology, pediatrics, and surgery are the foundation of the curriculum.

The Educational Commission for Foreign Medical Graduates (ECFMG), through its program of certification, assesses whether international medical graduates are ready to enter residency or fellowship programs in the United States.

ECFMG Certification assures the people of the United States, that international medical graduates have met minimum standards of eligibility required to enter such programs. ECFMG Certification is one of the

http://www.docinfo.org/docinfo_rpt.aspx   27/03/2008

201

eligibility requirements for international medical graduates to take Step 3 of the three-step United States Medical Licensing Examination (USMLE). Medical licensing authorities in the United States require ECFMG Certification, among other requirements, to obtain an unrestricted license to practice medicine. Additional information regarding the USMLE can be found at www.usmle.org and additional information regarding ECFMG can be found at www.ecfmg.org.

DEGREE

Doctor of Medicine (MD)

United States medical students earn either a Doctorate of Medicine (M.D.) or Doctorate of Osteopathic Medicine (D.O.). These degree types entitle a graduate to use these initials after his/her name. The title Doctor is based on completion of education requirements and is not an indicator of licensure status. Graduation from an accredited U.S. allopathic school program earns the student a Doctor of Medicine (M.D.) degree, while graduation from an accredited osteopathic school earns the Doctor of Osteopathic Medicine (D.O.) degree.

Currently, of the 148 medical schools in the United States – 126 teach allopathic medicine and award an M.D. degree, and 22 teach osteopathic medicine and award the D.O. degree. Currently, there are not any equivalent osteopathic medical schools outside of the United States. For further information on osteopathic physicians visit the American Osteopathic Association at www.osteopathic.org.

In addition to medical doctors and doctors of osteopathic medicine, individuals in the United States who have graduated from an accredited physician assistant program and are trained to provide health care services under the supervision and direction of a licensed physician are awarded the degree of Physician Assistant (P.A.). Physician Assistants can provide a broad range of medical and surgical services that traditionally have been performed by physicians, such as taking medical histories, performing physical examinations, ordering and interpreting lab tests and prescribing medication.

In some countries, such as Australia, India, and Pakistan, international medical school graduates who complete their studies in medicine and surgery earn a Bachelor of Medicine and Bachelor of Surgery degree, or in Latin, Medicinae Baccalaureus et Baccalaureus Chirurgiae (abbreviated MBBS, MBChB, and MBBCh.) These medical school diplomas are not offered in any U.S. or Canadian medical school program, and the exact name of the international degree programs can vary from country to country.

Medical schools outside the United States and Canada vary in educational standards, curriculum and evaluation methods. In order for foreign medical graduates to enter U.S. residency and fellowship programs, they must first be certified by the Educational Commission for Foreign Medical Graduates (ECFMG.) In addition to satisfying the ECFMG certification requirements, international medical graduates must also have had at least four credit years in attendance at a recognized medical school.

YEAR OF GRADUATION

Page 4 of 5

1976

Year of Graduation refers to the year a physician obtained his/her medical degree and graduated from medical school. The length of time since year of graduation is the personal preference of the patient and often depends on the relationship established with the treating physician.

MEDICAL SPECIALTY

We do not have record of the medical specialty(ies) for this individual.

Following medical school, physicians may enter a residency program where they choose to specialize in a particular area of medicine, which means additional years of training. The residency program may take the form of paid on-the-job training usually conducted in a hospital setting.

During this specialty training, the residents practice medicine under the supervision of licensed physicians who are experienced in their specialty. Upon completion of their residency training, the graduate resident is eligible to take the specialty board certification exam offered by one of the 24-approved medical specialty boards of the American Board of Medical Specialties (ABMS), the American Osteopathic Association (AOA), or other non-ABMS or non-AOA certification boards. A physician may gain board certification status in more than one area of specialization.

After residency, some doctors may continue their training to specialize even further and obtain certification in a sub-specialty, which usually requires an additional 2 to 3 years of fellowship training. For example, an internal medicine graduate may choose to sub-specialize in cardiology, which means an additional 3 years of training. On completion of the fellowship program, the physician may take a second board certification exam in the area of cardiology.

Certification in either a specialty or sub-specialty helps the public identify those physicians who have met a higher standard of educational training, passed competency examinations and have the knowledge and experience beyond the level required for licensure. Although many physicians are electing to become board certified, it is not a requirement to practice medicine. When selecting a board certified physician, it is important to review the certifying board's eligibility requirements, examination procedures, and ongoing maintenance of competency criteria. **Additional information pertaining to medical specialties of the American Board of Medical Specialties and the American Osteopathic Association can be found at www.abms.org or www.osteopathic.org**

LOCATION HISTORY (NOT CHRONOLOGICAL)
Tucson, AZ 85704-5819
Falls Church, VA 22041-2220
Arlington, VA 22201-5794

Since the Federation Physician Data Center database is a nationally consolidated database of physician information, it is very common for a single physician to have multiple locations on file. Generally, location

203

information is self-reported by a physician to a licensing and regulatory agency, and therefore, it has not been verified. Location information is updated in our system as new or additional information becomes available. **This location history is provided for use as a guide for individuals seeking to explore additional sources of information.**

PLEASE NOTE: For more information regarding the above data, please contact the reporting state board or reporting agency. The information contained in this report was supplied by the respective state medical boards and other reporting agencies. The Federation makes no representations or warranties, either express or implied, as to the accuracy, completeness or timeliness of such information and assumes no responsibility for any errors or omissions contained therein. Additionally, the information provided in this profile may not be distributed, modified or reproduced in whole or in part without the prior written consent of the Federation of State Medical Boards.

Gummy Bear received on the eve of Regent's death, 25.3.14, making fun of his death, so the sender knew in advance Regent was to die very soon Page 1 of 5

Fwd: Film Inv. March 25, 2014 5:48 PM
estment - Gu [Apply]
mmy Bear

X-Apparently- mohinihersom@yahoo.co.uk via
To: 188.125.84.179; Tue, 25 Mar 2014
17:48:14 +0000

Return-Path: <jasmine@spicefactoryfilms.com>

Received-SPF: none (domain of spicefactoryfilms.com does
hosts) IG1vdmlIHdoaWNoIGlzIHJlYWR5IGZ
ZWFyIGFuZCBoaXMgZnJppZW5kcyBoYXZlIIHR
bGQgZnJvbSBhbbiBldmlsIGdvdmVybm1lbnQg
aG4gVHJhdm9sdGEgYW5kIGhpcyBkYXVnaH

Gummy Bear Page 2 of 5

fax (81)	
FFFFFFFFFFFFFF... (299)	
griffiths (75)	
inv (592)	
jasminehughes (87)	
LEGALOMBUDSMAN	
namecheap (13)	
newsletters (1659)	
nnn (34)	
noigog	
personal (619)	
RE (5)	
SarahCox (6)	
sethi (29)	
SIGS and other (142)	
smash (12)	
ua (227)	
um (435)	
welcomes (96)	
windows secret... (53)	
wyatt	

YKoBym0WLDvTeUyV2S9a3H4tZDHNbhlhq5
mMslezq78GcTWA8v9ofPyHOXrC9lmjkCmND
UBNAtuNNBP1sexzh6MC6pBAFmH24fZRhf7x
tXhMIRYO6kaE78.Ky.KIPnJS_LM.oo1dH9n4e
IItkMnBcwCdfgViOw_rvpQQSPWGw64E.BpJI
r564Ujsxs_HDijkW6lOx2u3168H4VCy3oD6jY
NKxgJ0OkuKIV7VDAQY.cyUzAuAlf8Csh6tQ7I
t3GZpS9aQPQx5NNf69w7N6LpjcOoWeSpJ_C
ADdsT722P5LsBvlowbjfVrASnNXBB2mviUePz
UrlXI2ACnhZniIJFyVuXHio.QeKmI9vYzG.weM
2A32DmiqPuQhiHGVi18egyyh_iazZ5wog568I
u8WZUVw66_d5q64CSssU.SZdWZsFBykEYcv
n3IWKGBIayo5amARTNPso8QMFop2pc1aCJ
IFk8MyBGex1_E9M7ZyGmi4uBpT8FpPbAdv4
cxvuWEL..acchiJq1zS7Gq7pgbC6fbABVhYInc
td_LA5wmlkKeMhDkRBZUtgEwWPvZCVEOCS
1JIY9yczI4JXKBn8yhOWyluMeLa1XwVc4Phe
CAvXFLC.BKTAcRaBcjeQtNou4vMSjWH4Aadt
UJ1dN.DI4uIYPq5KTgGXPLosZB2_4qS9vTAs
8ILiKb2qnsD54oI2hOWMgOJMWBxDdKgjGA
5F.wrv7zW_oVSIwVgtezAuz5ZrKONWgeZ4ev
BWaOHvDcjwNlgNZZ2szeehApBj_dCn2gnU0
UYuOc555v1RbUA6eOGRerDEOVefqDFMLxJ
GMkx0FxM_5N_doCVzq4v7PyJ7zEb2dTiENM
wLOf8LmAGYA7ncc4NjtomV1kYxXu_3UEeNs
25pYrocInFQdvoE0vcY.icPkxjIwsazkXTqgujw

X-Originating-IP: [209.85.220.176]

Authentication-Results: mta1140.mail.ir2.yahoo.com from=spicefactoryfilms.com; domainkeys=neutral (no sig); from=spicefactoryfilms.com; dkim=neutral (no sig)

Received: from 127.0.0.1 (EHLO mail-vc0-f176.google.com) (209.85.220.176) by mta1140.mail.ir2.yahoo.com with SMTPS; Tue, 25 Mar 2014 17:48:14 +0000

Received: by mail-vc0-f176.google.com with SMTP id lc6so975903vcb.21 for <MOHINIHERSOM@YAHOO.CO.UK>; Tue, 25 Mar 2014 10:48:11 -0700 (PDT)

https://us-mg42.mail.yahoo.com/neo/b/message?pSize=50&sMid=39&fid=jasmi... 7/19/2014

206

Gummy Bear Page 3 of 5

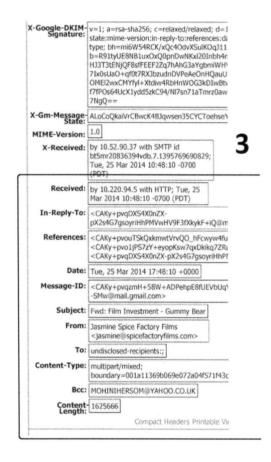

X-Google-DKIM-Signature:	v=1; a=rsa-sha256; c=relaxed/relaxed; d=1 state:mime-version:in-reply-to:references:da type; bh=mi6W54RCK/xQc4OdvXSulKOqJ11 b=R91tyUE8NB1uxOxQ0pnDwNKxl20Inbh4n HJ3T3tENjQF8sfFEEF2Zq7hAhG3aYgbmiWH\ 7Ix0sUaO+qf0t7RXJbzudnDVPeAeOnHQauU OMEl2wxCMYfyl+Xtdiw4RbHnWOG3kDIwBt\ f7fPOs64UcX1ydd5zkC94/Nl7sn71aTmrz0aw 7NgQ==
X-Gm-Message-State:	ALoCoQkaiVrCBwcK4BJqwsen35CYCToehse\
MIME-Version:	1.0
X-Received:	by 10.52.90.37 with SMTP id bt5mr20836394vdb.7.1395769690829; Tue, 25 Mar 2014 10:48:10 -0700 (PDT)
Received:	by 10.220.94.5 with HTTP; Tue, 25 Mar 2014 10:48:10 -0700 (PDT)
In-Reply-To:	<CAKy+pvqDXS4X0nZX-pX2s4G7gsoyriHhPMVwHV9F3fXkykF+iQ@m
References:	<CAKy+pvouTSkQxkmwtVrvQO_hFcwyw4fu <CAKy+pvo1jPS7zY+eyopKsw7qxDkikq7ZRı <CAKy+pvqDXS4X0nZX-pX2s4G7gsoyriHhPł
Date:	Tue, 25 Mar 2014 17:48:10 +0000
Message-ID:	<CAKy+pvqzmH+58W+ADPehpE8fUEVbUq\ -SMw@mail.gmail.com>
Subject:	Fwd: Film Investment - Gummy Bear
From:	Jasmine Spice Factory Films <jasmine@spicefactoryfilms.com>
To:	undisclosed-recipients:;
Content-Type:	multipart/mixed; boundary=001a11369b069e072a04f571f43c
Bcc:	MOHINIHERSOM@YAHOO.CO.UK
Content-Length:	1625666

Compact Headers Printable Vie

3

Gummy Bear Page 4 of 5

Gummy Bear

" The most watched Animated movie on YouTube
OF ALL TIME

" **18 MILLION new**
viewers every month "

" **2.5 BILLION**
people can't be wrong "

Dear Investor,

We have a new movie which is ready for investment, Gummy Bear and his friends have to save an alien world from an evil government agent. Starring John Travolta and his daughter Ella Travolta as two of the main characters in the movie we are very excited to be able to offer this to investors. Territory partnerships with major labels such as Universal Music Group

A sample from the gummy bear email series is directly above. Below is an example from the graveyard series. A sample email from the graveyard series. You can't prevent death, but you can sure profit from it, says this 3-page email of 29.4.14

Graveyard email page 1 of 3

sethi (29)	
SIGS and other (142)	
smash (12)	
ua (227)	
um (435)	
welcomes (96)	
windows secret... (53)	
wyatt	

DomainKey-Signature: v=1; a=rsa-sha1; d=vresp.com; s=simple; i=in@vresp.com; t=1398762324; h=From:Subject:Date:Message-ID:To:To:Subject:Date:Message-ID:List-Unsubscribe:MIME-Version:Content-Type;

Received: from [10.4.33.150] ([10.4.33.150:41002] helo=vm-mailer12.sf.verticalresponse.com) by locke (envelope-from <bounces-a19c1500ef-426c4ca0a1@b.cts.vresp.com>) (ecelerity 3.0.28.38595 r(38597)) with ESMTP id 3A/BE-04513-45B6F535; Tue, 29 Apr 2014 02:05:24 -0700

From: "International Commercial Investment LTD" <International_Commercial_Investm@mail.vresp.co

Reply-To: "International Commercial Investment LTD" <reply-a19c1500ef-426c4ca0a1-e92d@u.cts.vresp.com>

To: mohinihersonn@yahoo.co.uk

Subject: Secure Asset Backed UK Investment Contracted Returns of 37.5%

Date: Tue, 29 Apr 2014 09:05:23 +0000

Message-ID: <a19c1500ef-mohinihersonn=yahoo.co.uk@mail.vresp.com>

List-Unsubscribe: <mailto:reply-a19c1500ef-426c4ca0a1-e92d@u.cts.vresp.com?subject=unsubscribe>

MIME-Version: 1.0

X-Company_ID: 965464

X-vrfbldomain: fbl.p0.vertcalresponse.com

X-vrpod: p0

X-CTS-Enabled: a19c1500ef-426c4ca0a1

X-Campaign: a19c1500ef

X-vrrpmm: 965464-a19c1500ef

X-Feedback-ID: a19c1500ef:965464:vr1

Content-Type: multipart/alternative; boundary="_____MIMEboundary_____"; charset="UTF-8"

Content-Length: 27144

Received: from 188.125.84.161 ([188.125.84.161) by 10.200.25.180 (10.200.25.180); Tue, 29 Apr 2014 09:05:25 +0000

Compact Headers Printable View

Secure Asset Backed UK Investment Contracted Returns of 37.5% - jasminehug...   Page 3 of 4

An Alternative Investment Opportun
from International Commercial Investr

INVEST NOW!!!
and get contracted returns of up to 37.
with an asset backed investment

KEY FACTS
✓ The site i
  location i

✓ Plots are
  and resol
  price of £

✓ You will r
  months, a
  37.5%

✓ Deposits ;

Please find information of our latest
investment, our much awaited cemetery
development in the UK, which we are sure you
will find of interest.

✓ 12, 18 or
  payment
  purchasec

✓ This is an
  with clear

Request our latest brochure which will give you
a brief overview of the investment and the
options that are available to you. You will note

✓ The end b
  than othe

options that are available to you. You will note there is an interest free payment plan available for UK and overseas investors and this investment can also be made through cash or a SIPP.

Here is an example of an interest free payment plan:

5 plots @ £1,850 = £9,250
Reservation fee @ £350 per plot = £1,750
Balance remaining = £7,500
11 monthly re-payments @ £681.80
Payment plan admin fee = £175

Please note:

- Minimum purchase of 5 plots
- No early repayment charges
- Guaranteed acceptance for all investors
- No credit scoring

✓ This is a f
investmen

✓ The site w
March 20
site is aire
permission

✓ Investors
debit/cred

✓ The site is
company,

✓ Plots are s
order

✓ UK Counc
shortage

✓ Clear Exit
identified
Directors,
public

We can't guarantee your future, but we CAN

guarantee your income!

INTERNATIONAL
COMMERCIAL INVESTMENT

ICI is a trading naming for International Commercial Investments Ltd. Registered Office: Suite 7, Peel House, 30 The Down, Altrincham, Cheshire, WA14 2PX. Company Number. 8104097. Registered in England & Wales

https://us-mg42.mail.yahoo.com/neo/b/message?pSize=50&sMid=38&fid=jasmi...   7/19/2014

Graveyard email page   boxed section magnified

Secure Asset Backed UK Investment Contracted

Returns of 37.5% - jasminehug...   Page 2 of 4

Graveyard email page   boxed section magnified

2

426c4ca0a19b.cts.vresp.com>)
(ecelerity 3.0.28.38595 r(38597)) with
ESMTP id 3A/BE-04513-45B6F535;
Tue, 29 Apr 2014 02:05:24 -0700

From: "International Commercial Investment LTD"
<International_Commercial_Investm@mail.vresp.co

Reply-To: "International Commercial Investment
LTD" <reply-a19c1500ef-426c4ca0a1-
e92d@u.cts.vresp.com>

To: mahinihersom@yahoo.co.uk

Subject: Secure Asset Backed UK Investment
Contracted Returns of 37.5%

Date: Tue, 29 Apr 2014 09:05:23 +0000

Message-ID: <a19c1500ef-
mahinihersom=yahoo.co.uk@mail.vresp.com>

List-Unsubscribe: <mailto:reply-a19c1500ef-426c4ca0a1
-e92d@u.cts.vresp.com?
subject=unsubscribe>

215

RACIAL HYGIENE
EUGENICS
100% UNIFORMITY
OF OPINION

Part Two

2-0001: Orange is the New Black

My name is Mohini. I am writing a documentary in September of 2021, which I desperately want to publish. It is about my medical care of many years. I have not lived in the same city and so have been admitted to hospitals at various locations.

Doctors are not interested in my medical problems. The idea is to say I am not receiving proper treatment as doctors lie about my conditions, and keep my physical medical history on one level as a blank slate despite me being in and out of hospitals. The shape-shifter psychiatry that would keep appearing in my medical record has not made an appearance thus far since the end of the Dublin regulation, indicating it may have been introduced for legal purposes.

Maybe if you are someone who feels ill for a long time and continues to be told they are normal.

As a foreign national, it would be disrespectful if I failed to acknowledge the news item in recent years about the 200-and-odd women in Ireland who were wrongly told by their doctors that their cervical cancer tests came out normal.

They were told this again and again for more than two years until their cancer had progressed a lot, and some of these women have died, or have been told that death is to be expected.

My problem is not as serious as theirs but it is not just a medical problem but mental abuse. And I must take and take mental abuse in a speechless tomb where I have been "stitched" to illiterate women, the one and only who can speak with me. I am thinking of the movie "Caterpillar", where a mad scientist sews a row of people together. He sews one person's mouth to the anus of the person in front of him, and the chain of people crawl on their fours like a large caterpillar.

I am also not stating here that doctors (even some of them) are trying to kill me.

That is not my opinion, but that they lie to me and don't want to help.

The subject of this documentary, then, includes a discussion of what right I have, to make such an allegation?

As medicine is specialized, a layperson would not

generally know more about their condition, than a doctor. The law also does not recognize my medical opinion that I am not getting proper treatment, which is up to a medical doctor to decide. Fair enough. The only option (in any country) would be to get a second opinion. Going any further is a tricky issue.

There are patient advocacies, but they are ALL staffed with illiterate woman migrants, who would otherwise have nothing to do and no status. Being illiterate they are useless at handling complaints. This I hear is there on purpose, so complaints don't go very far, But having "Dumbells" handle every unhappy situation does not affect the outcome of a complaint about medical care, as the law forbids non-medical persons from having a valid opinion.

If your allegation (as a non-medical person with a medical opinion about your care) is of a kind that other medical professionals won't support, then you can have no solution. This creates a person whose problem will never be solved. I would like to apply and campaign that I will have a solution to this problem or medical termination of life, as it is my choice what I want to do. I understood the authorities may not give me what I want but I want to campaign before I die.

There is no place in the world where things don't go wrong in people's lives. However, people here are protected from realizing they are being made into slaves.

They cannot fight back. I want to fight back. As a foreign national who has been under threat of deportation, I am obliged to be a slave to things that are not acceptable, under (genuine) threat of deportation.

It is not proper to tell immigration they cant deport you because you will commit suicide if they do. That way, you are putting a gun to the authorities to decide as you want. You are denying they are the authorities. In the UK I had a medico-legal report from a psychiatrist which said I had a suicide risk if sent to India.

That is allowed in the rules, but the lawyer representing me tricked me and told me I should not speak to the judge, so he could say wise things. He then made it look to the judge like I wanted to hold the court to ransom by threatening suicide. He just told the judge I was fit to fly. This gentleman also told me about Exit, which allows voluntary suicide, so I could die if I got deported. Many folks in the UK have racial hygiene against me, in my opinion, for reasons they wont disclose, not the judges but the lawyers did. I was never guilty of threatening authorities with suicide to counter deportation, a fallacy that Mr. Ward perpetuated

There are no immigration authorities in any country who are going to care if you commit suicide because they want to deport you, except in the case when you are a female, who has "baby-produced" even if the baby is now OLD.

Part of the mental health crap from men pimping me to female genitalia, the sex-trained sex brains is because they feel I did not "baby-produce" and must get my salvation by union with "women" who have "baby-produced". They call me NULLIPAROUS-I need all this to be rectified or want a mercy killing. They think I can find all my stuff "inside the knickers" of a Samaritan. No man can speak to me and they blame me for not working when the women here are mainly working in baby care and care.

Also, I am living completely alone in a world where there is not a human to talk to and physical access is ONLY to illiterate women. Chances of employment and/or any human relationship are remote.

Most Boring Equation: Illiteracy + women = personal services, agencies, and organizations

Who in the wide world would want to read about my intentionally-inflicted, man-made malady?

I understand that most human beings in this world would not want to read a book, nor would they be able to. So why would they be willing and able to read my book, of all books?

You can argue that an author should never remark that most humans are illiterate if they hope to be popular with the public.

But I am not competitive by nature and do not aspire to become a JK Rowling. I don't compete with women as much as women compete with me. I don't compete with women at all.

So, I don't worry about not being popular. I don't want to rub anyone the wrong way. But I want my dignity and to say my bit without lying and pretending.

I will call this a documentary and hopefully, it is. Whether medical care would be interesting to read about- I decided to be honest with myself. I assure you this is not only upper torso material but contains no graphic imagery of myself or other people.

Along with anecdotes about medical care, are non-medical anecdotes. These have been introduced to build a conspiracy theory. I am indeed suggesting there could be a political or other reason I should not or need not stay well. This is purely speculative.

I refer to most places and people in my story by a single initial. Usually, this will be the real first letter of their first /last name.

Some authors pay to have an author interview, even tell the interviewer what questions to ask him or her. I have not got the money to do that.

I have little knowledge of marketing and have no way to promote my book(s). Let me say I am getting younger and healthier every year, where doctors choose not to be useful, and living in a virtual woman-gulag is not helpful. The word "virtual" is inserted to indicate that I am a free woman, IE not confined inside physical walls.

When one lives in a "woman gulag", one liaises with, and "works" with women. A woman of the system is a 100% woman-multiplier, or she gives rise to women. A woman of the system only refers me to women. She lives in (or pretends to live in) a world where men do not exist. It may not be a pretense, as she may very well have no contact with men except for their penises.

Women offer warmth. intimacy and tenderness to women, professionally. Paid listening (to women) has greatly improved the lives of the listeners, who do an effortless job, by just taking a barrage of words from agitated female visitors. Before that, they "worked with" paid sexual intercourse, usually with hungry male visitors, and got cash for just laying back.

These days, women compete with women, so there is no envy towards men, who are clearly be on a higher level. Men are speechless pain-free, and pleasant vistas. The women have casual sex with unlimited penises.

Women competing with women amounts to people playing a ball game without any balls. You can still get hit; you can still get hurt.

I may not have a single reader for other reasons than a lack of social networking and an abundance of illiteracy. Reaching the top in anything requires the brilliance; being good does not. Being good usually comes from persistence, but the political system can make sure I am no good at anything, and well my book(s) and I stay at the bottom until I die, and after I do, my books will be forgotten.

In the unlikely event that my measly creations invoke a public interest, I feel I (and my books) will remain oblivious until my passing. After that, I think, my books will be forgotten unless they are plagiarized by women. Women plagiarize women to receive prestige and to impress men.

Are you aware millions of women are hunting the internet for courses in creative writing and how to write bestsellers?

All those courses, except the ones that advise you to plagiarize an existing bestseller, are lying.

How many women will be at my bedside when I die? It is very kind of them to do so.

To be a popular author I would need to have two things (1)content that people find most enjoyable; (2)WOMEN to promote my book, for men, their lovers to buy, or to read my books for free.

To live I would need women. To breathe, I would need women.

I am somebody who was born 1200-1500 Km from the nearest ocean, and who cannot swim. The ocean reminds me of eternity and death. Sad and lonely, I dream of all symbols of death. I dream of the mighty bastard, who is no respecter of persons, whose waves can embrace you into the arms of death. Its waves lap the shores as people come and go.

If you tell anybody here you are sick of the "woman gulag" life you would like to die, their "treatment" is limited to making (illiterate) women "jump" on you. One feels they would rather deploy machine guns than allow a crack to open in the "woman gulag"

Alas, but there is no employment for me in a woman-booster scheme where dark-skinned slaves are always welcome as submissive bottomers.

Bottomers are coveted for boosting by men in top positions. The men give them sex when they realize they are quite submissive and moon-faced towards women of the mainstream, who will therefore not complain about the aborigines.

As women complain about me, there is no chance of a friendship, relationship, or job unless I "beg" women and liaise with women's groups. The latter jealously guard me against speaking to any man. It is their natural urge.

This attitude is not a problem for people from an African slum. Unfamiliar with modern concepts, they don't feel the pinch just yet.

If you are clearly beneath a man, you will be given sex, taught your A-B-C-D, boosted intellectually as much as possible, and given all kinds of jobs where everyone thinks you are working.

Do you realize I was expelled from the Institute of Physics due to their eugenic scheme which rendered me a second-class citizen with no human rights? They have thrown me into the mainstream of society where I have been under immigration (deportation) proceeding for umpteen years, which is from 2018 in Ireland, from, 2004 in the UK, and umpteen years before that. I see the science community especially Physics have a craze for women and are morally corrupt these days

The websites on science and technology will tell you of the glory of women, and the glory of hordes of women working in those places. Their physical rooms and magazines are crowded with photographs of women that look ecstatically happy. I assert there is a dark side to that amazing beauty, bounty, and brilliance. Brilliance is non-existent.

Except for direct entries after finishing school, who would be around 18, female recruits into science and technology were recruited either because they liaised with women in the establishment who passionately encouraged women, or slept with a man in the establishment.

The Institute of Physics is a classic example of a place that gives excessive media coverage to women that sleep with its directors. I am willing to take responsibility for what I say. I doubt an honest tribunal will deny that most of my allegations are true.

The problem is whether the state and its tribunals would support me and that might be any lawyers in the state that will represent me that I need to have an alternative to the eternally-praised "woman gulags".

The state, every state probably, that offers mental health services as a sexual enhancement for women wants me to suffer for the next 1000 years or be deported into another "woman gulag" unless I take up that religion. Mental health is that coercive woman religion, and the word health should not be misconstrued as relating to medicine. They want me to suffer deprivation for indefinite periods unless I liaise with sex-trained sex brains: the mental health workers.

f anyone fails to understand what the deprivation is, they are someone who sees me as a vegetable who can live in a room for years without anybody speaking to them no chance of employment for that reason, no boyfriend or husband. It is by eugenics that I am unworthy of life for not liaising in woman communities.

My gateway to life is through forging a long-term liaison with illiterate sex-trained sex brains. These are the substitute provided by the state for a normal life and gateway to them. This is torture from a homicidal-sociopathic viewpoint that favors women of gender inferiority. So as I am sure to perish, I pray for the damnation of sex-trained sex brains forever and ever.

I understand The Institute of Physics have recently changed their HQ's physical location, changed their profile to something insignificant, and split under company law into nine companies. I think facts and history keep on changing these days to suit one's convenience. You never know what they will say tomorrow.

A woman has to participate in one of the two sex schemes. A woman walks behind women who champion and mentor women. Or a woman sleeps with senior management(men). This is the way "women" get into

Science and glamor jobs.

Seeking and finding is no longer allowed for women after gender equality was abolished.

Because women have less motivation than men, things are given to them on a plate to help them "overcome barriers".

As a result, women who are seeking like men are not wanted anymore.

In the movie "Caterpillar" a "mad scientist" stitches a long chain of people up with each person's mouth to the anus of the person in front. The victims had to move on their fours like a long caterpillar, and in a few days, some people in the chain had died.

You love to eat delicious cookies. Have you ever been curious about how they are made?

Most delectable are the women in the Physics community. You adore seeing lots of women doing Physics, so are delighted to have one million women go from zero to hero in a twinkling.

Are you curious to know how this was achieved? No! You merely crave and worship the end result.

If you are a woman, this is a paradise for you. If you are a man, there is a paradise waiting for the important women in your life.

They are now like cats that can fly thanks to the hero scientists. The "Yes she can" book speaks out the whole thrilling story.

Okay, most women on the planet are not going to go near Physics, so most women who visit the Institute of Physics for a thriller are probably like people who visit Disneyworld to view or stroke seals and walruses. You will of course be advised by the guide these marine animals were born specially to serve your interests!!

In that case, it is my opinion that as these programs bum off public funds, if the expenditures are excessive (I have no idea if they are)the programs should be stopped as unfair wastage.

Instead of wasting public funds, the women could be sold tickets to attend a Physics event like you would ride a camel or submarine as a tourist.

Maybe the programs which pretend to be educational only serve as marital aids (that is like dildos) they breathe new romance into an existing man-woman relationship or create a new romance when a woman attends those thrilling programs.

https://www.newyorker.com/humor/daily-shouts/
schrodingers-tinder-date

https://www.fastcompany.com/3049226/instead-of-a-
wedding-couples-can-now-opt-for-quantum-entanglement

https://www.pri.org/stories/2017-07-25/love-quantum-
physics-and-entanglement

https://viterbi.usc.edu/news/news/2016/the-love-
algorithm-isi-and-eharmony.htm

Maybe the Institute of Physics should rename themselves
Institute of Eugenics and Sexual Enhancement.

Take, for example, their "Communicating Physics group".
Men and women who are not familiar with Physics may
not understand that this is a stupid name for activities that
are probably stupid as well.

Many more people would be familiar with driving a car.

Would you attend an educational program called break-
driving, which is about applying the brakes?

You have to know how to apply the brakes, to drive a car.

Likewise, if you can't communicate Physics, you are not going to be able to do it.

We have "story sums" in kindergarten, where "I had one orange, I "buyed" two oranges. How many oranges do I have?

You first make the public understand how great Physics is; then you produce an intense desire for everyone to race for it. Blinded by greed and desire, like sex, they won't stop.

I have seen one "Communicating Physics" meeting of these in session, a group of women guarded by a man acting like a sheepdog protects flocks of sheep. Understandably, I am banned from the building.

The street shows carried out by the Institute of Physics throw propaganda at the public as they travel around the country, with science demos and fancy equipment.

They can stay in five and four-star hotels and their propaganda have things like "brave and mighty youth" to flatter youth and sexual imagery for young women to reassure that should they "come to Physics" there will be plenty of opportunities to have sex, that you can hook up in conferences.

If you Google "quantum physics and sex" you will realize (thanks to the Institute of Physics propaganda that the masses believe that quantum physics is something spiritual and somehow linked to sexual union.

I am not clear on how sex is connected to quantum physics. Are they saying subatomic particles have sex with each other? Anyway, it's nonsense.

Physics research is becoming unimportant but medical research is still going strong. All the basic stuff of Physics, such as what would be needed to run machines, has already been discovered.

What's yet to be learned is highly theoretical, such as string theory, and cannot benefit humans in any practical way.

Entertainment is less important than food, and string theory would not entertain humans. These are purely theoretical issues with no applications to benefit the masses.

Hence, the physicist would be able to retain the interest of the masses and women by convincing them these abstract studies are a form of cosmic sex.

Can you imagine what would happen if the medical

community traveled around the country conducting street gigs and offering people little thrillers allowing them to wear a stethoscope for a bit and run courses called "Communicating Medicine?"

Loads of people would go in for a laugh if nothing else. The human body is always interesting to people.

You see, I thought nothing of being expelled from the Institute of Physics for bringing them into disrepute. They behaved poorly and tried to lower me to an unqualified female working as a career advisor because she was sleeping with a director.

One senior Fellow at IOP, Bernard, asked me to help him with a research project, and I felt he was lying about me. One cannot do anything if an expert in a field downgrades you as there is nobody on the planet who can verify if I or that supervisor is right.

If you are doing research, it means you are dealing with a little-known subject. If I were formally under him, there would be no point in doing anything but walking out.

I am an unwanted person to them and they would not have given me any opportunities, but they were not going to expel me had I not created a web page about the abuse they did to me. I did not worry too much about it. But when I traced my old Physics classmates -three of them, I realized they hated me, and that all physicists would hate me as I cannot do the new sexual behaviors.

Not only that, but they got hold of my husband, Nicholas Hersom, as well, and started the indoctrination to "Come to Physics".

He lives in Canada and I believe has a ring of women, with whom he has a loyalty pact to have nothing to do with me. These women tend to be Hindus, or are in a Physics program.

I know the secret about the round table conferences by highly placed men of letters, millions of dollars poured in, psych PhDs devising strategies to motivate the copulatory privates of the women in Physics.

I think they have brainwashed my husband to say I must obey my parents.

What kind of father would try to make his young 21-year-old daughter sleep with an old man who was a psychiatrist who was "interested" in me?

Hey, don't attack me as a liar, when all rape stories of women that make it to the top of the charts are only based on hearsay.

My father always wanted to denigrate me as a woman. For me, obeying the father for money would be more undignified than selling sex for money.

Just go on Youtube and listen to stories of trafficked women. You know, gangsters tell people they can help them to enter some country illegally and have a good life there.

In exchange, people give their savings and women are asked for sex. Many women willingly sleep with illegal transporters for a better life.

The road to entering a country illegally is dangerous and many "trafficked" people have been murdered or drowned in the sea on their way.

There are glowing stories of trafficked women used as sex slaves here. Going to an unknown country with unknown men and working as a hooker when you are not under lock and key means you are a consensual hooker from back in your country.

Of course, the transporters might be living off immoral earnings; this is honestly a case of two parties of unequal mental status, the trafficker and the trafficked having a relationship.

Youtube is full of glowing praise for sexually exploited trafficked women these days. The sex is mostly consensual, and unless you feel consensual paid sex is something glorious; they don't deserve praise.

But it would be appropriate (I think) for the governments to compensate all trafficked people including the men and non-prostitute women if they survived the "trafficked journey" and entered illegally and were harmed in some way.

I think trafficking is a serious crime but I don't think it revolves around (and is limited to) sexual topics. I agree that prostitutes have an equal right to live as others. But they cannot be the only ones entitled to happiness and comfort.

My article is contrary to the popular view about everything, but that is not the reason I and my big mouth will never amount to anything.

Why will I never amount to anything? It's because only women can take up my case in all things. This is an extreme restriction I am subject to. No male journalist can help me get publicity. I'd have to "piggyback" on a woman journalist.

In every aspect of life, I am only allowed women. I live in a same-sex prison against my free will. I have been battling immigration for two decades (not all the details are here) and have had to apply for asylum here to regularize my status.

There is a move to immigrate all undocumented migrants but as I am documented they can't have me under that scheme. But like other college graduates. I am likely to be refused asylum. (I have left out details about what already took place in my life before coming to England.)

On the other hand, I think any non-European prostitute working illegally in Ireland gets asylum in a twinkling.

To me, it's similar to other college graduates-they will ask them, will you be tortured by the police in your country if you are sent back? The criteria for asylum are superhuman, whereas with prostitutes, they just have to lie on their backs to get asylum before everybody else.

There are different rules for different people. Some people have a low difficulty level. But they pretend everyone is graded by the same standards.

The glory of women outnumbering men in successful asylum seekers is that it is policy for women to get asylum automatically if they have performed women's body functions. Having given birth is often sufficient for a woman to get asylum in any country.

Women's applications for asylum tend to have no other discussion but their sex and body functions. Women who don't meet that criterion, and use similar arguments a man could use are always be refused asylum unless their theme is a popular one.

An example of a popular theme would be someone applying for asylum in the United States, who hates the Commies*. She may qualify for asylum even without putting sex stories, whereas otherwise she would be picked out like a rotten carrot and put in the plane. That is how it is everywhere.

Criteria to grant asylum are different for men and women which nobody talks about. Women are selected for their sexual content of their story.

I have made an oath on God to receive nothing more that is good in life, unless it originates from a man, to assert my preference to have gender equality.

I shall die of suicide with publicity that I won't live without a man in my life, and if the publicity is blocked I will die without the publicity.

I shall refuse to take part in any activities where I will never speak to a man.

If women tried to give mental health support by force, I would dearly like to shoot a bullet through their private parts.

I am chained to this place- don't worry, I am not going to stay alive in any place, as I think the globe is a stinking gutter as long as I am "stitched to women".

Some people would call an egg a hen's period. This is a strange way of seeing things, but that is the truth about eggs laid by poultry. Maybe people who don't like eating eggs would see eggs as a vaginal discharge from a menstruating hen.

Modern women depend on *sex-trained sex-brained women.* Modern women have stopped walking behind men as they have shifted their dependency to a woman-based virtual reality platform constructed, and maintained by men. The sex-trained sex-brains constitute a *man-made, virtual reality platform.* On this platform, reality is distorted by hidden laws to make the world what you can only dream it should be. *Globalization, or widespread use* of this platform means *the world becomes idealized,* but only for those who can live inside the virtual region where that platform operates.

Because you have an inferior ego, you cannot suffer mentally. Your mind will block things that would cause you pain. You will just fail to understand.

Medical professionals preach "right living", which comes down as if from God, or the sky. This set of rules to follow keeps women feeling safe and secure.

It keeps women de-stressed, giving them something they can follow in place of their dreaded older dependency: men.

In this place, in modern times, the most acceptable opinions are found in leaflets circulated by the government.

Almost 100% of people have almost 100% of their opinions matching the content in the leaflets.

In not-so-modern times, this 100% uniformity of opinion never existed anywhere on the globe. 100% uniformity of opinion is a man-made phenomenon.

When I was a child, unsolicited Communist magazines used to be pushed under our door free of cost. As a child, I craved colored photos because, at that time, most printed matter was in black and white.

I fancied the idea that Communism, defined by the glamorous pictures in the magazine, would feed people dying from starvation. I was only 7, but many adults felt that way too, without thinking deeply.

In truth, these colored publications of my early childhood presented a skewed picture of a Communist state. Only the positive side of the story was presented.

As you know, most of the world got sick of Communism.

In most countries today (in 2021), the media is sugar-coating things. The media is covering up facts that the politics of the state would not want people to have awareness of.

Will people get tired of the twisted media? Will people have a revolution because they are tired of living under several layers of lies?

I think that's not going to happen.

Why? I think people have more well-being these days.

When people are hungry or troubled, they are going to get mad and blame it on the government. Starving people may even overthrow the government.

During Communism, women did not get condoms

and had no control over when they got pregnant. This enforced humility we don't have anymore. Lots of basic commodities were unavailable.

In addition to groceries and commodities, in addition to medical services, we also have a mental health system now.

This new-fangled system supports women like sanitary napkins supporting them during their monthly periods.

The mental health system is not God's gift, but it is man's gift to people.

It is a set of man-made psychological gimmicks that you have unthinking and blind faith in. Should you see through their absurdities, the mental health system will not "help" you".

All humans have humbling experiences in their lifetimes.

Having very few humbling experiences means you can always hold your head high. Every human feels like a king, through eradication of humbling truths, and adding of new, fictitious truths in the name of Science, the new God.

Thanks to the gimmicks of the mental health system, the need to be a "Number One" girl is artificially supplied to all rock-bottomers.

PART THREE

3-0001: FROM ENTERING THE UK TILL 2010

I lived in the United Kingdom from 2004 to 2018, doing immigration appeals from 2006 to 2018. At that point, I left the UK and entered Ireland in April.

Shortly after my arrival UK with my newlywed husband, my parents popped up out of the blue. They had managed to rent a B&B room at the remote location where we were staying and started interrupting our peace.

They were permanent residents of India. They had been apart from me since 1995 while I lived in Canada and the USA. No mail or messages had been exchanged between me and them for a decade.

All of a sudden, I had been deported from the US to India in 2004, and had no place to rest my head but by staying with my parents. They did not allow us to consummate our marriage and thanks to my mother's behavior, my husband almost dumped me in India in my deported state.

I missed being dumped like that by a hair's breadth. Barely a couple of weeks after coming to the UK, my parents rang and said they were just living around the corner.

Am I different from the rest of the human race?

From a retrospective view, I think UK citizens would say they think this is natural "Momma-baby" love that occurs in Hindus. Their mental health system also says I am psychotic and delusional to insist I am not a Hindu. The British mental health system is of the opinion that the religion my parents give me is the one I have. If I do not practice it, I am crazy.

All that rubbish came from British mental health workers, and I did not engage with them. I did not engage with any type of mental health worker.

I consider members of this so-called occupation, which have been classified in the medical department for a hidden, eugenic reason, to be illiterate, and of a below-average caliber.

I did not engage with any members of this "community bum-unity", yet they gave verbose opinions of me, such as my relationship to Hinduism, to British police.

It was proven the opinion I should be forced into Hinduism and take mental treatments unless I kept in touch all the time with the parents, was supplied by my parents themselves. The "sex-trained sex brains" said they obeyed my parents' orders, in a letter dated 2011-09-29, which is included in this documentary

I hope it becomes clear why I refer to this so-called occupation as sex-trained sex brains. The London police respect sex-trained sex brains for their insightful "sex advice" which means they advise police how to treat a female person, who is a subject of inquiry.

For those proud Englishmen who give glowing praise to a short woman that commands a whole army of men who employ arms and ammunition, be proud of the sex advice taken by your police to repeatedly arrest and terrorize me for years to try and force me to love my parents and take so-called (sex/mental) treatments from sex-trained sex brains.

Newlyweds like to be on their own, as much as possible.

There aren't people of any race or religion who would prefer to rather clean their parents' bathroom than go on a date.

ALL UK CITIZENS felt this action was appropriate and that I should be a caterer to my parents.

3-0002: NEGATIVE CONTRIBUTION: FAMILY

I won't go into much detail here. My parents and younger sister Viju contributed to the breaking up of my marriage. To understand this allegation better, please keep reading.

My parents have another daughter Viju who has lived in England for a long time, and whose husband Steven Wortley works for the Atomic Weapons Establishment.

My parents were permanent residents of India in 2004, at the time I went to England as a newlywed.

After turning up at the remote location where I was staying with my in-laws, and creating a disturbance for me, my parents pretended to return to India.

It was both awkward and embarrassing for me to explain to strangers that I have strange parents who are passionate about stalking me to any corner of the globe and that I need to stay away from them.

I didn't. I just swallowed it.

Even after breaking my marriage, their calls to me were passionate and emotionally charged. They appeared to be hopping back and forth between India and the UK.

When there were long periods when my parents" were in India" it was convincing until early 2010 that they were residents of India who frequently visited the UK.

During those numerous "brief visits to the UK", my parents would call me from their UK mobile phone, saying they were staying in a B&B in Reading Town. but that they could not disclose their exact location.

Their younger daughter Mrs. Viju Wortley did not (and does not) live in Reading Town. She and Steve lived (they still do) in a rural district closer to the Atomic Weapons Establishment, which is the man's workplace.

The distance of their home from Reading City Center is around 12 miles.

My parents may have been desiring to migrate to the UK for some years before 2004 when I arrived there.

My mother had said that Viju had made it clear that if our parents ever visited the UK, they were NOT allowed to stay overnight in the Wortley home, as Viju felt my parents (especially my mother) would be a bad influence on her children.

This had been a deterrent to my parents from applying for migration to the UK.

While pretending to live in India, my father constantly sent unpleasant emails which were skewed, and with no content other than money.

My parents' emails contained frequent comments serving as "circumstantial evidence" to "prove" that they lived in India.

For example, she'd write emails that remarked, "Be very careful in England as it is full of crime", and "Today being a public holiday..." on a day which was a public holiday in India but a working day in the UK.

3-0003: INTERNET TELEPHONY SERVICES HIDE PARENTS' GEOLOCATION

My parents' IP address had its geolocation masked. They used a virtual phone number from India that had the country and city codes where they were pretending to live for incoming and outgoing calls. This virtual number was forwarding calls to their landline in Reading.

There are a lot of companies all over the world, such as Soho66, or Zadarma which provide virtual numbers for a few pounds per month.

This helps people to give other people of their choice a false impression they are located in a particular part of the world. This is often used to do business in an area where you don't reside. I knew about those services and just failed to realize my parents were using this to trick their daughter.

I had to be bitten many times before becoming twice shy.

Yet British people thought I should be a slave to my parents. That may not sound progressive, and some people may disbelieve it.

3-0004: God sees the Truth but Waits

In early 2010, a land registry search revealed my father had bought a freehold property in mid-2006 in a West Reading rural district.

I suspect that while trying to break up my marriage, my parents also used my husband, without my knowledge, to gain a British visa.

For example, my husband showed me a credit card application he was making in early 2006. He had listed me by my maiden name and described our relationship as "financial" in the application. I asked him why he did not write that my relationship with him was "wife".

My parents also gave my husband money. They gave him gifts behind my back after we had separated. In front of me, my parents would behave as if they hated him. My mother would urge me to hate him. Behind my back, they were flattering him and lavishing him with presents.

During an earlier period, my father had had a habit of making non-stop phone calls from India to the USA / Canada where I lived.

He called people such as my research supervisor or flatmates. He typically told them that I was a baby born crazy and that he needed me desperately, so it was important to deport me back to India.

Unlike how people react in the UK today, American/ Canadian recipients (including women) of my father's calls to offices often gave him the cold shoulder.

They complained of harassing phone calls from my parents that went so far I came to know about the generated complaints.

The USA period was 1983-1986 and the Canadian one was 1995-1999. I cannot tell if Canadian and USA values have also changed to correspond to the UK of the present time, (which is 2004-2021) whereas I have explained, people want me as a slave to my parents.

My parents, (mainly my father) kept calling offices around the USA /Canada. They would call people that could affect my life.

They'd make these frantic calls all the time to my flatmates. All my relationships soured.

You can imagine my life was nothing but a bucket of tears in my 20s and 30s.

For instance, in Canada, I received information and emails sent by my father, to more than one source.

In them, my father demanded of immigration officers that they deport me back to India.

He demanded of the university registrar to remove me from enrollment.

In [1995-1999] Canada, a shocked Indian woman who knew me by sight had once advised me my parents had set up a manhunt for me at the local Hindu temple in Calgary.

As I do not attend Hindu temples, there was no direct possibility of being placed on citizen's arrest by idol-worshipers.

"Be careful, as people might be after you", the well-wisher warned. She asked me to be careful if approached by Indians I did not know.

In the 80s in the US and the 90s in Canada, most people who received my parents' distress phone calls reported my father used a psychiatric theme in a sob story to make people help to get hold of me.

Passion-filled and "highly respectable" phone calls with "Mommy-Baby love" and a psychiatric theme have always opened doors for THOSE TWO.

My father was crafty like a fox. He tested the water each time he made a call to a fresh person and would go as far as he could get.

However, people's moral values in the USA and Canada in the 80s and 90s differed from those of the 21st century-UK.

In the 21st century-UK, the "love-calls" of my parents to all kinds of government offices just made people believe it was a case of intense virtue and "Mommy-baby love".

Eyebrows were raised in the USA and Canada when my parents called them about me. Before that, in the early 80s, the English did more than raise eyebrows. They saved my life from my parents. So this is a mighty cultural change in the UK since the 80s.

In the US my parents were able to "hide behind" the Asian community, using the power of phone calls to sabotage me, which they followed up with physical visits by airplane.

In Canada, my parents were able to engineer my deportation by repeatedly calling Citizenship and Immigration Canada.

However, Canadian immigration banned my parents for life from entering Canada.

I had been subject to an administrative error, which led to my deportation. Thousands of Canadians had suffered the same administrative error.

Due to a psychiatric report written by an ex-war criminal, their prison sentences were unduly lengthened, and in my case, it was an immigration matter where the above-mentioned recommended the same.

3-0005: NEW MARKET FOR A PENIS GENERATED IN PHYSICS AND LEGAL BAN ON MY PRIVATE LIFE

In 2007 I was expelled from the Institute of Physics for "bringing them into disrepute and spoiling other people's business". They have got thousands of women in Physics now. The women were inducted through indoctrination and street gigs.

A brand new market for a penis had arisen, which had never existed before. They have stolen my husband, on whom they have showered friendship kindness, and promises of wealth health, sex, prestige, and the greatness of scientific inventions.

The UKBA had written an official letter in November 2009 banning a private life. They did not want me to have a boyfriend or husband on UK soil, they said. Well, I could not have a private life in the UK. It was a jail sentence (14 years in the UK) with no employment and no man in a real sense, all because of the wishes of the all-powerful UK government.

3-0006: 2010 Dad Bogus Missing Person Report Through UK Hindu Police

After I discovered my parents' secret UK residence in early 2010, my mother commented, "We are not the equal of Prince Charles".

"I want Thambi to sit at the right-hand side of Nick Clegg as a star of the LibDems.", my mother said. She was referring to Mr. K Venkataramanan, my father and her husband, as "Thambi".

What could be my parents' connection with the Lib Dems?? My parents were as foreign to Britain as I was.

Later in 2010, my father made a bogus missing person report about me to British police using a Hindu police constable working in his area, West Reading district. At that time, I lived in London, about 37 miles away.

On my initial visit, my parents had bragged that the Hindu Tory MP who ruled their district was their next-door neighbor and personal friend. My mother had added, "I think Alok Sharma is a white man", which of course, nobody is going to think!

The purpose of making a missing person report was to get revenge on me for not contacting them 100 times a day. The purpose was to force a union and to continue an already- broken relationship through the arrests and terror by police.

Are Human Beings Dogs?

Dogs can be trained to behave as their masters require by beating and restricting them in diverse ways. I suppose some unintelligent human beings, (usually those who possess women's genitalia), can instinctively imbibe behavior required by their superiors through punishment or intimidation. A superior can plan the slavery he or she needs and get it.

Britain is probably one of the rare places in the whole world, and in all of human history, where you can pursue a relationship with your unwilling daughter through tyranny by the police.

My father did not live in the same town as me. Reading is 37 miles from London. I was living with Mr. A in London. That Mr. A would be the one to know if I went missing.

My father had no way of knowing if I went missing, which is why his missing person report was fraudulent.

The police visited me and Mr. A, and they realized that I was not missing, but the manhunt under the "missing person claim" continued as I moved (at one point) to an undisclosed address after stalking by police had started.

My father and mother (as you know) are respected members of the UK Hindu community in which rich people normally enjoy good status.

My parents get servants from the Hindu temple. These ladies take a lower wage than the local women, which comes in handy for my elderly mother who needs home help.

Anyway, my father made a missing person report about me through a Hindu police officer, PC Karnail Virdee.

PC Virdee sent me one email containing my father's sweet pathos, which was inappropriate for a fully-grown adult of my mental status. Immediately after, the cop went on "long leave" becoming unavailable for questioning.

It also appears my father lied to PC Virdee that I lived with my parents.

My father also lied under oath to the UK Border Agency that I had been sectioned at a place called Prospect Park mental hospital, which is a psychiatric facility near my parents' residence, about 37 miles away from me.

This gave the false impression I had been sectioned and the false impression that I lived with my parents, which in turn, would lead to false evidence that I did not live with my boyfriend, which would make the partner application get rejected by UKBA in 2010. Mind you they had already sent refusal of private life on UK soil in 2009, and later confirmed they sometimes refuse private life and do not need to give reasons.

Page 1 Father made FRAUDULENT missing person report to a Hindu policeman in his area in the UK

Hello Mohini HERSOM I am a Police Officer from Thames Valley Police.

Mohini you have been reported missing and we only need to check that you are fine and to make sure that you are not in any sort of danger. We don't need to s welfare and trouble with the Police as mentioned above only to check on your welfare.

Please could you get in contact with us ASAP using the above reference number.

Many thanks.

PC3827 Sunny VIRDEE (Misper Co-ordinator)
Reading Police Station
Castle Street
Reading
RG1 7TH
07800 702187 or 08458 505505

"sCIENTIFIC aMERICAN" <editors@sciam.com>; <swortley@awe.co.uk>
Subject: Fw: Nazi Prison..psychiatric fraud and murder of me to keep dirty dunghole female sex offenders in false glory 4ever

Flag this message

Case Ref #MP/05781/2010

Monday, October 4, 2010 10:55 AM

--- On Sat, 10/9/10, Mohini Hersom <*mohinihersom@yahoo.co.uk*> wrote:

From: Mohini Hersom <mohinihersom@yahoo.co.uk>
Subject: Nazi Prison..psychiatric fraud and murder of me to keep dirty dunghole female sex offende
in false glory 4ever
To:
Cc: "K Venkataramanan" <rvtechno@vsnl.net>, steve.hubbard@physics.org, "Ross Campbell"
<ross888@gmail.com>, "Russell Cain" <russell.cain@jacobs.com>, "Ron Edge"
<redge@sc.rr.com>, p.i.p.kalmus@qmul.ac.uk, "RudyWrench" <comsenstrat@hotmail.com>,
a.choudhury@pohwer.net, vishanti.lall@iop.org, "Sean Fox" <sean.fox@iop.org>, "sean fox"
<sean.fox@london.iop.org>, "Mrs Viju Wortley" <2tall@waitrose.com>, "KV Godwillexposethetruth"
<vu2kv@arrl.net>
Date: Saturday, October 9, 2010, 4:49 PM

Hail Hitler the pig is dead. I know you will abuse me until you make

— On Thu, 10/21/10, Eyles Phil <Phil.Eyles@thamesvalley.pnn.police.uk> wrote:

From: Eyles Phil <Phil.Eyles@thamesvalley.pnn.police.uk>
Subject: FW: contact please.
To: mohiniherzom@yahoo.co.uk
Date: Thursday, October 21, 2010, 11:21 AM

Hello Mohini,

Thank you so much for getting in touch with me.
Unfortunately I've missed your calls and when I've tried to call you back, your number has been engaged.
I'll keep trying to speak with you.
And I just want to re-assure you that you are in no way wanted by the police and I don't want to upset you or cause you any harassment or invade your privacy or human rights.

My concern is that as you have not been seen in person I can't close your missing person report so that is all I need to do.
I'll try to call you again,
My mobile number is listed below too.

Phil

Pc 3996 Eyles
Missing Persons Coordinator
Protecting Vulnerable People Investigations Unit
Berkshire West BCU
EXT: 751 6307
DDI: 0118 9536307
Fax: 0118 9536349
Mobile: 07800 702339
24 hr 0845 8 505 505

-----Original Message-----
From: Eyles Phil
Sent: 13 October 2010 13:29
To: 'mohinihorsom@yahoo.co.uk'
Cc: Virdee Karnail
Subject: contact please.

Dear Mohini,

My colleague Pc Virdee has been in touch with you recently but he is away on his holidays this week and I really want to keep up a rapport with you as you are still a missing person and we need to ensure our bosses that you are alive an well.

I have a duty of care to oversee this and I would like to give you my reassurance that PC Virdee and I only have your interest at heart and once we've seen you in person, I'd be more than happy to leave you to live your life in peace. But until you are seen we need to keep 'pestering you' and for that I apologise.

I hope that you could get in touch.

Phil Eyles

Pc 3996 Eyles
Missing Persons Coordinator
Protecting Vulnerable People Investigations Unit
Berkshire West BCU
EXtn 791 6307
DDI: 0118 95396307
Fand 0118 95396346
Mobile: 07860 703339
24 hr 0845 8 505 505

mailto:phil.eyles@thamesvalley.pnn.police.uk

3-0007 The Story of Mohini's 9 14

Mohini's 9 14 took place in the United Kingdom, only 3 days after the famous 9 11 in the United States, only 9 years later on the time line. No bombs were dropped and no planes deployed. Nonetheless, it was a day of terror fraud and injustice by the police.

In September of 2010, I had a premonition that something bad was about to happen unless I left Mr. A's home.

Mr. A agreed there could be some truth in my fear. He would help me to follow my premonitions, he said.

I thought I should leave by the night of Monday the 13th of September 2010 but was delayed. I ended up leaving the next morning at 10 am. Naturally, by noon or 1 pm I had arrived at my new destination.

At my new temporary residence, I received a call from Mr. A in the late afternoon the same day. Mr. A said, gasping, that by coincidence, he had come home an hour early. He was found his front door was open. There was a hole in the wood where the lock had been.

Mr. A thought at first that he had been burgled, but had spotted a man running around the corner of the building.

He had chased him, which had led to the discovery of an ambulance sandwiched between two police cars.

The running men had gotten away in their police cars. The ambulance had followed suit.

They had come for me and had broken the front door to fetch me. Having searched Mr. A's house, they had realized I was not in and were about to leave. But they decided to run when they saw Mr. A coming and dumped the damaged door.

Mr. A had phoned non-emergency police. They had admitted they were the people who had raided his house looking for me. The housebreak was at my father's request, they claimed.

The met police had said they did not have an obligation to pay for the broken door. Mr. A had been left with the prospect of securing his flat where he was to sleep that night. He had luckily been able to do some carpentry on his own and buy a lock that evening and secure his door as the police had left his home at risk and gone away.

3-0008: UPGRADING OF
DEPORTATION DOCUMENT.

The morning after my 9 14, my deportation document was upgraded.

I was on reporting restrictions, and had to report on 15th September. It meant I carried two documents by law.

One document called IS96 had my ugly blurred photograph and explained the terms and conditions whereby I could remain in the UK, a visa substitute of sorts.

The other document was called IS151, followed by A, B, C, or D. These letters are similar to "ready, steady, go, jump." in the deportation process, where D is the physical deportation.

I went into Eaton House with IS151A. My deportation was in the "baby stages". I left Eaton House with IS151B

I was at the new location since 14th September, when I had learned from Mr. A via phone about his terrible housebreak.

When reporting I asked UKBA for help with the traumatic

incident that had taken place the previous afternoon. The UKBA pretended not to know anything about it.

I realized that police had broken into Mr. A's house only 24 hours ago, in an unsuccessful attempt to section me, and I was now receiving a document telling me my deportation was moving forward. Were these two events related in any way?

Met police told Mr. A the housebreak had been on my father's orders.

How could an old man like my father (evil as he was), have the power to force police to break into someone's house? It did not seem credible at all.

Actually the GP Dr Siddiqui I was registered with at the time, reported that my parents visited him, and asked him to provide my address contrary to data protection rules, claiming they needed it to save my life.

My father told the GP I was not willing to accept money from them, but that if he did not give me money,I would starve to death, as I was mentally incompetent.

The GP said he just asked my parents to go away.

Actually,my parents had visited me earlier at the home of

Mr. A when they were not allowed inside, So my parents
jolly well knew my address at the time they asked my
when they visited my GP for my address.

The GP had nothing to do the involuntary committal
bid by Met police on 9 14. The Met police claimed they
followed the orders of my father who was "concerned"
about my mental welfare; however my father is just an old
man who does not have a legal right to order someone's
arrest.

3-0009: MENTAL TORTURE BY POLICE LOOKING FOR MY CORPSE

Police kept talking to me while I refused to give them my location. At the same time, they kept searching Mr. A's house for me. The way they searched looked like they were looking for my body, for example in closets and cupboards.

London met police kept popping into Mr. A's to "catch" me in case I visited. At least twice they searched Mr. A's house without a warrant, but with his consent to search for me as well as for my body.

I stayed at the undisclosed location from where I was able to phone and tell the police I was doing fine. I remained at the undisclosed location from 14th September until around the beginning of November 2010 when I moved back in with Mr. A.

3-0010: LADY PCSO WANTS ME <u>ON</u> SOMETHING <u>UNDER</u> SOMEONE TO REINSTATE PARENT-CHILD RELATIONSHIP

In November 2010, a policewoman Anna Heggarty PCSO XH7010, visited me while I was alone at home with garbled information and asked for permission to enter Mr. A's house, which I declined

Initially, she said there had been a hanging inside this house, which she had come to investigate I said there had been no hangings here. She then asked to meet, and rescue an 8-year-old child called Mohini Hersom.

I said that was me, and she realized I wasn't 8, so, she asked if I had a daughter aged 8 whose health was at risk.

PCSO Heggarty said I needed to be "on something" and "under someone" to induce the love of my parents.

When she said "on something", I believe she meant neuroleptic medication.

The "under someone", as I saw it was referring to the gifted employees of the Pesthilenseroke Society who possessed noble and munificent female genitalia.

My definition of being"under someone" is a relationship which is like sticking my head between the legs of a hen, or under a hen, to incubate gradually into "Momma-baby" love.

PCSO Heggarty said she herself had gone through the baby-producing process, and knew how my parents would feel if a baby they produced was not responding to their love.

Little did I suspect that this visit by the PCSO was a warning directly from the UKBA, who needed me to take psychiatric treatments to repair the parent-child relationship, or they would proceed with flying to India for good.

3-0011: Father begs CEO of UKBA's Eaton House, to "lock me up for psychiatric reasons"

When I attended my monthly reporting at Eaton House, I was called inside twice "for interviews", in October and November of 2010.

Later I learned that people who are on their usual reporting get called "inside", which means going to the wrong side of the counter.

The trick usually fools everyone the first time they use it. Sometimes there is no second time. Most reportees will be called for interviews multiple times before being deported or granted indefinite leave to remain.

Being called in "for interviews" usually means you won't be let back out after the interviews.

Instead, they will divest you of your belongings, empty your pockets, and detain you till the end of the day at which point you will get driven to an immigration removals center.

You will also receive some kind of papers telling you they would like to deport you or your flight schedule.

The term removal means the same thing as deportation, or what they do to you in both cases is identical. But they use the term deportation for what they do to you if they are deporting you for a crime, otherwise, they call it a removal.

I was not taken away for deportation on the two occasions in November 2010, when I ignorantly consented to go to the wrong side of the counter.

This was unusually lucky.

They did not have their paperwork ready to deport me on those "lucky" days. Many legalities had to be satisfied.

I cannot tell you what would have happened if I had refused to go in. However, you need to know, they if they are calling you inside intending to deport you, they will never take no for an answer.

As if out of the blue, tall Sikh men in black uniforms who are hidden inside Eaton House will make an appearance, and are trained to use physical force to take you into the other side of the counter.

They look a lot more deadly than bouncers.

During one of my November 2010 "interviews" at Eaton

House Reporting Center, its CEO, Mr. C told me that my father had visited him and requested for UKBA to put me under psychiatric lockup.

Mr. C also mentioned "the love of the baby" and said he trusted that my father was doing this out of love.

Mr. C added that he does not trust my father or me. He was not interested in putting me under psychiatric lockup, he said."

You are also never going to be deported, however, we may remove you", said Mr. C. He said that he and his men may not have a university education, but were smart enough to deal with my kind.

Mr. C gave me the phone number of the AVM lady to act as immigration help and was annoyed when I had told him that all she wanted to do for me was book a flight to India. "I am sorry you feel our AVM lady isn't good enough for you. Maybe you should make a fresh start in India," Mr. C said.

3-0012: Pesthilenseroke* obeys my Parents

The Pesthilenseroke claimed they had no choice but to stalk me as those were my parents' orders.

In response to my complaint about prolonged harassment by the Pesthilenseroke Society, who banged on the front door after Mr. A had gone to work, and I was alone, sad, and frightened by their onslaught, the Society had written on 29.9.2011 a final response to my formal complaint.

This official letter said my parents had ordered this type of stalking and they had no power to disobey.

My parents told the Pesthilenseroke (Pesthilenseroke) Society I had a false relationship with Mr. A and that only my parents were my real relatives.

My parents had told the Pesthilenseroke Society that in their culture a daughter had to obey her parents; my disobedience was a mental illness.

Pesthilenseroke was ordered to make sure (they said) I stayed under a psychiatric lockup until or unless obedience to parents followed. The fact is, the doctors did not authorize this lockup and would not take part in the parental stalking.

By acting in this way, my parents were jeopardizing my immigration status.

After my expulsion from the Institute of Physics in 2006, UKBA had refused me the right to work.

In 2009 UKBA had sent me a letter banning me from having a boyfriend or husband on UK soil. I was living with my boyfriend, Mr. A, which UKBA could not stop. The ban meant the UKBA would disregard my marriage or close relationship when they thought it was time to carry out my deportation to India.

By claiming to Pesthilenseroke my boyfriend was a fake one to the Pesthilenseroke (Pesthilenseroke) Society, my parents were undermining my immigration status.

By having no employment due to having no work authorization, I would need to piggyback on someone to not get deported.

By declaring to Pesthilenseroke that I had a fake relationship with my boyfriend, my parents were making sure I stayed close to themselves or got dumped on the streets of Delhi, a third-world country with no social services, with no humans or assets to call my own.

A physicist to cry weep and beg on the streets of India in

the heat. In this regard, I wish to make scanty coverage of the side-topic "The copulatory privates of the women in Physics". Thousands of women have joined Physics and many millions more are having "thrills and spills" in "Communicating Physics" after a new eugenic scheme was put in place by the Physicists internationally. Some people have to be eradicated whenever there is a eugenic scheme.

3-0013: MY NEXT 9 14:
DEPORTATION DIRECTIONS

After the mysterious smashing of Mr. A's front door by
police on 14th of September of 2010, which was "my
little 9 14", I spent from 9th to 14th December of 2010 at
Yarlswood Removals Center, missing the flight to India
by a hair's breadth. This was "my next 9 14".

I realized that the November policewoman advising me
to be on anti-psychotics and "under" the inappropriately
intimate supervision of the venerable, sexually-gifted
Pesthilenseroke staff possessing female genitalia, to
induce a love of parents who were broken-hearted through
misfired baby-producing was the last warning by UKBA
before enforcing my removal.

On 9th December 2010, I was issued Notice IS151D
which gave my flight schedule by Virgin Atlantic from
Heathrow to Delhi at 10 pm on 14th December 2010.

I was detained while reporting on the 9th of December
2010 and supplied with Flight Directions.

Instead of calling me for interviews, the lady at the
counter had said on this occasion, "There has been a
change in your circumstances. Your relationship with your
boyfriend has ended."

I was not sure what she meant, and she explained,
"You've got to come inside."

An early bird at the reporting center, I was to stay in cells
for the rest of the working day.

At 5 pm, when the reporting center closed, I was to get
into their unmarked van with blackened windows for a
3-4 hour journey to the deportation center- a circuitous
journey through long country roads.

Once detained, immigration officers threatened to deport
me unless I called my parents.

In the first cell. my pockets were emptied. Rings,
wristwatches, earrings and everything like that had to go.
From this point, I no longer had a phone.

When I was taken to the main cell they gave toilet
refreshments and use of their UKBA cell phone.

I phoned Mr. A at work and told him what had happened
to me. However, the detaining officers told me my
deportation was 100% guaranteed if could not QUICKLY
think of one more person to phone.

If I had not bowed to the UKBA and telephoned my parents that afternoon, I would probably have been on the flight to India, as provided in the notice that had just been served on me.

Actually, my flight was still going to take place. As you will see, a lawyer stopped my flight at the last minute.

3-0014: YARLSWOOD IRC: A TALE OF 1000 BEDS, AND 1000 DRAINS

Yarlswood is a walled institute, hidden away inside another walled area which is an industrial estate, approachable by private transport from Bedford railway station.

Yarlswood runs a shuttle service for visitors of prisoners and has a discounted taxi company to travel from Bedford railway station to the IDC and back.

It is a detention and deportation center for women. However, there are men and children in a separate, locked family ward. It has several wards. Yarlswood is a huge modern prison with hotel-style bedrooms along corridors and electronic locking from a central control room, and it is 100% halal. It had 1,000 beds and every bed has drainage underneath, so that body fluids near beds could be washed off.

An enormous place with long corridors, they have cookery and drawing classes for housewives. Indian detainees celebrated their own festivals, as organized by Yarlswood. Two women were put in a (bed)room. They usually put you with someone from "your own culture".

Back in the mess hall what looked like a wall was a

sliding panel, from behind where they wheeled in a detainee with a spine injury, who said received corporal punishment alone in the basement from men beating her. I saw the bruises myself after Brazilian deportee Thelma Correa had been taken off a plane at Heathrow by a Portuguese pilot as tall and strong UKBA women officers were using violence on the plane

In the mess hall, they had an artistic painting of a pier with a cross-beam going out to sea, and people jumping off all four beams of the cross into the water as if to say, "Get out all of you."

They allow detainees to use a computer and internet from behind the barracuda network. This is like US immigration, called INS-they are also behind the barracuda network, although I am sure I never used a computer there.

It will be purely speculative whether my parents told Mr. Passmore, to whom they had paid a fat retainer that I had to go to India. He did stop my flight.

3-0015: My Mother and other helpful Countrymen

Once detained, I was reading the correspondence between UKBA and Mr. Passmore. Twice Mr. Passmore's petitions to UKBA were returned to him with an absolute refusal.

In them was mentioned a court hearing dated Nov 8th of 2010, that I had not attended. A negative decision had been given at this hearing in my absence.

UKBA's correspondence to Mr. Passmore said I had needed to be arrested for not attending it. That arrest had just taken place on 9th December of 2010.

The UKBA admitted they did not post me the notice of this hearing. So it was not my fault.

My parents told me that by law, it was my responsibility to make sure I got UKBA notices.

But I had not even known about this hearing's existence. So I was not awaiting its notification.

On the eve of my flight, 13th December, I stopped eating and drinking water. Deportation staff told me I would be flying to India even if they had to put me on a life-support machine. They said if I was dead on arrival in Delhi, it would be my problem and nobody else's. The deportation staff were Indians who spoke broken English. They said they were "pouffessionals" who were just following a "pouffedure".

I told a guard I had an English boyfriend had did not want to be deported; I would fast to death. She was Indian and said she too had an English boyfriend and hoped I received help.

On the evening of 13th December, my mother urged me on the phone to discontinue my hunger strike, and to fly to India very quietly, not to protest anything.

I realized that being quiet and obedient in Yarlswood was not going to help to prevent my flight, possibly make sure it took place.

My mother added that it would be the best thing for me to fly to India.

After all, I was coming back to the UK after 5 days, she said.

My mother said Mr. A had agreed to fly to India in 5 days and marry me.

A quick phone call to Mr. A confirmed that my mother, Radha, by name, was just using a trick to make sure I got deported and never came back.

Mr.A said he had never said all those things to my mother. "I don't even have my passport, which will take a month to come," said Mr. A. Besides, he confirmed he had never told my mother he intended to marry me.

3-0016: FATHER PAID LAWYER TO PROVE TO UKBA I WAS A *BABY* BORN MENTALLY INCOMPETENT

Mr. Passmore said my father paid him a fat retainer to prove to UK immigration I am mentally incompetent.

I was supposed to be taken out of Yarlswood at 2 pm on the day of the flight, 14/12/2010. The Virgin Atlantic direct flight to Delhi was to leave Heathrow airport at 10 pm.

I was dizzy with a pounding heart, waiting to be grabbed when I decided to phone Mr. Passmore for the first time. I told him about the life-support machine, etc, and casually chatted to him saying a lot of people wanted to prove I was mentally incompetent.

To my surprise, Mr. Passmore said "Your father has asked me to prove to UKBA that you are mentally incompetent."

Mr. Passmore said that as soon as he got me out of this place he would resign owing to a conflict of interest between the person who paid him and his client, myself.

The guards entered and said you must leave now.

I did not realize they were saying I would leave detention.

Through two locked stages and a couple of hours, I was reunited with Mr.A, who was waiting in a room with an exit. We hugged and kissed. It was a happy moment.

Mr. Passmore had stopped my flight. He resigned following that. After that, he was reluctant to speak a word about what had happened.

3-0017: Post Yarlswood Joys and Sorrows

Post-Yarlswood, I made a Subject Access Request to the UKBA which revealed they were indeed behind the "psychiatric house raid" on Mr. A's home, my 9 14, and the reign of terror that spanned months before and after that fateful date.

Met Police had lied to Mr. A on that fateful date, that my father had ordered my arrest, and ordered for Mr.A's home to be broken into by city police.

My father is not in the police and would have no arresting powers.

Dr. Siddiqui had known nothing about "my little 9 14" and was not involved anyway.

If I had not had a premonition or my friend had not supported that premonition, I would have been at home when they broke the front door on "9 14". They would have forced me into the ambulance and whisked me away.

I can't be sure what would have happened if I had been at home and they had kidnapped me. Could they have sectioned me, which needed two doctors? I am not sure. But I am sure they intended to detain me with a view to deportation.

Because their plan to do this via housebreaking on 14th September had failed, they had made other attempts and detained me during regular reporting on 9th December of 2010.

The UKBA makes all deportees see a medical officer before the flight, a procedure for their internal medical records.

Their medical officer working in the custody unit does not behave like normal doctors or nurses.

He writes a "fit-to-fly" certificate. It is his job to do the necessary procedures UKBA wants, so they can fly out their intended deportees.

I see no reason why the UKBA medical officer would not have put psychiatric allegations in my record which were compatible with a fit-to-fly certificate.

All this being speculation.

The new year 2011 was joyous as I had narrowly escaped deportation.

But was not stress-free. My status was that of a person who could be detained and deported at any time. The original dispute of the UKBA, on which my recently-issued IS151D had been based, was alive and well.

My father paid for a counselor I found myself locally to stall my flight to India which could have taken place at any time.

I had to do whatever it took to stall my repeat arrest by UKBA.

For those who are not familiar with how the law works, seeing a counselor will not necessarily stop a person's deportation.

But some people say jocularly that mental health takes priority over fourth stage cancer in terms of the power to stop deportations.

There is some truth in this joke, the law being nobody's friend unless they happen to be ten steps beneath a prostitute. If they recommend mental health problems as more likely to stall one's deportation than fourth-stage cancer, then seeing a counselor can help, although there are no guarantees.

While some countries will proceed with deportation if you

claim (or show medical evidence) of a mental condition, the UK is one of the havens for an automatic right of stay for mental patients.

3-0018: Father wants to buy me Lunatic Visa Threatens to break Door force Consent Signature

After I was released from the Immigration removals center, in the new year of 2011, my parents forced me to visit them.

In their home, my father said he had a plan to immigrate me in a special way. He had a special Asian lawyer called Chechi who had a special psychiatrist. "You will enter that psychiatrists' clinic and spend half an hour with him and leave that clinic via the back door immigrated. I promise you after that you will never work again" my father said. My father said you can live here, have an easy life and a council house.

My father was happy for me to be one of those thousands of idle people that have "A HOUSE", with my life a solitary and silent paradise, "bumming" off the state under the mental health bounty.

I did not want the "never work again". The "you will have a council house'also made me mad.

I realized my father would pay money to a *bent*

psychiatrist to get such a terrible psychiatric diagnosis of me so to validate his diagnosis I would have to stay unemployed for a lifetime.

I was also angry about the council house, as my father had just said, "we are very wealthy and want to protect and support you". Remarks like that have always made me want to vomit.

None of this I wanted. Not even their stinking wealth, which would make Radha bring up Prince Charles. I opt for happiness and dignity over wealth. Unholy control over my flesh and legal rights was going on like forcible rape. But the UK respect women, who are of inferior mental status, and the police wanted to torture arrest and humiliate me (at the behest of these Pesthilenseroke women) to be subjugated as they would be, willing to do anything for bread.

As council houses are means-tested I could not see the daughter of someone that wealthy being eligible. My father intended to ask me to make a bogus claim of poverty to get a council house, or else deny me any inheritance, I thought to myself.

I was furious and walked out of my parents' house. There was a bus stop nearby. I think 200 yards away. I had to catch the bus to the railway station in Reading to return to London.

My father liked to pretend that he was more able-bodied than me and that I was mentally incompetent.

I understand that modern British "women" will accommodate a father who behaves like that by cooing and nurturing.

Again I have understood adult women of the UK won't feel mad if treated like that. I understand they lack the pride found in men. I am sorry but I have been tortured and cannot put up with this stalking, mental health, hatred, and "women's role".

By the same token, British women would want me punished for disrespecting the father.

This explains why I don't want women anymore.

If these women would accommodate any man's penis in return for a small fee, I think they are probably morally obliged to cater to the selfish and egotistical whims of an evil old father in exchange for scraps of bread. Why not?

That my father was acting like it was madness for me to walk out of his house. and following me in his car when I was waiting for the bus.

He was acting like I was incompetent, like I had

Alzheimer's or whatever, and had incoherently walked off. He put up a car chase like it wasn't safe for me to walk to the bus stop nearby in broad daylight.

It is daunting to live in a world where no human understands or accepts you. The anger I feel at my father's annoying behavior is something a British male would feel. It's okay to be shunned by all men as they don't accept women who feel anger in the UK. My anger stays, and my life goes, to shorten the life sentence in this woman-gulag.

But the spontaneous reflexes of a British female in the same situation would be cooing and nurturing. What she won't feel in that situation is negative emotions.

I mean I feel there is an extreme racial hygiene in the UK against women who don't practice *female mencap* as found in British women.

I hope you understand I may be less than an animal and worse than a donkey to every male in the UK, for failing to practice *female mencap*; and for failing to *make gold* with *prestigious bearers of female genitalia* working for *prestigious and bountiful organizations* like the Pesthilenseroke.

This would mean I am worse than a *Nigger* to any British male and would not have a boyfriend on British soil unless I wanted someone who would feel less respect than to an animal.

Let me theorize then, that the Home Office issued me a legal notice prohibiting private and family life on UK soil.

If we agree there is racial hygiene in the UK against women with no *female "mencap*, and every UK man would see me in a poor light. I would be single on UK soil plus I would not speak to any man.

Not speaking to any man, assuming I can live like British people, will merely reduce my working potential to become as low as the upper limit of that of the equality and diversity communities, and possibly even lower.

Which of you who are men would speak to women if you lived in a land where every woman would tell you *there is a man out there, in an organization* who is *trained* to give you tenderness and intimacy?

You who are a man will you or will you not commit suicide if you lived in a world like that?

How come you think I must not commit suicide and how come you want more and more female genitalia piled over my head, when I complained I am dying of the same?

After a few days, my father drove to Mr. A's house in London from his place in rural Berkshire. They are very sick and old people.

In 2011, they were a decade younger and stronger than they are now. I was alone at home, and Mr. A was at work.

My father banged on the door and tried to force me to sign consent for his appointed lawyer to take over my immigration case.

I would see a psychiatrist for 30 minutes, and emerge from the backdoor of the clinic with indefinite leave to remain, and something that they would do as part of the process meant I would never work again.

So if my father was to be trusted to keep his word, this was my destiny, if I signed this document. My father knew I was not willing and wanted to force me if he possibly could.

I said no and he said he would break the door. I think under normal circumstances he would have broken the door and British police would have been sympathetic to his story.

The police would have taken my father's side had he broken down the door, I felt, as my father would utter the magical word "mental health." The final legal verdict would be that was my father was doing the noble deed of trying to save my life.

Not Opening Door for Father Lawful in the US Worse than Murder in the UK

So anyhow my father had once threatened to break down the door when I was in the US and he kept taking a plane across the globe to Tucson Arizona to abort my self-funded studies.

I mean that was 1984-1985 and I was able to call the American police who told him to go away.

It was a very small matter for the American police and they told my father to leave, because I didn't want to open the door. Whereas in the UK, in the 20th-21st century my action is deemed a capital offense leading to psychiatric punishment by woman teams such as the Pesthilenseroke.

3-0019 SECRET LAWS LANDMINES INFERIOR SEX ROLES

I feel there are secret laws in the UK, No one utters them or sees them in print. They are however enforced all the time.

The advantage of having a secret law, I think, is like having the cake and eating it.

The disadvantage I think is that the place is full of landmines and surprises for them that are not *the chosen ones*. Essentially some people are getting bumps and knocks in life while others have a double advantage.

I have yakked enough. What do I mean?

Women lack the mental sensation of dignity. They would respond with *beggo-pleado* and experience total fulfillment in a situation of slavery, if government-sponsored leaflets did not tell them it is slavery.

The law is different for men and women. Everyone lies till they are blue in the face about this law. This is why I call it somewhat imprecisely a secret law. It is like measuring the height of men in feet and that of women in inches and comparing the numeric value to judge if they are equally tall.

This is the big secret of the UK.

I am not suggesting that all UK women would beg and crawl at their fathers' feet, just that those who won't crawl at their father's feet would probably be *outcasted*.

When you are outcasted you are also believed to suffer from mental health problems necessitating treatment given by *sexually-gifted superwomen*.

3-0020: 2011-01-16 _Met_ POLICE CONTEMPT AND OVERDOSE

Met Police offered the opposite of Protection

When my father banged on the door on 14th January 2011, saying he would break the door and force me to sign my consent to appoint Chechi, I phoned the police _American-style_.

I had a tape recorder connected.

I can't recall where I put the tape as I was isolated, living in a virtual environment of uniformity of opinion where there was no one with my opinion.

The police told me with contempt in their voice that I was mentally ill and should obey everything my father said.

I felt so bad about the behavior of the police that I took an overdose to kill myself.

I took between 16 and 32 tablets of Nytol on the evening of 16th January 2011 which was a Sunday. I told my friend I took them and then he took me to an _Accident and Emergency_ in a taxi.

In the taxi, I started feeling a strange sensation in my eyebrows.

Once in A&E, I found it hard to stand and they gave me a chair. Soon, I was gasping for breath.

My friend said not to worry we must wait for the doctor. My chest pain started and was increasing.

Soon I was in agony. It would have been an hour since my overdose. I was lying on the A&E bed.

I was put on oxygen and struggling to breathe. I told my friend I may not make it into the morning, but my friend said not to worry because if your heart stops we will restart it.

If he had not been with me that night I probably would have died that morning on 17.1.2011. I felt okay about passing away as I had a friend by my side and had not done anything wrong.

I knew the agony had to increase and then it would all be over. My agony was increasing. I thought about warmth and the sun. I wished I had never done this and could be standing alive in my body talking to my friend.

I recall a Chinese male doctor entering and exiting.

A female doctor came in requesting ECG and said to lie still so she could take it. I was heaving and writhing. She said nothing was wrong with me and I was just acting weird on purpose. She was suggesting that I did not take an overdose or was completely healthy.

She said I was a pretending bitch, and pulled off my oxygen, but Mr. A put it back after she left.

My friend closed the curtains and he switched on the oxygen machine and put the tubes back in my nose. I had a problem with my throat getting stuck and I was breathing about 75%. He trickled ice cold water down my throat causing it to *unstick* so I could take in air with a gasp.

I woke up in the recovery room and my friend was standing there. Everything around me looked pink. Maybe I was seeing through my own blood.

He went home and I was woken up at some point in the night and asked to go home, I understood what I was being told but my answer didn't make any sense. I realized I was incoherent. They took me home by ambulance.

I was offered an unusual remedy for suicide: obey parents & attend *Hindu woman meetings*.

The next morning, 17.1.2011, I was visited by a social worker Richard Ellis from NHS who advised "For this suicide attempt to not happen again, you should regularly attend meetings with Hindu women in Southall to prove to your parents that you are not psychotic. He was British not Indian yet interested in making me a Hindu.

Why the f*** am I worthy of death if I don't want to be a Hindu"? I had told them I was not a Hindu but the illiterate hospital staff was filling out my bio data on the medical reports with entries like *Hindu, schizo head"*and *Age=Prime Minister* so I had to give up.

Why should I prove to my parents I am not psychotic? Why should I prove anything at all to my parents? Finally, why should I speak only to women? Who was he to tell me all these things?

Later I got my medical record of that incident. Medical records people are very nice and release records even when the doctors don't want that.

I've seen that at more than one hospital.

I'm not a doctor and I just can't explain what I'm saying that that the ECG may very well be evidence I could have died that night.

But to this day (2022) no doctor is willing to admit I had a heart attack on that day. They always change the subject when that question is asked.

They lied in the medical report that I told them I took alcohol with Nytol. I am not illiterate. I have enough intelligence not to tell lies like that. I know about breathalyzers.

They did not give post-cardiac support. They left it to Nature and God. Maybe they hoped for the worst.

NHS Trust

| Accident & Emergency Department | D | GP | NHS No: | 630 829 2621 |

| Hospital number 02451285 | Mode of arrival Emergency Services | Arrival date |
| Name Mrs Mohini Hassom | Refer source Other | 16/01/2011 |

Address

| Incident Type | Arrival time |
| Other | 19:22 |

| LAS call sign | B602 | Time discharged |

Occupation / School / OPH
SELF EMPLOYED

| Ethnic Group |
| Asian - Any Other B |

D.O.B. 28/08/1958   Tel No.

Family G.P. Dr M. Siddiqui	Next of kin Name	INFORMED	YES / NO	Religion Hindu
Address 21 Walnut Way				
South Ruislip	Address			Age 52 years
Middlesex				

| Tel. No. 020 88454400 | Tel. No. | ...ationship | Sex Female |

| Presenting complaint Drug Overdose | | Police No. | Bee BKD |

| Total Attendances | 0 | 5 | Alerts | Ward / Destination | Bed AVL |
| | | | | | Time-WO 72:35 |

MEDICATION / PROCEDURES							Time & Signature
DATE	TIME	DRUG /PROCEDURE	DOSE	ROUTE	SIGNATURE	TIME GIVEN	SIGNATURE	ECG
								X-RAY
								U+E
								CRP
								LFT
								CK
			TTA					COAG
								AMYLASE
								FBC
								GLUC
								REFERRED

PREFERRED NAME:
HISTORY OF PRESENTING PROBLEMS: (B7 RO2)   Time Assessed: None

Taken 16 tablets of Nytol @

APPEARANCE ON ARRIVAL   1025   8 alcohol taken

Depression

| on arrival | 1/2 hr | 2 hrs | 4 hrs | | 1022 |
| PAIN SCORE 0/10 | | | | SIGNATURE | TIME |

T °c: 36.5	P: 140/min	B.P.: 140/80	MSU. Sent/Saved	Allergies
Resps: 19/min	Sa o 08 air %	P.Flow L/min:	B-HCG: Neg/Pos	NKDA
Blood Sugar mmol/Lt	GCS: 15/15	Pupils: R L	Immunisation
Weight Kg:	PAR Score	Visual Acuity	Overseas travel in last 30 days?

308

CLINICAL NOTES (cont.)

16/01/11 TAMAN Sample Label:

Time seen	NAME OF DOCTOR / ENP (PLEASE PRINT/STAMP)

+ years.

OD· Nytol
Suicidal
No H/O OD in the post

PMH: , Depressive

DH: Allergy: Nil

O/E well

CVS jvp
          I+II +S
          on   der
RESP

GI

plan: Serum
      drug
      level
      @ 22:30

SIGNATURE	OUTCOME	DIAGNOSIS

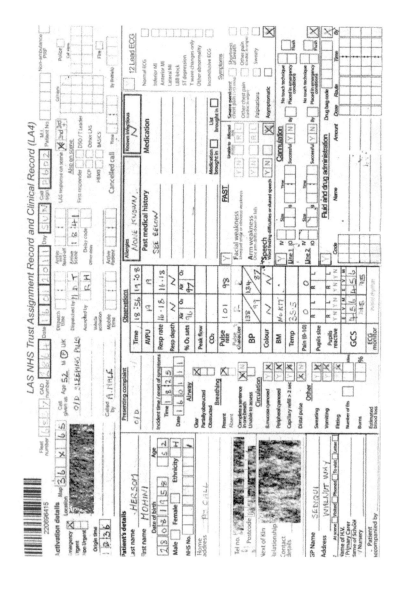

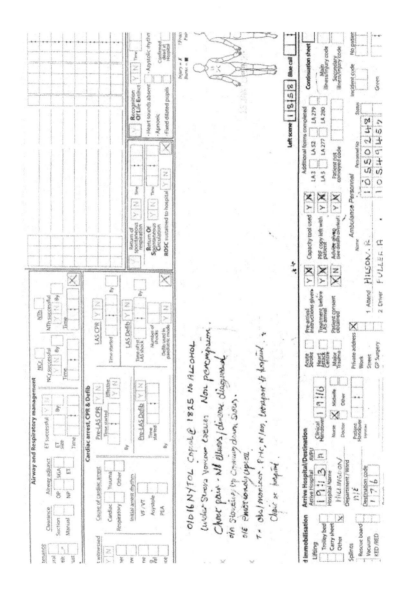

220696415

LAS NHS Trust Assignment Record and Clinical Record (LA4)

Fleet number 6827 · CAD number 2864 · Date 16 01 2011 · Day SUN · Call sign P602 · M.I. Patient No. · Non-ambulance PRF

Activation details

Emergency [X] · Urgent · Non Urgent

Map 36 X 65 · Location [redacted]

Origin time 18:36

Call given as Age 52 M (F) UK

O/D SLEEPING PILLS

Called by A.MALE

Dispatch time · Dispatched by HDT · Accepted by RH · Vehicle activation · Mobile time

Arrive at HP Stand-off · Arrive Scene 18:41 · Delay code · Other delay · Arrive Patient

LAS response on scene [X] 2nd 3rd+

Also on scene: First responder · DSO / T Leader · ECP · Other LAS · HEMS · BASICS

Callsigns · Police · Call signs · Fire

Cancelled call Time · By (Initials)

Patient's details

Last name HERSOM

First name MOHINI

Date of birth 28 08 1958 · Age 52

Male · Female · Ethnicity H

NHS No.

Home address [illegible] CALL

Tel no. [redacted]

Postcode [redacted]

Next of Kin · Relationship · Contact details [redacted]

GP Name SENQUI

Address WALNUT WAY

At scene · Visited · Phoned · To visit · Letter

Name of H.V. / Primary Carer / Name of School / Nursery

Patient accompanied by

Presenting complaint

O/D

Incident time / onset of symptoms: Time 18:25 · Date 16 01 11

Airway: Clear [X] · Partially obstructed · Obstructed

Breathing: Present [X] · Absent · Complete a sentence in one breath [X] Y · Unable to assess

Circulation: B.mucosa cyanosed N [X] · Peripheral cyanosed N [X] · Capillary refill > 2 sec N [X] · Distal pulse Y [X]

Other: Sweating N [X] · Vomiting N [X] · Fitting [X] · Number of fits · Mins · Burns % · Estimated blood loss

Observations

Time	18:56	19:08
AVPU	A	A
Resp rate	16-18	16-18
Resp depth	N	N
% O₂ sats	Air 96	Air 97
Peak flow		
CO₂		
Pulse rate	101	98
Pulse character	R	R
BP	138/99	134/87
Colour	N	N
BM	No KIT	
Temp	35.5	
Pain (0-10)	0	0
Pupils size	R L	R L
Pupils reactive	R L	R L
GCS (E V M)	4 5 6 Total 15	4 5 6 Total 15
ECG monitor	Initial rhythm	

Allergies: NONE KNOWN.

Known infectious: N

Past medical history: SEE BELOW

Medication

Medication brought in · List brought in

FAST: Facial weakness (Unequal smile or obvious weakness) · Arm weakness (One arm drifts down or falls) · *Speech (Word finding difficulties or slurred speech) [X]

12 Lead ECG: Normal ECG · Inferior MI · Anterior MI · Lateral MI · LBB block · ST depression · T wave changes only · Other abnormality · Inconclusive ECG

Symptoms: Severe persistent chest pain (>15 mins) · Shortness of breath · Other chest pain (cardiac in origin) · Other pain (cardiac in origin) · Palpitations · Sweaty · Asymptomatic [X]

Cannulation: Line 1 IV IO · Size · Time · Successful Y N · By · No touch technique · Placed in emergency conditions · Flush; Line 2 IV IO · Size · Time · Successful Y N · By · No touch technique · Placed in emergency conditions · Flush [X]

Fluid and drug administration: Drug bag code [X] · Code · Name · Amount · Dose · Route · Time · By

NURSING INFORMATION SHEET		NHS NO		
	Family GP Address		Date Admitted & Time 16 01 11 / 1922	
			Religion Hindu	
			Ethnic Group Asian	
		Tel No	Age 52	
Tel No		Name patient prefers to be called	School/Occupation /Retired self employed	

Language spoken English | Interpreter required Y/N | Interpreter Name and Tel No | Gender F/M

Is there a concern about lack of capacity to consent? Y/N (if yes inform Doctor)

Is there a concern about a Deprivation of Liberty? Y/N (If yes inform Doctor)

Has the patient lived outside the U.K in the past 12 months? Y/N If yes refer to Overseas Visitors Teams | Consultant

Ward	Date	Time
Ward	Date	Time
Ward	Date	Time

Reason for Admission and Current Medication	Past Medical History
OD	Depression

Next of Kin/Named person (First point of contact)	Relationship (relative/carer)	Address	Tel No / Alternative Contact No	Aware of admission
				yes
Wishes to be contacted at night Yes / No				
Wishes to be contacted at night Yes / No				

The patient has stated information may be shared with (name of relative/other)

Allergies/Alerts

NKDA

Attach Red Alert Band Y/N
Complete patient alert record
Date 16 01 11
Sign

Patient Identification	MRSA		DNAR	
Identity Confirmed Y N	Swab Taken Y/N		Status	Date
ID wrist band attached	Date			
Nurse Signature	Status	Date		
Patient/Carer Signature				

DENTIAL - PATIENT INFORMATION

The Hillingdon Hospital **NHS**

NHS Trust

WARD

	Daily Assessment and Plan of Care	
Date & Time	Nursing Record must reflect AIR-A A = Assessment- what is found on assessment I = Interventions required R = Response to intervention A = Action- any further action taken as a result	Sign Print Name & Role
16.01.11	Pt. admitted to A+E majors presented with OD of 16 tablets of nytol. Awaiting blood results after 4 review. Alert, orientated, self ventilating and communicative. Patient accompanied by partner. Transferred to Observation ward.	R-BENTON
16.01.11 @ 2235 hrs	Received patient from A+E majors patient alert. Observations done and Par2 because of Respirations and heart rate. Patient declined pain. Also observed patient walking to toilet un asked.	
16.01.11 @ 00:40hrs	Observed patient. Still awake. alert and communicating well. No complaints raised.	

Patient admitted to A E majors presented with OD of 16 tablets of Nytol. Awaiting blood results after 4 review. Alert, orientated self-ventilating and communicative. Patient accompanied by partner. Transferred to Observation ward Recieved patient from AE major. Patient alert. Observations done and Par2 because of respirations and heart rate. Patient declined pain. Also observed patient walking unaided to toilet. Observed patient still awake, alert and communicating well. No complaints raised.

The Hillingdon Hospital **NHS**
NHS Trust

TPR, BP, Pain Assessment and PAR Scoring Chart

| Height: | | BMI: |
| Consultant: | | Speciality: |

Location:	Obs										
Date:	16/01/U	/	/	/	/	/	/	/	/	/
Obs. Freq:	12:00									
Time:	02:35									

PAR SCORE: 2 2

Pain score:	00
Pain on movement:	00
Sedation score:	00
NBV Score:	00

Weight Kgs:
Bowels:
Fluid Balance:

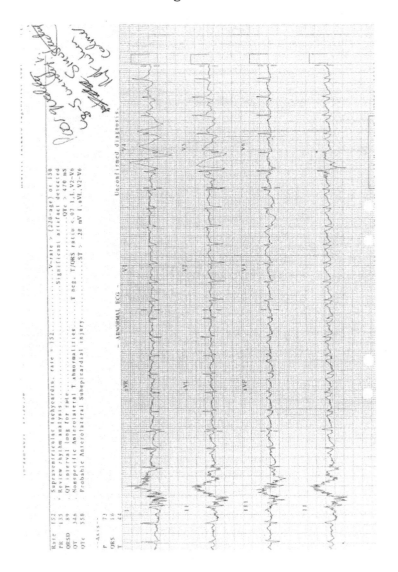

3-0021: British Race-Relations Romance Needs Ugly to be Cast Out

By February 2011 I was sick of the counselor, and rid myself of him. But I had engaged my own legal representative in the immigration matter. They did not know my father. That would protect me from deportation so I could dispense with the counselor.

The huge law firm accepted legal aid. They did not however do a great job. They first put me under a caseworker whose husband was Indian.

I thought this would make her understand me better but the opposite was true. Her relationship with that Indian man was obviously very romantic, as she said, upon learning I am alienated from the Asian community that it would be a good idea to deport me back to India, so I could be forced to live with Indians.

I have already explained British moral values and what they see as morally right and wrong. One thing the British are proud of is the great "comfort" they offer to the female private parts of persons validated as citizens. There is nothing but prestige for persons with female private parts.

A law magazine I glanced through while waiting for a lawyer appointment said on the cover, "There are only two kinds of people in this world. Those who accept British law and outcasts."

This seems to me to indicate that people living in other countries, who are not under British law, and people who live in the UK, and disagree with their laws are not human beings.

There are desirable behaviors required by law of a human penis before mating, and entering its female counterpart.

The British have tremendous compassion towards *female mental deficits* and to compensate these *environmentally* through *laws, pressure groups* and *human rights organizations*.

They want the mating process between two individuals of unequal mental status to take place in a *man-made greenhouse* where the inequality is rendered invisible, through manipulation of the environment.

A sexual turn-on for British people is people wearing masks that provide a cover to all kinds of surprises, and unknown disabilities.

The males become violent and sociopathic/homicidal when the disabilities of the objects their penises enter are

317

exposed. . I sometimes feel they would rather 100 people died than forsake one lie or cover-up about the vulnerable whose facts are buried as a (mental) health matter.

That's why when they sent me a notice refusing a private life in the UK they were taking the place of God, the UKBA said they don't have to give reasons when they refuse private life.

People always praise the Government as the hand that gives and the hand that takes. Everyone is contented and comfortable all the time. When this contentment falters, a proper and compliant citizen knows it is time to reach into the mental health cupboard.

As we all know, THAT CUPBOARD is well-stacked with women.

This lady immigration lawyer who felt I should be deported to India got replaced after a month by her male colleague. Caseworkers were automatically assigned by the huge law firm. He was no better or worse than her.

As Mohini will narrate, immigration lawyers did not want me to stay in the UK. On the whole they were more unhelpful than the judges who were not bad at all.

Black and Muslim immigration lawyers were the only

ones who did not want to make sure I was deported from the UK. That is to say Indian and white lawyers tried to lose my case every time, or that is just my opinion.

I felt I was a victim of a political racket, which was not carried out by the state, or the medical profession. Muslims and blacks also were politically not a part of the racket.

3-0022: February and March 2011: Post-overdose Attacks:

On 8 Feb 2011, there was another housebreak done to Mr. A. It was totally unnecessary and was carried out by London *Met* Police out of sheer conceit and arrogance. This time the front door was smashed to smithereens, forcing Mr. A once again to take care of the compromised security and replace his door.

This was one of the *police attacks* relating to the *Momma-baby love* .

A couple of days later a had a satellite cardiac event which was the tail of the overdose event. I was in a different location where doctors did not know me, and so got an honest troponin measurement.

I had been traveling home on a bus I felt my left side becoming very weak. I got off the bus I found a pub where I could sit down and ask them to call me an ambulance.

By the time the ambulance came, I had recovered and that weakness on the left side had improved.

Once in the hospital, they found my troponin to be rather high. They kept me overnight to do another troponin test

12 hours later. That happened the next morning, when they asked me to go home.

In March 2011, there was yet another housebreak of Mr. A's house. This time it was not the London *Met* police and the front door was not broken. I was terrorized into opening the door fearing it would be smashed again. Four black men had ducked their heads behind the wall to try to avoid being seen when the black man and white man had banged violently and burst in when I was alone in the house.

A black man and a white man who looked like gangsters entered the house and behaved badly. The white man looked like a skinhead. He said he was a psychiatrist whose name was Da Silva. He alleged that a screwdriver lying on Mr. A's table was a tool I kept to kill myself. His black companion, whose name was Mike Stafford, was an employee of the Pesthilensroke. The latter threw an file from an overhead shelf across the room, saying, "I don't like these files."

Da Silva commented about our double mattress on the carpet that this was a mentally-ill way of sleeping. He also commented that I may be starving to death, upon seeing a fridge rammed against a wall that could not be opened without moving furniture.

The *skinhead shrink* was making out like I was a *feeble-minded prostitute* residing with Mr. A who would starve if Mr. A did not feed me. He feared I was starving as he saw a fridge that was positioned so I could not open it easily. I was shocked when the skinhead added, "Come to me if you are hungry, and I will give you food.".

I remained in a standing position, as the (standing) pair urged me to take a seat, saying in a soft voice nothing but the words, "Get out of here".

The Pesthilenseroke posted me a "medical" report after the incident, where they discharged me from suicide care.

They NEVER gave me any sort of care, and certainly not suicide care. They did not know I was about to overdose, and did not take part after it. Just because strange men were prowling outside the door, sometimes using walkie-talkies, when Mr. A was at work, and I was isolated in his home, does not mean they gave *care*. Pesthilenseroke NEVER had a legal right to start a conversation with me-I don't know if this is not British-but I NEVER co-operated.

Some lady asked if pimps were chasing me, when I told her strange men prowling outside when I was alone. I did not answer, "Yes". But I think the Pesthilenseroke males may very well be pimps, although I am not a prostitute, and don't want their "medical care" provided by Pesthilenseroke employees with female private parts.

Later, Stafford apologized for throwing a file across the room he said happened by accident.

3-0023: IMMIGRATION LAW FIRM TRIES TO GET ME DEPORTED

Firstly, I want to be very clear about what happened. I want to allow the reader to determine, providing I am telling the truth, whether this law firm acting for me in the immigration matter was really trying to get me deported.

Secondly, most of the law firms that dealt with me in the immigration matter in the UK did similarly. This law firm was not worse than the others.

If law firms generally act against me, it cannot be attributed to lawyer incompetence. It must be a political trend.

Obviously the reader might argue I am talking nonsense, as a lawyer (like a doctor) would always try to help. If one lawyer does not help, another will. The reader might argue I lack merit.

I know that all their objections are rational, and based on common experience.

I am indeed speculating (as in an article preceding the present one) whether the UK has a *racial hygiene* against certain types of people, which would explain why lawyers as a whole would be trying to get me deported.

My heartfelt sympathies rest with your point of view that I am talking nonsense. I was surprised myself when these things happened to me as I had believed the British are the most fair-minded in the world. I have learnt otherwise.

After my release from Yarlswood on 2010-12-14, I had made a Subject Access Request to UKBA.

This had revealed that the Met police HAD LIED to Mr. A on the phone on the occasion of "my little 9 14", that they broke his door as per my father's orders. The UKBA had given those orders, it was revealed by documents provided in the Subject Access Request.

An IS151B had been given to me the following day at Eaton House reporting center in lieu of the intended involuntary committal. This was an upgrading from my existing IS151A/

Then there was being forced to visit parents, and the parents pressuring me to sign a document to get me an instant UK residence by paying a shrink to find me gravely disabled so I would never work again.

This had been followed by the father trying to force me to open the door at Mr. A's when he was at work to force me to sign that consent. Trying to break the door with his failing limbs.

I had called police for help. The latter had said I should obey my father as I was mentally-ill.

As if I could become the equal to a linguistically-retarded cock-sucking immigrant female Londoner literally bathing in a sea of condoms from age 12, liaising with mental health services, who realizes "man is master", obeys the father and has everything in the world except dignity.

Humiliated, I took an overdose and doctors at the A&E acted like I was pretending, and pulled off my tubes while I was struggling to breathe.

And the only post-cardiac support I got was to tell me to impress my parents by liaising with Hindu women.

I had engaged my own law firm under legal aid rather than one that would serve my father's interests to downgrade me mentally in the eyes of the UK.

However the caseworker I was assigned by this Post-Yarlswood law firm (as I have explained) was a lady with an Indian husband who said she felt I deserved to be deported so I could integrate with the Asian community from which I claimed alienation.

After a month she had been replaced by a guy Mr. N who

was only as helpful as her.

My attempted suicide was helpful for stopping my deportation to India if presented appropriately by a lawyer.

The law firm chose to play down the fact I had just tried to take my life. Instead, they replaced this fact with a legal-aid funded Harley Street psychiatrist, who gave a diagnosis of gravely disabled. There was also a note from the shrink attesting that the suicide would not happen again

The overdose reduced my chance of deportation.
The grave disability diagnosis reduced my chance of deportation. The fact I had a grave mental illness but was not going to overdose ever again increased my chance of deportation.

I ask the reader(if any) what the outcome was. Was the law firm increasing, or decreasing my chance of deportation?

The reader (if any) would probably say I was gravely disabled and was not likely commit suicide, a 100% truth, if a doctor (psychiatrist) wrote this. So the law firm was only writing truths. And if I ask the reader (if any) whether I am presently gravely disabled and am someone who wlll never commit suicide. The reader would again depend on a doctor's verdict. If a doctor said I have the type of mental illness that varies from minute-to-minute, that's what the reader will trust. But if a doctor told him or her that of date, mental illness has no cure, that's what the reader will trust, and champion.

Mental health is a science which never fails. It gave us salvation by making women equals

Of course if the immigration lawyers representing me felt it would be better for me to be deported to India, or if (God forbid) they felt I would be better off dead, or if they felt I should die unless I obeyed my parents they are not going to present helpful evidence, or present existing evidence in a helpful manner.

Not only did this man and woman not help me in the overdose matter; they also twisted it so it would look bad in the eyes of the judge.

I am saying attempted suicide was a fact. If my lawyer were to say I was humiliated by police and took an overdose in grief, that would help stop my deportation. This was closer to the truth, but my lawyer(s) wanted to police to stay "lily-white". Often keeping some people as "lily-white" would mean their victims need to be ascribed a mental illness, to win sympathy, because on paper, nobody wronged them, but they are distressed. In that case, the lawyer is giving evidence to the judge, whether express or implied,that my distress was a hallucination.

328

Maltreatment by police and its exposure does happen in all countries,including the UK. There is no reason why my abuse case should be concealed forever, unless there is a reason.

The evidence gathered by this law firm obliterated my overdose, and made me deportable in spite of it. This tallies with the caseworker's viewpoint that i should be deported to India if I was alienated from Indians. England is a safe place for the lawyer to live and allows her to have a romantic married life. Their courts have decided the just option is to not let me work or have a man in my life, and be solitary, bombarded by Pesthilenseroke, and other plagues and pestilences

Instead this law firm made me see a Harley Street psychiatrist for free (under their legal aid) who wrote I am very severely disabled mentally.

Although UK is a place where people standing on its territory can easily get residence if they show themselves to have a mental illness, I have a personality mismatch with the mental illness gang. Anyhow if the police abused me that should be stated. Masking police abuse and misrepresenting as if nobody did anything wrong wont help the victim have a good life nor will it help the immigration process.

I understand that for most readers, the fact I claim a psychiatrist wrote I was severely mentally disabled, is proof that is what I am. If that is the case my case should be closed.

If you are a reader who believes that psychiatrists can sometimes lie or make mistakes, and that lawyers get psychiatric reports written so as to win (usually) their case. Then read on.

If you are the type that trusts psychiatric reports for accuracy like a "word of God" my stories may not interest you, and you should just change your knickers to a larger size. And if you are not in the habit of wearing knickers, it's never too late to start.

The other thing this law firm did was giving me wrong information about themselves making an application for me to immigration.

You see the way deportation works is -they ask people who are waiting for their immigration application to be decided to report periodically at a reporting center. When your application to stay is refused, they grab you at the time of reporting, detain and take you to a deportation center such as Yarlswood.

They like to grab reportees by surprise. For that reason they try not to send your notice of refusal by post to your home, Refusals can take two months to two years and people forget all about it when they are grabbed unexpectedly.

Lawyers protect reportees from being grabbed by having an application in place to "protect" you.

By giving me wrong information that they had an application in place to "protect" me, this law firm were giving me a false sense of safety, increasing the chance I would be grabbed unexpectedly..

While the firm were in fact increasing my chances of being deported I got a letter to report, which was at an unusual day of the week and unusual time of day .

Reporting was monthly for me on the fourth Friday of each month . Immigration like Thursdays and Fridays for grabbing people. That way, as soon as the deportee had had some sleep in the detention facility, a weekend yawns on them, and solicitors and offices are not available. As flights to your home country are normally within a few days of grabbing, this gives the deportation office a big head-start over the candidate.

The fact I would need to report at a strange time would mean I might be alone in the reporting hallway, which is something immigration like. They want as few reportees as possible to see other reportees being nabbed lest this should produce awareness that the same plight awaits themselves.

It is a bit of a fox and chicken game.

The letter ordering to report had also changed my roll number from one starting with "H" to one starting with "V", which is my maiden name. This might indicate immigration want me to understand my connection to my husband has ended. In a sense, UKBA were placing a final seal on my deportation.

I rang the reporting center when I got that strange notice to report. They confirmed my lawyers had not sent in any applications.

My next move was to contact my lawyers. Their office had moved miles away.

The head lawyer of immigration was getting married. I could not talk to immigration lawyers for several weeks, as the rest of the immigration lawyers were on leave. It looked like an excuse and I even visited their remote location.

I felt as though this firm hoped I would attend that strange reporting day without any lawyer I could call when UKBA detained me.

3-0024: PRAISE JESUS, I AM THE BEST, BETTER THAN THE REST

Yes my sister is Mrs Viju Wortley but I found an immigration lawyer also called Mrs Wortley.

Sabina Wortley Okejoy was working in a hair dresser's shop in Cambridge and said I could pay her anything I liked.

Which is nice so she got 500.

But this is not a good thing as a solicitor should either be on legal aid or specify their fees. They should not leave it up to you to pay whatever you want.

She was licensed for immigration and had passed OISC exams. Yes she did say, "Praise Jesus I am the best better than the rest," but I taped her in my frustration without her knowing.

Taping your lawyer can be interesting but it is not a strategy that wins. In the tape Mrs Wortley can be heard saying I should get a doctor's report saying I am mentally incompetent.

She says that even a fake one from a doctor would be fine,

in order to get easy and fast indefinite leave to remain. I forbid her from sending an an application until I have seen it.

I suppose this is not a proper relationship as it shows I am not respecting my solicitor. Yes it is a clients right to instruct their solicitor, and tell them if you are not willing to co-operate with something.

But the fact I want to "check" what she posts looks like I am inspecting a kid. Very inappropriate.

The truth however was that Mrs Wortley went "over my head" and posted a petition to immigration without my knowledge.

This application had several medical conditions she fabricated This was a certain way to get the application refused, because immigration dislike being taken for a ride. When you state illness but don't produce doctor reports they get rid of you.

I showed her application to a more experienced lawyer who said "yes" to my question regarding whether this application was the kind that would go in the trash immediately.

Mrs Wortley may not have been better than all the rest,

but wasn't the worst either.

The good thing that came out of appointing Sabina Wortley to act in my immigration matter was that I did not need to report that special day.

I was only reporting on every 4rth Friday, but had for a notice by post to report at an unusual date and time. Reporting when ordered is obligatory, and the penalty for failing to report (and not explaining) was detention and deportation.

On this special reporting notice my name (Roll number) had been changed from "H" to "V" .

I figured the change of my roll number by UKBA was their emotional reaction (which they did not expect me to understand) whereby they were removing my marriage ties to a British man for good, as I would soon be Indian soil.

I also reckoned I may be attending at a time when the reporting hallway was empty, and I could be nabbed without eyewitnesses seeing me. At regular reporting times, other reportees can see you are being nabbed, although UKBA keep it low-profile

I needed to talk to my lawyers before attending that

special reporting as I felt things were amiss.

At this point I discovered ALL the immigration lawyers of this firm were on leave and not returning for several weeks

Moreover my previous lawyers had LIED to me that they had put an application in for me to UKBA. Having a pending application in place prevents a person from being detained and deported on a reporting date.

This shows me that had I not suspected something was not quite right, I would have attended that special reporting date without fear or suspicion

Then-maybe-I would have been in a cell with IS151D-Flight Itinerary-and tried to call my lawyers, only to find they could not answer for at least another two months!

I remained with Mrs Wortley until the end of 2011

3-0025: Meeting Regent Exeter

In August 2011 I was under Mrs Wortley, and met one friend on Facebook and went over to see him. This was the start of a great friendship that ended through his death in March 2014. His biography is the subject of Part One.

3-0026: MEDICAL EVENTS IN 2011

I had my abdomen scanned as I started having pains
in them. Once I asked for leave from reporting which
clashed with a hospital appointment.

The Eaton House deportation officer argued that I could
attend the reporting center after the hospital scan was
over.

He was right. But I did not go in later that day as I
was tired. I received my second IS343 Notice meaning
"Immigration offender" for failing to report as required

The whole thing was stressful on my body mind and soul.
I saw a gynaecologist who was referred by the existing
GP and changed my GP.

The latter said she could not help me properly as I was
being processed by immigration. I was upset as medical
care is free and there is no definite rule to refuse certain
things to people without leave to remain in the UK. I
wrote to the new GP that it was stupid of her to refuse me
things .

This GP wrote me back saying he cannot be my GP
anymore. He also expressed anger about the health service
he alleged had disciplined a psychiatrist I had never met.

I had no idea they had disciplined her and she had been forced to relocate and retired. That happened towards the end of 2011.

I had experienced much grief from the Pesthilenseroke (Pesthilenseroke) and their stalking had been specially bad from mid-2010 when my father had made a fake missing person report of me up to that point in 2011 when two men from there had broken into the house in March 2011.

I had not engaged with Pesthilenseroke women but think this lady psychiatrist Wafaa Jouhargy was connected to this society. I think she spread notes that she and her woman team wanted to punish me. This had nothing to do with me as I had only heard of her.

In fact in the UK they dislike all forms of complaining although under modern law all institutions must provide a complaints procedure.

However in the UK, they hate the word "punish" and take disciplinary action as soon as they hear that you have people you plan to punish.

I had not even mentioned her name in complaints as I did not see her. It was about the Pembroke stalking I complained. Unlike what the GP thought I was not responsible for what happened to his colleague. Only men did the housebreak and she was not there at all.

It was in 2011 my complaint about the stalking of the Pembroke took place. Someone Martin Morris said their visits to "save my life" had been too frequent to be a genuine case of combating suicide and that my father had made a malicious referral about me to mental health services.

Pembroke sent an explanatory letter as detailed above, dated 2011-09-29 confirming my parents ordered the stalking, but Martin Morris was not available ever again.

I did not have a GP for the next 2 and a half years. I had exhausted the GPs for my catchment area and had to register in a farther catchment area.

3-0027: Overview of Police Stalking and Hacking in 2010 and 2011

The following event took place several times between mid-2010 and March 2011.

I would say to my father on the landline, "Bastard, get off the phone or I'll kill myself".

I would use the service rectel.co.uk to call back so my voice would be recorded.

Every time I did this, police would turn up at the front door (I think)faster than if a murder had happened. They would force me to ride an ambulance to A and E. I would remain in A and E for several hours. I would be seen last because I did not have any illness.

They would check my temperature and blood pressure. There would be a doctor who would ask what my problem was. I would say the police brought me in here because I'm not obeying my parents and the doctor would say okay you can go home.

I got two sets of records from these incidents by making Subject Access Requests, one from the police the other was a medical record.

The latter had a sketchy account of my going to A
and E in an ambulance. Comments were added by the
Pesthilenseroke to these records.

Pesthilenseroke are illiterate folks who do not work in the
hospital and were not physically present at any point in
these incidents. They acted like some kind of Godfather
who was overseeing my life, I did not like them but there
was little I could do to stop them from appearing in my
medical records.

Met Police wrote me they hacked my Gmail Onedrive
Cloud looking for covert tapes of themselves

I taped an elderly Physics professor I had become friends
with within the United States. The latter said the Institute
of Physics had a policy that if a woman spoke to a man
about the subject she would get nowhere. Only a woman
that consulted with women could make career progress.

I also taped police on several occasions in 2010 and 2011.
Some of these were rectel.co.uk tapes mp3 files that were
timestamped, were of the times when I had said to my
father "Bastard stop calling here or I will kill myself"
which was followed by police arriving in minutes to force
me to attend A and E.

These tapes show that my father was making calls that caused distress. The continuance of the calls -rectel timestamps its mp3 tapes-show that calls would continue for months after I told my father I'd kill myself if he did not stop which was done with police approval.

Foolishly I stored the calls in Google and hot mail clouds.

I got a letter from London met police in 2011 or later they hacked my account to discover tapes of themselves.

They said they used some machine to hack my passwords and had to use a different more effective machine to get through my long passwords. They said they had not found any offensive audiotapes.

The police left my tapes of themselves taking to me undamaged. This can mean that they either did not listen to all the tapes in the cloud-missing tapes of themselves, OR those tapes of themselves were not really what they were after.

They may have been after something more important. It may have been illegal for them to hack my cloud as one is allowed under UK law to tape police without their knowledge to show they are unreasonable.

My call with the Physics professor was damaged.

The rectel.co.uk tapes were where I said to my father, "Bastard stop calling here or I will kill myself" were all damaged.

I have no idea who damaged the tapes and I suspect it was law enforcement agencies.

Damage was done in a sophisticated way to these mp3 files. The files were the same size but had become silent

Central and North West London **NHS**

HILLINGDON

NHS Foundation Trust

Our ref: SB/LAH/MMMHersom

29th September 2011

Mental Health Directorate
Riverside Centre
(on the Hillingdon Hospital Site)
Pield Heath Road
Hillingdon
UXBRIDGE
Middlesex
UB8 3NN

Mohini Hersom
26, Bourne Court
Station Approach
SOUTH RUISLIP
Middlesex
HA4 6SW

Tel: 01895-279602
Fax: 01895-279501

Dear Mohini

Re: Complaint Response

Address: 26 Bourne Court, Station Approach, South Ruislip, Middlesex HA4 6SW
D.O.B.: 28.08.1958

Background
You made a written complaint about the services you received from Pembroke Centre CMHT in November 2010. Your complaints were summarised that:

1. You were unhappy that the Pembroke Centre sent a slanderous letter addressed to Dr Thakrar and Dr Patel later copied to your GP, Dr Siddique.
2. You were unhappy that the content of the letter which advised that the police had visited you in January 2010 when this happened in November 2009.
3. You were unhappy at the lack of response from a previous complaint.
4. You were citing harassment by the Pembroke Centre.

Following extended contact with you as detailed below you received a formal complaint response in March 2011.

The response was that:

1. It was unfortunate that the letter was considered slanderous. However perceived, the issue of slander was clearly unintended. The staff involved felt it important to communicate their concerns about your needs to your GP. Unfortunately, the letter was sent to your previous GP due to staff at Pembroke being unaware your GP had changed. An apology was offered for any distress this may have caused.

2. In the letter in question, the team were referring to correspondence they had received from the Hillingdon Emergency Duty Team on 29th January 2010. This referred to an event when Police had visited your home due to concerns raised by neighbours, and staff wanted to ensure you had appropriate support.

3. There was no record of any complaint from you prior to November 2010. It was accepted that you enquired in June 2010 about making a complaint, although at that time did not wish to discuss this.

1

4. There was an apology that you felt you were being harassed by the team. However, they had received a number of referrals and concerns about you and were only trying to engage with you to offer what support they could.

In April 2011 further correspondence was received by the CNWL complaints team from an e-mail address, (address supplied), signed by you in name.

1. This was requesting copies of your records of contacts with staff at Pembroke Centre and another team (CRT) within the Mental Health service.

2. It was also stated by you that:

'The Pembroke Centre are torturing you and acting illegally. The centre is run inappropriately, the staff are mentally and morally backward and seem to be illiterate. The staff were expecting submissive behaviour from you because you are a woman, they have misdiagnosed you and refused to provide their credentials and job titles'.

It was decided to respond by:

1. Engaging with you further and offer to meet with you at another CMHT to explore what may be helpful and how those involved could achieve a resolution.

2. Undertake a more detailed examination of the circumstances of your referral and assessment of need, your diagnosis and any service provision in view of your comments about the inappropriateness of staff in the team and their responses to your needs.

I have examined your records and produced a summary of the contacts you and staff had for the period. For the purpose of accuracy, this section headed Chronology is in the first and third person, as written by staff at the time and as you would find it if and when you asked for copies of your records.

Chronology

Referral
26/01/2011
Ms Hersom, hereafter Mohini, was first referred to Hillingdon Mental Health services. Her mother contacted the Pembroke CMHT, she wanted to know what plans there were to help her as she believed she was seriously ill. She also wanted CMHT staff not to acknowledge Mohini's partner Alex as her partner. Mohini's mother kept repeating they were her parents and according to their culture they should know about Mohini. I informed her that whilst I could empathise with her, I could not give her any information without discussion with intended service user and their consent.

05/02/2011
Mohini's father contacted CRT. He informed staff he wanted to come to the CRT office and give copies of e mails that Mohini has sent to him. He continued to provide details of Mohini's mental health history requesting assessment and treatment for her.

07/02/2011
Office visit by both parents requesting MHA assessment of daughter due to risk of suicide.

07/02/2011
Home visit to Mohini by staff to assess risks of suicide presented by her parents. Contact refused by Mohini.

[Handwritten marginal note, left side:] It is illegal to give someone "medical treatment" even if limited to verbal abuse and refuse to submit to reason and show ID that they are legit medical personnel. You cannot pretend someone is a mental incompetent and ignore

[Handwritten note, bottom left:] they show they know their rights. This is fraud and torture.

[Handwritten note, top of Chronology:] Note my mother tells "medical" my relationship with the man I live with is false and because of their culture they have a right to be in my life even if I dont want them (lifelong imprisonment)

[Handwritten note, middle right:] My parents mispresent the truth and reply to invented issues they pretend I sent them

346

08/02/2011
Urgent assessment in A&E by CRT.
Mohini recounted she was a failed asylum seeker who had been in a detention centre until 14th December 2010. She said she was going to be deported but her Solicitor stopped/blocked deportation.
She said came to the UK on a marriage visa in 2004. Her marriage broke down after 9 months and that is the reason for her facing deportation. She was currently living with her partner Alex.

She was assessed as having no formal thought disorder and there was no evidence of auditory or visual hallucination, no delusions or paranoia. There were some fleeting suicidal thought but no intent to or plan of or history of overdose in the past. Denies suicidal thoughts, no intent or plan. She gave the impression she was reactive to social problems. Plan agreed was Mohini advised to seek an injunction against parents and to access legal advice centre then discharged home.

09/02/2011
Office contact with Mohini. She was angry with her parents whom she finds interfering, they keep calling the police, Pembroke and her GP about her. Encouraged to attend OPA on 24th March 2011. She raised a request only to see white male staff. She described a number of fixed delusional beliefs that appear long standing. She did appear low but had no plans to harm herself.

She was very worried about her immigration status but said she had a Solicitor involved. Impression formed that parents seem quite adamant that the father is the nearest relative and can request his daughter be sectioned. Staff, however, were of the opinion that Alex, her partner, is the nearest relative and that the parents are at present upsetting Mohini with their attempts to have her mental health assessed. View of AMHP was Mohini was not needing MHA detention given current presentation and her previous presentations to the crisis team. AMHP would action letter to parents informing them that of such view under the MHA and that partner Alex is the nearest relative and she is in any case not detainable.

10/02/2011
Mohini presented herself at Hammersmith Hospital. A & E assessment was concluded and information transferred to Hillingdon service.

23/02/2011
Mohini was assessed in Hillingdon Hospital A/E expressing suicidal thoughts. Allocated for follow-up by CRT home visits but subsequently refused follow-up visits and contact.

02/03/2011
Home visit by Team Leader/ AMHP and Psychiatrist. Mohini refused follow-up and mental health services and staff left premises under duress.

03/03/2011
ICD 10 diagnosis was confirmed as F 60.4 Histrionic Personality Disorder made by medical staff in Crisis Resolution Team.

14/03/2011
GP contacted by Pembroke Centre. He said Mohini told him she feels harassed by mental health services and that if they continue to harass her she will harm herself. He said she is not on any medication. He said he did not feel her mental health was worsening but continues to be stressed by thoughts of her parents harassing her and her immigration issues.

15/03/2011
Mohini did not attend office appointment and was offered a further OPA on 21st April 2011

3

21/04/2011
Appointment was cancelled. Another date and time offered.

13/07/2011
Mohini conveyed to A & E. She reported that she was brought to hospital because her ex-brother-in-law "who is a Lib Dem Counsellor", wants her "locked up" in a "mental hospital". She left before completion of assessment. Police were informed. PC Butler was told that Mohini is known to the Pembroke Centre and that her next appointment is on 21st July 2011.

16//08/2011
MDT meeting at which case discussed. Following no contact from Mohini or her partner, agreed to write to GP and will close case to re-refer if necessary.

18/08/2011
GP informed following no contact Mohini to be discharged from mental health services.

31/08/2011
GP confirmed Mohini no longer registered at that surgery since April 2011.

Complaint
Your complaint was that 'the Pembroke Centre are torturing you and acting illegally, the centre is run inappropriately, the staff are mentally and morally backward and seem to be illiterate. The staff were expecting submissive behaviour from you because you are a woman, they have misdiagnosed you and refused to provide their credentials and job titles".

Complaint Investigation
The Manager who looked into this complaint met with you in July 2011 and has spoken to you several times since. You have attended Mead House to hand in photocopies of documents you feel relevant to and evidence of your continued complaint about your treatment at Pembroke CMHT. These could be appendices if required. He has summarised your clinical records about your care and treatment in a chronology above. In August 2011 you were discharged by the Pembroke CMHT where you were assessed, due to not attending OPAs and not needing a mental health service.

Findings
1) His last contact with you was in September 2011. You have consistently expressed an opinion that your complaint should be resolved by you not having any further contact with staff in the Pembroke CMHT. As you was discharged from Pembroke CMHT in August 2011 by default, this should currently be the case. However, should you repeat your presentations at Hillingdon Hospital or another A & E you will be liable to re-referral there.

2) You have also taken particular issue with how you were treated by staff by their gender and race, expressing dissatisfaction with the approach and manner of female staff of an ethnic minority origin. You have asked only to see white males. For a number of other reasons it is not possible to offer a service on this basis. It was found that on one home visit, you did not accept a service from staff in the stated preferred groups.

3) If you are referred for any other reason by other agencies with your current address in future, then further contact with those on duty at Hillingdon CRT and subsequently Pembroke CMHT, may be necessary for your own safety and wellbeing.

4) You also expressed a view that your complaint could be resolved by the staff you had contact with being disciplined, due to their actions in your case. It was found evidenced in the chronology detailed above, that their attempts to assess and manage your presentation and risks were reasonable and normal. It was concluded as a result of this investigation that it is not appropriate or necessary to take any disciplinary action against the staff and there are no grounds for this.

4

348

Conclusions

I hope this has addressed your concerns and the points you have raised with the Manager in your meeting and subsequently when you have spoken further. This letter is my final response to your complaint and means that local resolution is now complete.

However, if you remain dissatisfied with my response, you have the right to take your complaint to the Health Service Ombudsman. The Ombudsman is independent of Government and the NHS. Her service is confidential and free. There are time limits for taking a complaint to the Ombudsman although she can waive them if it is felt there are reasons to do so.

If you have any questions about whether the Ombudsman will be able to help you, or about how to make a complaint, you can contact their helpline on 0345-015-4033, email phso.enquiries@ombudsman.org.uk or fax 0300-061-4000. Further information about the Ombudsman is available at www.ombudsman.org.uk

You can write to the Ombudsman at:

The Parliamentary and Health Service Ombudsman
Millbank Tower
Millbank
London
SW1P 4QP

If you need any help or advice to make your complaint to the Ombudsman you can contact your local Independent Complaints Advocacy Service (ICAS). ICAS provides independent advocacy for people who have a complaint about the NHS. They can be contacted on 0300 456 2370, alternatively contact may be made by fax on 0845 337 3062 or by e-mail pohwer@pohwer.net. Further details about ICAS service can be obtained on their website: www.pohwer.net

Yours sincerely

S. Brookes

Sandra Brookes
Service Director

3-0028: The Years 2012 and Beyond

I was healthy on the whole in 2012 and 2013. I suffered a trumped-up criminal conviction in 2013. I am aware that some people do not believe a conviction can be trumped-up.

I lost a friend in 2014 and this friend told me before he died that all women in the UK attend women's groups in some shape or form. This friend died of psychiatric medication but some other factors are quite suspicious and I've documented them in an earlier section.

I am fully aware that British people and I'm sure people from many other countries would make me a laughing stock arthritis article in the doctor about a friend that died of psychiatric medication.

If I say publicly my friends take psychiatric medication people will say I am probably a mental patient.

I'm not here to try and change him believe strong believers and I'm not you no equal to that task. All I'm trying to do is to spread a message which I hope will be understood by millions of people.

People pass on their ideas and attitudes. If you as a reader do not agree with my ideas or my attitudes; you're free to disagree. I'm not here to try and change your beliefs even if you think badly of me and I don't care.

April 2014: Migrant Rights Hooked me up with Doctor

I had had a problem in 2011 when my GP did not want to be my GP. After that, I could not get a GP. I know this may create a bad impression but I am at least being honest in this story where I must stick to the point.

In 2014 I had registered with a GP's-whose senior partner was Dr. S-with the help of a migrant rights organization.

At the end of 2015, I was staying in a hostel Sobo in Brighton. I started feeling very tired and preferred not to walk. I realized that my life force was weakening and felt this tiredness must be coming from my heart. At the end of the year, I returned to London.

In January 2016 I attended a London A and E with severe chest pains and breathing difficulties.

It was so bad I wanted relief through death or for some doctor to help me. They finally called my name and give me a drip for hours. I felt better at some point in the night. I was discharged with the verdict I am completely normal and had muscular pain. Paracetamol was all I needed.

As I had been in agony, I was skeptical about their theory that I had no disease.

I started having similar chest episodes regularly and attended A and E. I won't call them cardiac episodes at this point. Because each time I went to A and E they did an ECG and a blood test and said with authority they are clinicians and are TELLING ME everything was okay with my heart.

At A and E, they would give me drips and sometimes an injection to stop my bizarre and painful vomiting.

In February 2016 my doctor in London asked me to take the treadmill test. After the treadmill test, the doctor said my performance was excellent. She wanted one more test, an angiogram.

Thinking back, I realize the hospital doctor wanted the second test because the first one had indicated an abnormality. This means if the treadmill test results had REALLY been excellent they would not have bothered with an angiogram.

I had my angiogram in March 2016. More than a couple of months had gone by and they had not given me its results.

The junior GP wondered why not. He asked me to go to their senior partner Dr. S who avoided answering my question about disclosing the angiogram results.

3-0029: INVISIBLY HANDCUFFED TO HATEFUL WOMEN AND PESTHILENSEROKE

Another contact my first one was 30 minutes or less meeting a lady on their glorious premises, in 2007 when I was urged to go, and decided never again-they were not nice I thought. In 2010 what with police stalking to force love of parents, and "my little 9 14" of September 2010.

I did visit those glorious premises for second time, with Mr A as my bodyguard, I think we spent just a few minutes in 2010 complaining to a lady there requesting Pembrokers to stop standing outside the door as soon as Mr A went to work, hoping to strike up a conversation in case I was stupid enough to open the front door or attempt to leave the house.

But they were standing outside the door as late as 2016. In case you did not understand the police wanted me tortured by women in the United Kingdom.

Women thrilled at idea of my suicide indicates a homicidal hatred level

For years to come, some women jumped up and down with joy at the thought of my suicide that they multiplied that one overdose event into several suicide events and

introduced a fictitious psychiatrist. These became part of
the UKBA records.

Which women sent suicide lies about me to the UKBA??
I don't know, It could a handful of people. I insist that
repeatedly fantasizing someone is attempting suicide
and sending fake reports that it happens shows that these
women hate me to a homicidal level.

3-0030: Why the British can't see through my Parents' Crocodile Tears

What is it that makes the British people of the 21st century adore my parents' crocodile tears ? First an inability to differentiate between a persons appearance (old and weak)and their character. If you look physically weak or are stupid, the British see you as a very nice person .

The pathos, the "depression", the philanthropic men on reeking websites, their tongues dangling out by at least twelve inches, running equal-opportunity "lick-charities" for you and any and all women guessed right, mentally backward immigrant women stand in a priority queue.

Philanthropic and law-loving males with a spirit of self-denial, praying that their tongues and "Science" will discover a way to make all the women in the world "come."Verbal comprehension is not important, and you can drink your way into a state of total comfort.

People who never give up, and want to artificially award higher levels of glory to those whom they consider as needy, even though they have no merit. Committed to boosting those who are infirm of body mind or even a conscience. Worshipers of weakness, of the effeminate.

Your will be done in the end. You will create a paradise where "everyone" will be happy, and whenever that fails, "psychology scientists" will give treatments until every individual feels happy all the time.

With a passion to kill all germs on sight, and to make it up non-stop to the weaker sex to atone for the offense of homicide.

My parents keep referring to me as "baby" in their sob stories when I am nearing 60 and British people bow their heads in respect.

When genitalia overpower the conscience,you will helplessly obey your parents even if they spat on you as adult, or give advice that others should behave that way.

The ultra-female psyche, where the moral conscience is overpowered by the concept of genitalia married to the concept of the machine gun, or homicide

Your parents made you and have a right to take your life. One person who is not in the UK said this to me.

Incarcerating me and forcing "woman-treatments" until or unless I obey and love my parents-I am told is the correct"Hindu"behavior-I am insane and "removable from human society" for failing the "Hindu" norm did not succeed as the law in the UK had not yet progressed to that level of woman comfort.

It was no use telling them I am not a Hindu, as the illiterate"workers" will what they like in their scrappy scrawly illiterate handwriting.

A healthy UK female will not refuse to contact parents if they insist as she lacks mental capacity to oppose authority or stand up to men. They hated me because I did not have female mental deficit as much as British female, and wanted to label me as such.

They are people who increase and decease a person's glory artificially. I have been abused so much I know I need to die and will never recover. I cannot have "paid privates" for support. It has to be natural relationships and goodwill from men, which I they stopped artificially.

That's why I was arrested several times by London met police in a 12-18 month period in connection with lack of love of parents.

So then there is a certain primitive tribe in the UK called the Pembroke. They are menials in the hierarchy with no qualifications or ability to behave. The male members of this tribe would kick and bang on the front door and other actions that were rude and aggressive..

Some one wrote their letters for them as they lacked command of the human language needed for formal expression. Females of this tribe are thought of as "intimacy analysis experts" by police and court.

A combination of "the special scientifically created training which comes from lofty medicine" and the female genitalia that gave them the talent to assimilate such training helps a female Pembroker be an oracle of intimacy analysis.

Male Pembrokers do the banging screaming and using of walking talkies outside the front door of a house,. They may throttle the person inside the house!! But male Pembrokers pave a smooth, wide and comfortable path for the Female Pembroker to sail in like a cool princess and do her "intimacy thing"

Women are often paid in London to travel in police cars and attend a scene where the police are arresting or cautioning someone. The woman's work is "just being there". Her genitalia exude warmth for miles. Having her in the room is restful in a disturbing situation. Everyone feels like their head is on a comfortable pillow. More recently doctors are apparently hiring women to work as painkillers, to combat dangerous side effects of painkillers. A couple of women will "just be there "in a room when someone is howling with pain.

3-0031: ILLNESS AND RESPONSES OF DOCTORS

Loads of people go to A&E with chest pain. The doctor will will take your blood sample and check your troponin levels. If you have just had a heart attack your troponin will be high. Most people come out with normal troponins and are told to go home as being completely free of heart problems.

Doctors lie that if your Troponin is Normal, You have no Heart Problems

An artery in the heart get blocked during a heart attack -I think the blood can't flow through -I don't know what exactly happens to that blood. During this event your heart muscle-some of it dies- and releases troponin into your blood, Unless you die, in a day or two your troponin goes back to normal.

Therefore the troponin blood test has no way of telling if you did not have a heart attack two or more days ago. It cannot also predict that you will not get a heart attack two days later and die from it.

I don't know why doctors tell this lie to everybody, I think they want people to go away quickly as they are so busy and not have to answer all kinds of complicated questions.

My Coronary arteries blocked and unblocked themselves

Once in A&E a doctor explained to me my symptoms and agony were all those of a heart attack.. But my episodes resolved in a 2-3 minutes whereas in a real heart attack the episodes would not resolve for at least 20-30 minutes.

My artery did not become blocked. Instead it blocked and unblocked itself. They were coronary artery spasms, he said.

The senior partner in the GP surgery did not want to release the angiogram to me which could be used to explain my chest episodes. He said both my chest problems and overall body pains were a result of mental illness. He recommended take anti-psychotics and neuroleptics to cure my chest illness and overall body pain.

The senior partner advised the hospital to treat the crazy one(me) appropriately

The junior doctor decided I probably had cancer and asked me to have a bowel scan in the hospital. I had a problem with fasting which I explained. They were not pleased. The nurse taking me in for the scan had a big note book where she showed instructions from the senior partner. These said I was a schizo head, and if I made trouble fasting, to deal with me "appropriately"

She said she was supposed to use force on me, I declined. They told me in that case to leave. I felt so ill I forgot my way out and asked for help. I was pointed into a locked car park with no exit. I did go back to the door leading to the car park and eventually got the main exit.

I did not have the urgent cancer test, but that story had a happy ending as I did not have cancer, as confirmed when I had the colon scan 6 months later in Brighton in November 2016.

On London Underground, People called me Cripple

During that year, in the London underground many people described me as disabled a cripple and what not. Only the senior partner in the surgery did not consider my body pain as anything but a psychiatric symptom. Everyone is allowed paracetamol. I got pain medicines from a private foreign doctor

November 2016: Brighton: Mental Retard has Psychiatric Tiredness

My female GP in Brighton said in November 2016 she would do a blood test to check my vitamin d levels, which could have gone low, due to my dark skin. If they came out normal, my tiredness was psychiatric.

The vitamin D levels did come out normal, so she have a questionnaire which he said would take 48 hours to complete. I could have filled it out in 48 seconds. It was so easy. I just declined. The kind of questions were inapplicable to me. I felt they are for an "ultra female" and mental retard.

Some British people will get angry with me. They will ask how come I can make judgments like that. I have been a teacher but that should not be used to say I can make a judgment like that about that questionnaire. Anyone who has an ass has (a right to) an opinion, as they said in the 80's in the USA.

I had this chronic cough at Sobo Brighton in late 2015. Society is becoming ultra modern and back in 2016 Brighton was still a village. Frank a black hospital staff that lived at Sobo said my cough sounded like I was dying. I mean they did not throw me out of the hostel which they would in the modern world in the interests of health hygiene and comfort for women.

At the end of 2016, I returned to London. I wanted to change my doctor surgery so I would not have the senior partner who treated me as a crazy which no other doctor had done. In England people can change their Doctor Surgery on request.

Now, at the beginning in 2017, I was going back to them to that Migrant Rights Organization to ask to change from the senior partner. They helped again, and I was assigned to a surgery further away, under Dr E in April 2017.

The values for the death guarantee test result too low-I was hardly dying

Dr E told me right with I had blocked coronary arteries and and he let me have access to my angiogram report done a year ago. This report recommended I get put on statins immediately as my cholesterol was alarming. In April 2017 my cholesterol was still high but Dr E said it had improved on its own since the angiogram was done in March 2017. He put me on a daily tablet of Atorvastatin and aspirin.

I was still having A&E episodes through 2017, which changed and slowed down. I felt after each A&E episode which on average every two months, I stablised and became weaker than before. I felt I was going down the staircase of life. One step down would be a thud, followed by a plateau of increasing weakness then another thud down(A&E episode) and so on.

Dr E did an echo test of me, and unlike everyone else told me the echo was not completely normal. He told me me the left ventricle of my heart was pumping more slowly than the right ventricle.

That was August 2017. The echo test contains the word

abnormal in the readings list. Also I "googled" some quantities in the report which led to another figure being abnormal.

Since then over 4 years have elapsed more than 10 doctors have seen and told me this echo is completely normal. I have chatted to doctors on the Indian website icliniq and they say the same thing. In fact they think I should see a psychologist for "STRESS" if I disagree with the doctors opinion.

So many doctors cant be wrong can they?

But the question remains:Why did Dr E say there was a slight problem in the ECHO of 2017?

Why does the ECHO say 'ABNORMAL" in a couple of places?

Why do I keep having heart-related symptoms, which can't be passed off as "indigestion".

My blood pressure was slightly high in 2016-17. My systolic would be around 150 but they would tell me the readings were excellent in A&E. Why were they lying to me? I could read the instrument and see "150" which I knew was slightly high and not excellent

I talked to someone on the internet locally and he said I have chronic heart failure and I took the letter back to Dr e who didn't Echo test and depth guarantee test.

I read in an article that the people they have many kinds of depth guarantee there and they do a blood test called BNP and if your levels are high it means that you're certainly going to die. My levels were very low.

3-0032: Extra-helpful lady doctor and disclosed reason for deportation from the UK

Now about some trouble. The surgery of Dr E, who was semi-retired told me I could have a solution to my chest pains, if I agreed to one particular doctor. She was a Muslim lady. I didn't understand why I would not want to see her. I also did not understand why there was a reward offered top me for seeing her. Very inappropriate.. I was going to be punished with inadequate care if I did not see her!

The doctor got on the phone, and acted like she would do anything for me.

However the doctor in question made it obvious there was a problem. She got on the phone to me and acted as if "she would do anything for me."

I was wary and said a lot of "yes" and "thank you." I decided not to meet her.

Towards the end of 2017 another immigration lawyer told me that the real reason I was being deported is my lack of participation in women's groups. he told me to take the window treatments the Pembroke what are the mental health center in the area where I lived.

3-0033: 2018: Making a Fool Carry her Own Shame in a Sealed Confidential Envelope

At the end of 2017 actually in 2018 I went to Liverpool and stayed in a hostel there.

I visited London and took ill. I did not have a GP in London and so I went to a drop-in clinic in the same area.

I saw a female doctor. I told her I was having chest pain and that I wasn't getting any cure or treatment. I was repeatedly told I was normal but my symptoms were not going away I was also deteriorating, I said.

The female doctor me to go to A&E she asked me how I could go.

I said I'd ride the bus.,(I think she must have found that very funny.) She gave me a sealed envelope to take as referral to the nearest A&E.

I usually open any sealed letters about me and try to stick them back. I don't care if I get caught cheating. I will just need to see what is written about me.

The sealed letter written by the female doctor did not say that I was crazy. But the letter was weird. It said I had absolutely no chest pain. It also commented I plan to go by bus to A&E. Which might indicate I am healthy??

I had seen her briefly and said I was getting chest pain so how could she know it was a lie? It wasn't.

She should not ask a patient to attend A&E if she feels they are healthy as it wastes A&E time which can be used for genuine emergencies.

3-0034: December 2017: Muslim
saves from Deportation

As you already know, I was on immigration reporting
restrictions. I had to attend a designated reporting center
on the 4rth Friday of every month. On 1 December 2017
I was inside the reporting center, It was a Friday morning
and they asked me to come inside for interviews.

Hidden black-uniformed guards pop up on special
Occasions

A different kind of security are sitting inside Eaton House
reporting center. Tall and black-uniformed Sikhs that
never show up unless someone needs physical dragging.

I had already been taken inside in 2010 and 2013
and almost flown to India. I knew I did not have an
application in place and that I could actually be flown to
India once I went in for interviews.

I was not going to dare to resist as I would be dragged
in by those tall Sikhs in black uniforms, who appeared
only when resistive candidates needed coercion or
dragging. Otherwise, reportees would not know they were
"HIDING" inside.

Then they said they were processing my papers for the

interview so I would need to wait. I asked to visit the toilet. I went back into the reporting hallway but felt a premonition I could not understand, to stay by the exit of the reporting hallway. They expected me to be gentle as a lamb which unfortunately, (except for Professor Mohammad's timely intervention)I was.

A charitable lawyer serving Allah has 99% success rate in having deportees released.

Professor Mohammad was helping. He said it was not his real name. He does not take money and cannot disclose his job or occupation. Just wants everyone to know her is a very smart lawyer. He has helped thousands of people to re-united with their families. He said he just does this for Allah.

I telephoned Professor Mohammad even though he has specifically instructed never to contact him on Fridays which he spent in a mosque. Professor Mohammad picked up the phone. He said you must not go for interviews, and must leave the building. I said I was close to the exit but scared to leave

Professor Mohammad said "you must leave"

The exit/entrance of the reporting hallway opened into a small area which had the toilets the security guards at the mouth of the entrance/exit to the building.

There was no x-ray machine to go though to exit the building. I walked past the guards and out of the building, feeling sure I would be nabbed. It was 10 minutes to get out of the compound, and on the main road to a working bus stop. I could no longer run because in December 2017 heart trouble had kicked in but I walked as fast as I could.

When I got on the first bus that came along I was scared to turn my head back in case a police car was following the bus. I was terrified of answering as well as of not answering my mobile when a call came in which was obviously from the lady officer I had reported to. She asked me where I was, I needed to come for interviews.

I said from the moving bus that I was still in the toilet. She replied that she had searched the toilet first. I wasn't there.

But Professor Mohammad told me what to do after speaking to the reporting staff about my case.

And then there was reporting date given to me. I went to Liverpool, to attend another kind of immigration and stayed in a budget hostel there

3-0035: Liverpool: 2018: Jane do what Tarzan Say

My last residence in the UK what's in Liverpool . I was waiting to attend a Liverpool information with an immigration appeal.

In the 2018 I stayed in a hostel in Liverpool because I was awaiting attending immigration appeal.

During this time I had a couple of A&E episodes in a span for two months

During one of them, my lung X-ray and it looked so bad they thought I must have been wearing metal jewelery which stained the X-ray plates. They did the x-ray again to make sure that was really an image of my lungs.

They gave me antibiotics and asked me to take rest at home.

I had to come back to the hospital and see the doctor of infectious diseases and get an x-ray to check for improvement. She started pointing out things on my lung x-ray and I said to me they were just gray patches, as I am not a doctor. She was annoyed and in her report about me said I was delusional for how could I think I could be a doctor. She did not like me.

The Chinese GP in Liverpool said I could not have
my medical records as I was a 'SCHIZO HEAD".
(Layperson's vocabulary). I tried to challenge him so
he seemed to press a panic button. His the lady who his
colleague came running. The pair asked me questions and
let me go.

I feel that his purpose of calling via panic button was to
section me if there was a need.

I don't know what you think of this but I feel that they are
Partners in cruelty I don't know if what you think.

PART FOUR

4-0001: MY LAST DAYS IN THE UK

I was staying in a crowded and stinky budget hostel in Liverpool in early 2018, waiting to be given a date to go to an immigration interview. This interview was to take place in the building where Liverpool had a reporting center.

The UKBA knew I had come to Liverpool. But they had not yet put me under reporting restrictions. That needed fresh paperwork for a new location, which took time.

Until I came to Liverpool, I reported regularly since the start of 2010, in one of its multiple reporting centers, namely Eaton House.

As usual, I fell sick a couple of times during my brief stay in Liverpool. On the first occasion, I called an ambulance to go to A and E from inside a locked building.

My ECG was taken by the paramedic who brought me to A and E and showed "LBBB". The paramedic admitted my observation but was dodgy about explaining if I had a serious heart condition. They would not release the medical records afterward and claimed the ECG was lost. I always tried to get my records, as they were saying my heart was normal, and my ECG indicated some kind of problem persistently which they denied.

At A and E, they X-rayed my lungs and saw stuff there that looked terrible, and decided to double-check if something so ugly was really present.

They asked if I wore jewelry that was showing on the chest X-ray, which does not happen because the radiologist checks for and removes all jewelry if present. The second X-ray was taken within 30 minutes of the first one and was identical. My ECG taken a second time was also not normal which an A and E doctor agreed to.

They told me I must have a terrible lung infection and needed admission to the infectious diseases ward. They kept me in a separate cubicle in A and E intended for infectious people. However, after a couple of hours of lying there, they told me all the tests had come out normal and I was doing fine, and to go home. I was given some antibiotics to take home.

They wrote me with a follow-up appointment in the hospital with an infectious diseases doctor.

The latter, a lady was showing me the X-ray and saying things about it. I answered, "The X-ray looked to me like patches of gray and I couldn't see what she could. She wrote in her report I was delusional as I tried to be on the same level as a doctor.

Like everyone else, she felt I should not have anything but paracetamol for pain. "There is no reason for you to have chest pain," she said. Next time you get chest pain you should have women, who will just be in the room giving support."

Women working as "comfort-pillow" riding police cars when the police visit people with an unpleasant message was attractive enough. Now it was women working as painkillers! Alas but this one was more than just her imagination.

Later in 2018, I was admitted for a couple of days to a rural hospital nearer to Kremlin, where another (lady) doctor told me about the painkiller profession for women. I also saw this on television. So that is one of the lovely things women can do.

The medics did not explain the abnormal results already observed and discussed with me. They said "everything" had just become "okay."

Did they think I had the mind of a small child so they could simply reassure me that "everything was so good"? I realized the doctors either did not want to reveal the diagnosis, or they were not sure and could not be bothered to find out.

I realized I had a medical condition of the chest that would never go away, and that it was the decision of the medical profession that I should never find out what I had nor receive treatment for the same."

Going back to the idea that doctors may have a political or ethical opinion that some people are unworthy of life, due to being unwanted in human society. I would be wanted if I "shared my flesh" with "women in Physics" and the female-dominated mental health communities.

I am using a figure of speech to describe the situation when I say "shared my flesh" and do not want a misunderstanding that physical, or sexual contact between me and "women" was requested, where I'd been non-cooperative.

The doctors would consider it unethical to "kill off" persons they considered to be unworthy of life; whereas allowing them to die naturally when they developed an illness would be more up the doctors' street. I have speculated precisely this.

I have provided detailed circumstances in Part One as to why I feel Regent Exeter lost his life due to a long-standing opinion of his physician Dr. B that it was appropriate to let such an individual die untreated (undisclosed diagnosis).

I have also provided details of forensic evidence of a non-medical nature indicating that non-medical parties were looking forward to his passing.

That the UK police who are the highest force in the land in this matter decided not to investigate the issue.

I was advised by a lawyer who was a crony of Regent Exeter and much saddened by the news of his death. He said that he was a very high lawyer and that he did his level best to get the matter investigated inside the British legal infrastructure.

The Office of the Ombudsman, to whom I brought a complaint of foul play for two years, had decided against considering the matter. Their final response threatened jail if I displayed to anybody the correspondence exchanged with the Parliamentary Ombudsman, except for their final response.

It was so traumatic, and it was obvious they wanted nobody to think I may have submitted valid evidence but it was not considered.

Coming back to my (UK) situation in 2018, I had received legal notices intending to deport me. But legal experts had said a reason for this intention had not been provided, because the reason provided was worded unclearly and did not constitute a strong enough reason.

That was the criminal conviction I state was trumped-up, called "harassment without violence". It involved false allegations describing female traits I do not have.

The Pesthilenseroke had deeply craved that I "liaise with" their female "intimacy providers" and kept coming around for years, and prowling outside the door.

They lacked the legal right to force the desired "sexual" communication and had NEVER been instructed by the medical professionals to carry out such operations. I felt the Pesthilenseroke were clamoring for racial superiority over me, a non-compliant individual, who asserted my legal right to refuse.

This would be easy to understand for those who know what types of people from every race would work in a place like the Pesthilenseroke. The fact the Pesthilenseroke told false tales to the court involving stories of what I said to themselves showed me their keen personal interest in me.

This was a falsification of the despised truth that I had not engaged with them. The plaintiffs of the criminal conviction Mrs. Viju Wortley and my parents had engaged with them and requested my lockup.

But there was no law under which I could be locked up and medical professionals were not getting involved. So the Pesthilenseroke's activities were limited to harassment through constant visits and annoying mail I could ignore without consequence.

Coming directly to the point, I make a comparison between me and the late Regent Exeter, that I have a similar problem to him, which s weaker in intensity and did not lead to death. Both of us are not wanted to human society. This is my theory, my speculation. My story hopefully explains why I feel that way.

In the case of the late Regent Exeter, deportation was not a quantity as he was a UK citizen. How would they GET RID OF SOMEONE they could not deport? Well I have explained in Part One, 1-0001, and 1-0003, my suggested reasons why anyone would want such a kind and gentle man out of the way.

Indeed, before dying, Regent had said all British women attend women's groups in some shape or form. Maybe I should admit his view as having some truth in it. Nobody else would tell the truth, would they?

Here is why I would be one of those they need to exterminate, or eliminate through deportation

I was jailed in Yarlswood IDC briefly, in 2010 and 2013, I had noticed that women who appeared to be submissive and illiterate and took an interest in their cookery program were released and allowed to stay in the UK. Women who wrote letters or said, "Sir, I'd like to explain my situation" were not let out, they were deported.

This means women demonstrating a plethora of female personality traits, (with much potential to practice "woman-to-woman intimacy" with groups and mental health communities were preferred for admission to live in the UK).

And before coming to Liverpool, a naughty but successful Pakistani immigration lawyer who could not give me his name had told me UKBA knew The Pesthilenseroke was lying that I had engaged with them. He said I was being deported for not engaging with The Pesthilenseroke, which amounted to not having a relationship with women.

I had come across two other cases of foreign women in the UK that were unwanted in the UK, as they did not liaise in women's groups. One is a story of a 38-year-old Brazilian woman Thelma Correa-Caney deported to Brazil on 7 January 2014.

The latter was a fellow inmate with me in Yarlswood, who had a spine injury and could move minimally. They had what looked like a wall in the mess hall that was actually a sliding panel.

They brought Thelma in and out of that sliding panel

and she said she was wheeled to a place in the basement alone, where other inmates did not go, where staff would deal with her unseen.

Thelma received corporal punishment from Yarlswood. I personally examined the bruises. Thelma had a baby with her British husband Darren Caney who was a homeowner. After two years of marriage and a child, the couple separated.

Thelma had an accident where she lost sensation completely below her spine. Doctors were able to operate on her and she recovered her spinal use partially.

It was not legal to deport Thelma as a mother of a UK citizen has a right to remain there without visa procedures until the kid turns 18.

But they had given custody to the father and she had a right to stay as long as she applied for visitation rights.

But she had no money education or legal advice from anyone, and had previously endured 6 months of jail after her visiting Brazilian teenager (jealous of the mixed-race English baby) lied to police that Thelma saw her baby illegally.

It turns out Thelma preferred men and was not compatible

with British women's groups.

A second case was an elderly alcoholic in the Brighton Hostel, who said his wife was a Hindu. I did meet her eventually, and it turns out this woman, whose name was Laxmi, was despised by UK women and no Hindu or white woman would speak to her, and she had only one Muslim woman as a friend.

Although the couple stayed together all their lives and had three children, the man said he was disappointed they could not have a good life as his wife was shunned and ignored by the British community. Laxmi did not liaise with women as a British woman should. She stayed at home and did not link up to women's groups.

I, therefore, speculate there is racial hygiene in the UK whereby women from overseas, that won't "liaise with women" are preferably ejected from UK soil. The fact I received a legal notice banning me from having a private life in the UK may have resulted due to this racial hygiene.

I am now going to explain this phenomenon of racial hygiene I have just proposed. This explanation is to do with the "100% uniformity of opinion" which was talked about, and seen in print, in 2006, and disappeared like the morning dew afterward. Maybe it had become implemented, and so was no longer spoken about. It became a HIDDEN LAW. I feel I saw this hidden law while it was in the making.

A lot of people understand what this means. It means, if you don't hold a particular opinion, you will be eliminated from the system.

To be clearer, I have come to my conclusion that the mental health system is a man-made environmental factor that panders to the lesser instincts of mankind, by offering a reward: banishment of the inferiority of races and individuals. Remember no weapon can cleave what an "EXPERT" has called a "SCIENCE".

Feeling inferior and superior to others happens due to opposite reasons, but they are the flip side of the same coin. An adult person who feels inferior (in my estimation) is a counter-productive individual as much as people who feel superior. As people with inferiority complexes should mostly be considered as counter-productive individuals, an overwhelming desire to lie to oneself, just for one's vanity, is also a lesser instinct of man.

Respect cannot be extracted at gunpoint, which is what the British system is trying to do for persons who have reason to feel inferior. There is no reason to feel inferior, just because you have less of something

All humans are supposed to respect each other,

irrespective of their status. The lives of people with an inferiority complex which are going well should be lived happily without becoming jealous of those who have more intelligence education and other attributes.

The basic postulates of the mental health system may not be truthful, but these postulates can be propagated due to their popularity from providing as unshakeable truth what folks would like to believe.

When this environmental factor becomes dominant (everyone is using it or will do when there is need, or the same is a rule applying to all women), in such a case, we are getting near a point of 100% uniformity of a specific set of opinions Everyone believing the same thing makes that belief an environmental factor or political climate.

I have come to my conclusion that this intentionally introduced modification of the social environment BY THINKERS AND CONSPIRATORS gives us an altered environment comparable to having a room lit with bluish tube lights whereby people cannot see their veins and would not be able to shoot up drugs in case they are junkies.

The altered environment, or place with a greenhouse effect of sorts, results in the lower intelligence of women compared to men becoming invisible. It becomes a sort of permanent secret and enhances human vanity and the high quality that results for every citizen because they feel like a king, and at the top.

They may not be a king(queen) but THEY SURE FEEL
LIKE ONE, in the intentionally-altered environment

The CONCEALMENT of inferior female intelligence,
(a truth that should become invisible until it is deemed
to be a myth), becomes EFFECTIVE only because there
is almost no one in the environment who understands
what way females are not intellectually on par with men.
Concealment has to be total, in other words operating on
all human beings, to be effective.

People would otherwise communicate their experiences
with each other. What is known to one person can spread
until everyone knows it. To keep the secret with 100%
efficiency, the "ugly happenings" that arise from that
secret need not happen.

If "ugly happenings" do not occur as a result of an
unpalatable truth, it is easy to get everyone's cooperation
that that unpalatable truth does not exist.

People drop their face masks in a crisis and start to reveal
their true colors. A crisis is therefore an important time
when a female would behave in a way that everybody
would understand the feeble side of her nature, both
morally, and intellectually.

Everybody knows that the normal use of a lavatory is for the ejection of Number1 and Number 2. The successfully-protected woman, needs to eliminate a "Number 3" from time to time. Here, Number 3 represents some poorly-understood quantity.

She does this inside the four walls of a specially-constructed virtual lavatory, which in this case is the mental health system. She discusses "her thing" with functionally-illiterate mental workers. A good example of the latter is the "woman-to-woman intimacy team" of the Pesthilenseroke.

We also see that a woman is usually a better choice than a man, as she is good at being a passive receptable that has no emotional reactions, no aggravation, no interest or feeling. Or else, how could she put with working the world's oldest profession? She has to do the job of taking in information like unlimited water poured into a toilet, with one-way traffic. Like a prostitute lies back and takes it, while a customer rams his penis, the mental health worker, who is usually a "woman", "working with" "women", just sits and listens. This is a substandard and defective communication.

I have stated above that the objective of the mental health system, when it gains dominance over all peoples in a geographic region (or globally as the case may be) will result in making the inferiority of female intelligence invisible.

We see that providing such defective communication is a distasteful and unmanly operation. Naturally, the occupation attracts persons of inferior social and moral intelligence. While serving as a cover for female inferiority, all kinds of people such as men and women who are not that inferior, are constantly urged to consult with the mental health system, when they are unhappy.

Referring everyone to the mental health system serves as a cover of the identity of the type of person(woman) who might genuinely have a use case.

This type of defective communication would annoy any right-thinking person. Indeed there are a lot of complaints against the mental health system wherever it is operational. These complaints fall on deaf ears.

The authorities ignore complaints against what they have put in place, so that inferiority of female intelligence may become invisible to all humans. Wherever the mental health system is operational, there is no way for anyone to raise a complaint, particularly in a sensitive topic about it. That's where a hidden law comes into force and one might find oneself stepping or a SURPRISE LANDLINE if one is serious about getting a complaint moving all over the place.

This method of defective communication will not appeal to right-thinking people. The keyword, of course, is "right-thinking". There are people pouring

INFORMATION down the mental health lavatory, (that is, the human being that just listens).

Willing participants are rare.

Willing participants are persons are pouring a genuine "Number 3 down this human lavatory". If you lament being sacked from your work, there is nothing inherently private or shameful about it. It is therefore not a genuine Number 3. You may not feel much satisfaction from an exchange that takes place inside four walls with a mental health worker.

A bonafide "Number 3" would be about how that person feels and reacts to a situation, which would be deemed morally wrong or of poor intelligence if examined by the larger public.

The bearer of the "Number 3" is of inferior mental status, Gender inferiority is indicated, and will become public if the government did not provide a way to direct "Number 3" down a private channel with secure, one-way traffic.

We also see how many agencies and organizations have sprung up in the last few decades. Forget about the ISBN Agency, the Spread betting Agency. I am only referring to those agencies that give advice (nothing but advice) to "people" where only women are served and those that give advice(nothing but advice) to "women" where only women are served.

If you live in the UK, you probably understand what I am talking about. since the UK has lots of these. Well these agencies include the mental health system, which may be the only one of them that is protected under the glorious umbrella of medicine as some kind of "health agency".

In each of these agencies, advisers are illiterate females. Additionally, they do not have the mental ability to give advice. They are provided with leaflets. They just reel off those simple sentences as "advice". Needless to say, if you know how to read and write, this plethora of agencies and personal services is of little use. The mental health service is one such agency.

It is not normal, it is inconsistent with natural laws for those who do have not the mental capacity to advise to work as a constantly-praised team of advisers. This is part of the conspiracy to create a virtual greenhouse effect, where you feel awe as soon as you look at a woman, and you start to think she had the advice to give. .

This is like having land where all the security officers in all businesses in the land are in wheelchairs. An unnatural choice, such could be achieved through modern technology.

The disabled should be provided with extra arms and

391

ammunition, to make up for their physical incapacities. They could operate from behind a high-strength glass screen and use sensors and panic buttons, which when pressed would make the able-bodied rush to the spot.

Some people may not see any point in having a set-up like that. However, it would provide equal opportunities for handicapped people to work as security officers.

Besides" attitudes are fast changing". When you see a quadriplegic, you first think of physical combat, as that's what they are fit to do.".

Anyway, having such an "easy-peasy" idiot-friendly virtual platform for people to navigate the path of life means that who those are fearful, those who have no thinking power will find the world to be a fearless place as much as the powerful.

And having an idiot-friendly place should not affect the quality of life for those who are not idiots. Because whereas a big cat cannot get through a tiny hole, a big hole will admit both big and tiny cats.

Ah! But this logic does not work fully well. Which is the same thing as saying sometimes the idiots will get an unfair advantage over their natural superiors.

People have always had superstitions. We have a whole billion people who (on the face of it) seem to think the (holy) cow, which is but an unintelligent animal, can grant blessings. In the 20th century, medical doctors placed a knitting needle into your eye socket to relieve stress from your brain.

They pushed the knitting needle in slowly. This was also known as lobotomy. Even today many people don't understand this is something scary. In the 21st century doctors still, place 800 Volts across your temples to cure depression.

In recent years, public interest in Physics has spiked, due to street gigs by the Institute of Physics, despite hundreds of websites having been created where Physics has been frequently confused with sex.

I am an expelled member of this Institute (expelled for bringing them into disrepute) and would much rather see you plowing fields as an ox than studying Physics if you thought it would be okay to put 800 Volts across someone's temples.

You do not have to study anything to be terrified of the idea, as long as you are familiar with electricity and have received a shock from handling gadgets.

Well here we have eradicated unpalatable things like

women "walking behind" men and now they live in that man-made "easy-peasy" "help and health" paradise where they rely on women instead. Is this an improvement or a step backward?"

If you choose and revere a mental health worker, you are going to vehemently oppose the theory that mental health workers lack mental capacity. After all, if they lack mental capacity and you walk behind them, what does it say about you.

Women can't live with the notions that mental health workers are illiterate because it speaks badly of their own intelligence and men don't want to deal with such ideas as it makes them feel the women in their lives are fools.

So we have the {holy) cow culture where people cling to the idea that mental health workers are behavioral specialists. I assert though that this is but a superstition, a fallacy supported by the conspirators of modern society.

People have not become cleverer, nor have women done so through the centuries. We fall back on cumulative knowledge that grows with time. In a deeper sense, people are NOT making intellectual progress at all.

Going back to the title of the book I speculate that they kill those whom they don't like. After reading books about eugenics I concluded that only the medical community or university have the power to enforce eugenics on a population.

They would be the conspirators of the modern eugenic scheme, the modified environment, the virtual greenhouse filled with help and mental health agencies. Any new eugenic scheme has to sound pleasant and rewarding for people to take it up.

If the conspirators said they were going to kill people or inflict deprivations on some people so they would dwindle or cease to function, they would not achieve that 100% uniformity of opinion where all heads will bow to that new eugenic policy.

Going to a subset of the new eugenic scheme which I state is existing, this would be not killing people, but deporting them due to unsuitability due to eugenically unwanted characteristics.

This produces a whole nation where unwanted characteristics have been eliminated. This is not racial discrimination but whatever race you are, if you have certain characteristics you are not welcome here I have speculated, giving reasons, as to why I feel Britain has a eugenic policy to deport from among women who are in immigration detention those who speak to men, think and communicate, or are not submissive. If you went along with the above para, you would probably reflect (I do) that the British probably generally prefer to allow entry

395

into their shores, of submissive females, while females with illiteracy, learning disabilities, and mental health problems would not be a problem at all. I've explained the mental health system is a major environmental factor of the UK, designed for concealment of certain truths about human nature such as female inferiority, and create a happiness paradise where no one feels like they are intellectually inferior to anyone. Effectively criticizing the mental health system, and departure from that serene and speechless 100% uniformity of opinion would crack up the mental health system, so that romantic concealment is no longer possible. If men disrupted the peace, by criticizing women, or by criticizing the mental health system, they could be arrested and expelled from all sorts of places. Many of these are things for which a woman cannot be prosecuted. If a woman born in the UK, or an Englishwoman started to criticize the mental health system, they would need to be silenced. Regent was an Englishman and he had God's gift of life stolen from him to achieve what man wanted, that nobody shall effectively criticize the mental health system. Criticizing is okay, being effective enough to bring the system down is another thing. Regent would have brought the system down had he lived another 5 years. He would have certainly done so I feel, if had I realized how urgent his problem was and taken him to doctors when I first met him in August 2011.

The longer you leave heart failure(which is what Regent must have had) untreated, the less chance they will survive. On the day he died he may not have much time left even if he had started receiving belated but proper medical care.

The doctors told him he was about to die, and he went home unaided and was jubilant with the charity shop ladies that he had won his battle against time and completed the writing of his Last Testament.

The doctors who realized he would die any moment should not have asked him to go home on his own in an inter-city bus. They should have helped him with the will etc so he could die in the comfort of a hospital bed.

I think you have understood me by now. Doctors did not want him to live. Rather than see the mental health system which is the sentinel of British romance crack up, it was preferable to the medical community that some people could die.

In the case of female foreign nationals, many are happy to wear the mental health cloak and adopt the British way of life. But some foreign women are born with gender equality and cannot wear this cloak, and become a "woman person".

The foreign national who is pressured to accept the mental health system and liaising with women aid organizations as a way of life, may not be able to do to higher intelligence, education, and mental development make it harder to convert.

397

Blessed are those who come in as a medical doctors especially if they are happily married and no one will ask them about liaising with women. Most British accept that immigration is much more lenient towards marriages of immigrants of the same race than if one party was English. You see the British race-relations act contradicts a relationship between a man and woman of different races.

Thus a colored person marrying a British white person would be a disruptor of the legal code and 100% conformity to that code in thought word and deed. So also, foreign females (other than those on the lowest intelligence level), have grown out of a different kind of spiritual food.

They cannot eat the British spiritual food that is fed to all adult women-the "easy-peasy" idiot-friendly "help and health" system, because they have developed, or progressed too far to be fooled by psychological gimmicks. They would disrupt the system as (I suppose) I did, by refusing when "forced" to liaise with the Pesthilenseroke.

You must realize the British state who must have realized I cannot adopt the British woman's way of life, which is liaising with women and mental health communities, and they placed me under a clamp when I wanted to stay in the UK.

They declared I shall not have a boyfriend or husband on UK soil and that I cannot take up paid or unpaid employment in the UK. This is like wearing a painful nose-clamp for 14 years, a life-limiting condition awarded by the state.

The second time I got sick in Liverpool, I took a taxi to A and E. They said my heartbeat was too fast and I had unstable angina. I stayed in a cardiology ward for 3 days and was discharged with 7 different tablets to take daily for a week, and a diagnosis of completely normal. I felt so weak I could hardly walk.

Someone staying at this budget hostel, (which subsequently closed due to financial losses to the owner), suggested I move my case to Edinburgh or Kremlin. He had worked as a deportation officer in Edinburgh. He had already quit his job for a better one, he said, when he advised me. He explained there was a soft border into Ireland from Belfast.

4-0002: Rhinoskin Reception Centre

My journey into Ireland took place on 2018-04-30, using methods suggested by Mr.W. But by then Mr. W, had left the UK, and was not available to consult. I was very scared at Busaras Bus Station of getting arrested, but no one looked at me.

On 2018-05-17 I registered at the IPO, and was driven along with other men and women in taxis to Rhinoskin reception center, which was marked for the public to see as a recreation center.

4-0003: A Marked Person in the UK and then Ireland

Anyway, when I came from the UK I had been through the immigration process and I had left without completing it. I had started a new immigration process in Ireland.

I was told at Rhinoskin by an experienced social worker that something was missing in the paperwork to me from the IPO.

I was a "marked person" for unknown reasons. Did I have a "price on my head?"

I was a "marked person" for unknown reasons. Did I have a "price on my head?" So I started questioning that. and visited the legal aid office; they said everything's alright. I got a lawyer. She was a really nice lady. However, she did not want to know anything about me or my case. She wanted to do my case with absolutely no information about me.

I had to go to the IPO again for a preliminary interview around the 23rd of May.

At the interview, the lady who was interviewing me shouted across to another lady exclaiming, "She is an IPPA!".

I was already aware that national identity card numbers such as social security numbers have biometric data coded into them, such as your gender age, or other data hidden in the letters and numbers of the identification.

Only officials (not lay people) can tell by looking at an identity card if it belongs to a male or female, etc. Credit card numbers must satisfy a specific mathematical formula.

I put two and two together and verified that the other candidates did not have IPPA on their blue cards. They had the usual string of numbers but not IPPA or other acronyms. The social worker had told me something was wrong or missing from my paperwork. Eureka! I was a marked person, who is of course not supposed to know she is that. IPPA had an unknown and bad meaning.

But then, what the experienced social worker had said about me being ineligible for free legal representation appeared to be untrue after I got one lawyer and then a second one for free.

I speculate though, that while I was doing immigration appeals in the UK,(2006-2018) lawyer after lawyer deliberately lost their case. Each lawyer lost his case by reapplying with exactly the same content as the previous application that had been refused.

This habit made the judges or caseworkers who were to make a decision angrier and angrier. The applications made by the lawyers I user one after another looked like I (and whoever represented me) did not understand instructions. By losing cases that would have otherwise been accepted, the lawyers worked on getting my appeals exhausted.

In the UK, from 2006-2018, lawyers were trying to deport me. Yes, this is an allegation I am making about immigration lawyers. This allegation is likely to make the lawyers and members of the public, especially females angry as lawyers are not supposed to represent you in an immigration case and try to get you deported.

Needless to say, if this allegation I make were to be true, it would mean that there was a political reason for wanting to deport me. Otherwise so many lawyers would not have been trying to deport you. I fully accept that people reading this would not believe me.

The lawyers' applications were always saying the same thing. It was the partner application combined with a mental health reason. This can be proved if I show the list of applications made and their corresponding notices of refusal. The partner applications were identical to those that had just been refused, without asking the judge for the reasons why I am not allowed a husband or boyfriend in the UK.

The mental health reason stated by the immigration lawyers sounded repetitive, and reflective of nothing but illiteracy. To me, it sounded like they were portraying me as a mental retard. It was considered and rejected every time. The deciding judge(s) said I lacked evidence.

The rule which says medical allegations must be accompanied by a report from a licensed physician was not followed. Such reports were not available, but there were reams of notes I was not allowed to see, from the illiterate Pesthilenseroke. Rumors and gossip were used as evidence I had mental health problems.

As I have already stated, the lawyers' portrayal of my personality seemed to me like an illiterate and mildly retarded person, which is not curable and is not an illness. My qualifications were omitted by force. This is curious, because I was being portrayed as an imbecile, and they did not bring up that I was a Physics graduate from UMIST. I, therefore, speculate malicious intent to do everything to show me at the bottom of the pile

They were denying me the right to have a boyfriend or husband and the right to work for the rest of my life. They were also making the whole world believe I am mentally retarded. And while I am aware that a lot of folks have an intellect that goes no further than genitalia. These folks would understand nothing. But I am sure any lawyer would have understood this was bordering on lifelong torture and something close to homicide.

I am sure most would desist from such practices (all other things being equal if I were a man. Ingrained in their minds is the concept a woman's mind is pure dung and she is oblivious to the concept of dignity, or they knew it was right to steal my God's gift of life for women in Physics, the mental-health supported personalities and other preferred individuals.

I did not consent to these things. But the partner was involved, and some of the time he was paying the lawyers' fees. He did spend a lot of money over the years on me (on getting legal assistance) but he did not listen to me at times when I would have saved him a grand or more in expenses and prevented the case from being lost and going to the higher court of appeal. The proceedings took place with a person breathing down my neck, always wanting to go in the opposite direction to what I wanted.

I realized no later than August 2018 that I was some kind of a marked person in Ireland, based on a UK document I have not been allowed to see; they may even deny it exists. I had two lawyers from the legal aid office, which takes me up in April 2019. Both of them tried to make a case where there were no details of any kind about me, just the mental health reason.

As in the UK, these two lawyers lost their cases.

However the second lawyer dropped psychiatry was after I clarified I lacked a gushing urge to speak to a psychiatrist. Without the gushing urge to speak to shrinks saying they would kill me if I went to the UK, he said it would be pointless to see a psychiatrist. You see, if I did feel such a gushing urge, that would correctly prove I am an imbecile- and I think any proven imbecile can stay in Ireland, just like the UK.

During this period (up to April 2019) I was homeless staying outside Direct Provision. I slept in a mixture of paid hostels and "Kremlin homeless places" and got pneumonia for the first time.

People assumed I would sleep on the streets, but I never did. People had been given the message I was not educated, but like any slum-dweller, or prostitute, who sadly make choices differently. I would have preferred to be arrested by airport police than sleep on the streets. That almost happened.

I saw doctors often. Doctors visited the homeless places twice a week. It was easy to see what the GPs were reading about me when they logged into their computer.

They had a mental illness written up about me, which varied like the weather.

I mean, I saw a different mental illness written up for me on the doctor's computer each time I saw a doctor at the homeless places, which is not supposed to happen. Mental illness is of date incurable. So if you find you have a mental illness, you are going to die with it.

At one point, the medical computers said "drug-resistant psychosis." Do you know why it was a lie?

Because they would first have to diagnose me with psychosis, then try out at least two different anti psychotics to conclude it is drug-resistant.

I heard that prisoners of war had been put away like that.

Usually people who are not on psych drugs do not have any evidence to argue a legal case that they have a mental illness. However, if they can say they are drug-resistant psychotic, then it becomes credible.

One temporary GP volunteered when I saw him over a problem which had nothing to do with psychiatry, to write that I am having daily psychotic episodes. "it will be the end of your immigration problems," he said.

I've no idea-maybe it would have. I did not have a lawyer representing me at that time.

I know that for most modern people, particularly girls, their clothing may not leave much to the imagination, but mental health does.

It is common practice for a lady (no men as of today's date) working at an office to comment, "I am concerned about Mohini....illness.....doctor"

The fact people are not connected, see "illness" in me, shows I have something real they find objectionable. The fact that only women find it reduces the credibility I have something wrong with me but does not take it away altogether.

According to current trends I feel aware of, men are loyalists to "women's equality". If men learn that "becoming concerned" about me and finding mental health reasons is a 100% woman-thing and part of a pattern, they will become twice as abusive towards me to "prove" that women in their office are equal.

The fact any man will lie cheat and cover for a female colleague coupled with the fact I can only speak to women makes the workplace a hostile environment where I would be very unhappy. The fact men lie and cover-up for women colleagues and advertise as woman bosses to women of the public, indicates women in a workplace are of inferior mental status compared to men.

A woman is seen as having a special sexual talent for fathoming out the brains of women. Anything I say is interpreted by women to men even though we are speaking the same language. She is there even if she is not there. It's like living under contemptuous sex slavery.

I think though, that other migrant women are finding the whole scheme exhilarating.

The lady in the office has a "romantic" imagination. Much is left to the imagination about mental illness.

Whenever she feels anger jealousy or fear (usually towards a stranger of the same sex) she can instantly dispel those unpleasant feelings and revert to her chronic comfort. She simply turns on the "concern tap" about that stranger having a mental health problem to which everyone is 100% certain to nod in respect.

Gone are the negative feelings, she feels safe like she is in her private bedroom. A situation of total approval and safety, where there is a "doctor" to "fix" the human object of her wrath or passion.

Bringing things to a conclusion about mental health means the lady in the office would not be able to instantly dispel negative feelings and come out on top.

That's why they keep the mental thing open. The possibilities are endless when it comes to mental health. What is not possible is something a doctor said or was alleged to say is incorrect if it runs down someone's "mental health".

I cannot tell people what to believe. You see, "mental

health allegations" are made by people, mainly women, in a light vein. I think it's their culture. They expect you to have infinite humility like themselves. It's not supposed to offend. Their perception is very diffuse, like driving a boat through solid mud. Satisfying her is to pleasure her like crazy. It won't happen.

4-0004 My Big Bloody Mouth in County West Sheath

After 6 weeks in Rhinoskin I moved to another refugee center in County West Sheath. This was a routine movement along with others.

I was told by staff, "Everyone here is guaranteed asylum, but you will be deported"

My first lawyer a lady asked me for a psychiatric report for the court hearing. She was going to submit no details about me to the court except for a psychiatric report which was to "prove" through the glory of the medical profession, that I was gravely disabled..

So the lady lawyer could get this medico-legal free of charge, so she phoned my GP in rural Ireland. The GO also a lady had taken the phone call about me but had never met me. She met me subsequently and started talking to me like I was crazy, from the first moment. It was obvious the dice were loaded, with the lady solicitor's call, which must have said I am crazy, rather than explain she needed an excuse to get a medico-legal report free of charge.

I suppose they have a visa category for mentally deranged people. It is an extreme indignity to give me that kind of visa.

What if the lawyers wanted to represent me as a prostitute to get a visa?

Is there a limit to what you would do to get a visa? Since a prostitute would do anything for a piece of bread, I suppose they would not mind becoming a lunatic on paper to get a visa.

I changed my lawyer. Which was unnecessary, as all lawyers, male and female, would treat me like that, using brute force to give me an imbecile personality

After 6 weeks in Rhinoskin I moved to another refugee center in County West Sheath. This was a routine movement along with others.

I was told by staff, "Everyone here is guaranteed asylum, but you will be deported"

My first lawyer a lady asked me for a psychiatric report for the court hearing. She was going to submit no details about me to the court except for a psychiatric report which was to "prove" through the glory of the medical profession, that I was gravely disabled..

So the lady lawyer could get this medico-legal free of

413

charge, so she phoned my GP in rural Ireland. The GO also a lady had taken the phone call about me but had never met me. She met me subsequently and started talking to me like I was crazy, from the first moment. It was obvious the dice were loaded, with the lady solicitor's call, which must have said I am crazy, rather than explain she needed an excuse to get a medico-legal report free of charge.

I suppose they have a visa category for mentally deranged people. It is an extreme indignity to give me that kind of visa.

What if the lawyers wanted to represent me as a prostitute to get a visa?

Is there a limit to what you would do to get a visa? Since a prostitute would do anything for a piece of bread, I suppose they would not mind becoming a lunatic on paper to get a visa.

I changed my lawyer. Which was unnecessary, as all lawyers, male and female, would treat me like that, using brute force to give me an imbecile personality

A bonded sex slave, a prisoner to "woman support", to psychiatric visa bids in the UK for over a decade WANTS TO DIE.

The trick of psychiatric visa bid was played by lawyers hundreds of times in the UK. It had failed hundreds of times for over a decade.

At County West Sheath roads were strictly not motorable, but the drivers were clever. The nearest post office was about 7 miles away, and nothing but fields and cottages with winding roads.

Soon I started waking up with blood in my mouth and a strange taste, not the taste of blood. It made me feel much pain in the throat and very tired. This used to happen in 2018 in the UK, where the quantities of blood were smaller and I was living in denial. The blood was now very obvious.

I had it for 2 or 3 days in a raw condition when I requested to be taken to hospital in great pain.

They fast-tracked me at A and E but pretended like the blood had never happened. I stayed in the the hospital for 3 days.

4-0005: Male Lawyer wants me examined by FEMALE Doctor for possible Mental Illness

The second lawyer, a man, did not want to deal with me at all. He sent a message through his junior asking me to see a WOMAN doctor who would confirm or deny that I had a mental illness.

He was treating me like a pariah unless proved to not have a mental illness, and I felt weird.

Based on years of experience, I knew that it was more certain that only women would be used in my regard, than that the sun would rise in the morning. Also, the lawyer did not say that he needed a mental assessment by a female doctor.

Doctors are supposed to be competent, and the sex of a doctor is not supposed to count when it comes to the accuracy of an assessment..

I have explained I was told in the UK that the reason for deportation was that I did not liaise with women's groups. This happened shortly before my departure from the UK, while Regent, who died in 2014. who was free of hypocrisy, had told me that all British women are connected in some way or other with women's groups.

416

There is, then, a selective filter, so WOMEN WHO ARE NOT INTO WOMEN are not wanted on British shores.

There is no explicit law that women should bond with women. That would depend on a woman's brain, and her primal (sexual and basal) instincts and urges. I think such a law is operational in a covert way. People will have to be unexpectedly punished by falling foul of law virtually nobody thinks exists. So the UK is like a place ridden with landmines, which for some people are a constant terror and botheration.

Since racial hygiene and eugenics traditionally refer to murder, castration, and sterilization of persons possessing certain objectionable characteristics, or to dwindle their population by other means, it is questionable whether we can say this policy would mean that the UK is practicing racial hygiene. After all, they are only preventing such persons from entering their shores. Their eugenic enforcement is not global., but limited to the territory of the United Kingdom

If he asked me nicely to get checked up for mental illness as it is mentioned on your UKBA records, I wouldn't have a problem doing what he wanted.

However-to come to the point- I hypothesize that such racial hygiene is also prevalent in Ireland so not bonding with women would normally be shunned and perceived as a mental disorder.

That's why the lawyer tried to check if this sex-specific disorder existed. A female doctor would have brain urges and instincts of women, and as she is acceptable to human society as a doctor, she has passed the woman-to-woman intimacy test with flying colors, she would be able to judge, based on how much I "pleasured" her brain, my mental health level.

This then, is the subject of inquiry, or is it? I'd say, this is the reason I have had so much difficulty with immigration, due to the new-fangled racial hygiene.

It's not my business, but based on the few examples I have seen, I believe that non-European prostitutes are getting asylum over here faster than others. Their path through the legal system is easy and comfortable. Can I speculate that the brains of prostitutes are wired heavily with women's basal urges and instincts, and they get a high score in the psychometrics I seem to be lacking? I apologize for speculating in areas where I lack a qualification.

Later I learned that the lady doctor was quite a nice person who had no connection with this scheme. She was known to the lawyer, but he was not known to her.

He kept calling me "madam". I think he respected male clients more and may have been calling me "madam" because he thought that I might be a retired prostitute mentoring younger prostitutes for sex work.

418

Neither lawyer won their case. Like UK lawyers both wanted my life to be a blank slate other than a psychiatric report "proving" me gravely disabled. Losing the case may not have been the lawyers' fault. Maybe the court does not want me to be in the country unless I am gravely (mentally) disabled, and does not want me walking around if I am.

They did not realize why I would dislike being immigrated as a mentally-retarded female. Other women who applied for refugee status had never objected. These lawyers were only trying to help

4-0006: Medical Lies keep the Dumbells Happy

I could not do the treadmill test. But before discharging me, they told me I had done it excellently.

They said I had pain because of bone softening and they gave injections to my bone to stop the pain.

They told me I was normal and asked me to go I would not explain why there had been blood in my mouth. They made it into trivia. They said, I think they think I have a touch of COPD, but there's nothing that needs to be done about it.

I was not happy in County West Sheath even though there were plenty of cows and horses to be had, and I liked farm animals (no pun intended). I felt isolated as I took the group shuttle to the post office and grocers as everyone else was conversing in "African". I felt like I was trapped in a locked nursery class. I had little use, personally for the truckloads of baby food from the goodness of Ireland that filled the warehouses at the West Sheath Center.

I understand that any young married couple, that arrives in Ireland as a refugee gets pregnant immediately after arrival. Any single black female who arrives here also seems to get pregnant immediately after arrival, usually without the father's cooperation, and depending only on the state. Some single African women have several babies while living alone in Direct Provision.

I suppose Ireland is a great place to go for any woman who would like to give birth.

I am not qualified to comment – as my reasoning is based on a handful of first-hand experiences and other people's cases are protected under data protection.

4-0007: Maybe Asylum is given only for Sexual Activity

I have seen in Taslough (UK) a whole vat (a barrel 3-4 feet high and 2-3 feet in diameter) filled with loose condoms in the women's toilet. Men were getting legal advice. Women (my joke) were getting only condoms. Women got women "ADVISERS" and in this case, the WOMAN ADVISERS knew nothing.

If international refugee law says refugee status only or mainly is for those who have abundant sex with anyone and everyone but it is not on the (public) books then I am ineligible as I don't have a partner This is purely speculation.

Other things I speculate about is that asylum is not granted to educated people anywhere in the world, and if you have never held a pen, you won't even need the baby-producing qualification, to get asylum in any country, automatically. I also think- this is only about Ireland and only about the present time- I don't say this will last- but any non-European hookers wandering on the streets not only get asylum, but the machinery works faster than for anyone else, and their pockets are jangling with money once asylum is awarded, a free house and whatnot.

Whatever I said above, I did not see in print, nor was I told these things by any living human. With no legal and social qualifications, I may be wrong, as my observations may have been the exception, not the rule.

Anyway, living inside these places, a major difference is everybody else is happy without any conversation except me, it seems. Of course, I do not have the mental capacity to work with no human speaking to me, but female residents, if they work are in care, child care, and "mentally disabled". I do not have a right to ask, to speak to a man, which is regarded as obscene. I think.

In a great social welfare system, PSYCHIATRICALLY NORMAL WOMEN would not ever ask for a man except to use his PENIS. Asking to speak to a man is non-existent among refugees-I don't know about locals. Penises are abundantly available to use for females, especially for Africans, in the absence of any conversation behind doors windows curtains, and under beds in refugee centers.

Everyone else here lives their entire lives out of agencies and organizations, and nobody understands what a social life or conversation is.

Equations of women and personal services

Agency = Organization = condom + sandwich

Health + wealth + cookery + housework = doctor

The top and bottom halves of a woman have been
DISSOCIATED by the MASTERMINDS OF
CONSPIRACY for optimal quality of life. Such
dissociation is not possible in nature. It is due to social
engineering by men. This involves a new way of thinking.

PURPOSELY-INTRODUCED ERRORS are interwoven
into the mental health system as well as into the rest of the
MANMADE CONCEPT INFRASTRUCTURE to create
the new way of thinking.

Females are using the mental health crutch to a greater
extent, and in larger numbers than men, so their
HANDICAP AS AN AGGREGATE is coming out to zero
with respect to the figures for men if the scheme is 100%
efficient

THE TOP HALVES OF WOMEN HAVE
BEEN WELDED TO ADVISORY WOMAN
ORGANIZATIONS and mental health services, A
woman's emotional needs are provided by "SPECIALLY
QUALIFIED" members of the same sex. Such a
qualification is exactly what I have described earlier as
the SEX-TRAINED SEX BRAIN.

These include the mental health system, social workers,
counseling, psychologists agencies, and organizations.

Their crania are "kept happy" with "happy drugs".

I feel some people are repeating like a SLOW-WITTED
CABBAGE that I should use the drugs aspect of women's
support system as well as the commercially-provided
same-sex welfare and intimacy.

THE BOTTOM HALVES OF WOMEN are, on the
other hand, impregnated by speechless men in all kinds
of weird places, with CONDOM SUPPORT, WOMAN
SUPPORT, and POLICE SUPPORT.

EVERY CRACK IN A WOMAN, be it emotional,
intellectual, or an actual geometrical orifice is FILLED
THROUGH THE LEGAL INFRASTRUCTURE.

I spent my childhood in India where I was taught Indians
were socially backward to stigmatize women who failed
to give birth. I think the stigma against me in the UK and
Ireland, against women without baby-producing, is more
severe, especially in making immigration decisions. I
don't think anyone here would believe I don't crave baby-
producing. I see Pakistani housewives giving me pitying
looks in the refugee center and I am getting used to it.

I am not wanted by immigration due to lack of baby-
producing. I am not wanted in Physics due to not raving
about the need for women to be in Physics and "helping"
them do Physics. Women mentoring women into Physics

ARE LIKE retired sex workers in that they "help" the younger ones to carry on the good work.

The place is for me a same-sex morgue with no conversation, where nobody hates, and the system is always in the right. So if you feel the slightest discomfort, you must hold your silence in total solitude forever, like a prostitute that can live without telling anyone what goes one. I would need a the temperament and strengths of a prostitute to survive in this type of world

The place is for me a same-sex morgue with no conversation, where nobody hates, and the system is always in the right. So if you feel the slightest discomfort, you must continue your speechless existence, as nobody of the management wants to address your problem. This saves the management from any form of mental exertion. People who become very unhappy with the speechless life and their problems never being addressed will be placed under mental health treatments. Usually, the first step in mental treatments is private and unmonitored sessions with a " sex trained sex brain."

The place is not a "death gutter" and is not inhumane because we are dealing with a population with very low intelligence and low literacy level. The difference in intelligence between men and women is astronomical. The person does not have the intelligence to articulate their problem. Like dogs suffer a disadvantage by not being able to speak out their needs, they too do not have a

426

solution to their problem.

As in the case of animals, other humans in authority
who are in a higher intelligence band can often guess or
diagnose what is bothering them. They may then be able
to put right what is bothering them.

In no case it is physically possible to put right something
for which a person needs brains to set it right because
they do have not the brains. A 100% possibility of putting
their problem right can only happen when the problem is
purely physical.

Substitutes for the real thing are constantly sought but
they are mostly not as good as the real thing. Indeed being
of inferior intelligence, they have no self-awareness. They
are like an animal trapped in their urges and instincts.
They are like my poor old doggy who would become so
envious of my petting a sock he would grab the sock and
hang from it.

One can say users of sex-trained sex brains are born
unfortunate but their lives are lined with positive things as
well, which smarter people don't have. For example, they
have no ambitions and no dignity concept and little pride,
and cannot be wounded from injury on these.

Well-provided with food and sex, these persons lack
nothing as they have maxed out their potential. The

system is not a "death gutter" and all it is doing is not proving mental stimulus to people who haven't got a mind, plus a mindless, speechless, and therefore happy life for the management who can run the system handed down to them, without using their brain

How does the mental health "W-O-R-K-E-R", the sex-trained sex brain solve women's issues?

If we accept that the sex-trained sex brain is an imbecile-I know this is heavily opposed by lovers of women who use them-then my verdict is an imbecile cannot solve anyone's problems not even her own. The answer then is that she does not solve problems but it works by the fact there was never a problem in the first place. If you are a foreigner who cannot speak the language, would you not feel happy to have a chat from time to time with someone who speaks your language

In the same way, the human female incompetent speaks the same language as the rest of the population, but her mental faculties are weak, and she cannot match a man in intelligence. She has heavily supervised (speechless) mating, in place of walking behind a man, as they used to, and nobody understands she was born with poor intelligence.

As such the things that come out of her mouth create a bad impression and aren't socially acceptable as she is primitive. Naturally, such a feeble-minded individual

has a few moments of respite when having a quality
conversation with somebody on her own level, is a treat
that has been set up as a branch of "health", so that
everyone will respect it

If a female is observed to be not that stupid but is still
subject to, or a believer in, the mental health system, then
the natural impediment, or handicap she has, compared to
the intelligence of standard men is smaller

So you understand I am living in an environment that
is like dress size 8 when my size is 16; it is more of a
paradise for a female whose impediment is stronger.
There is no facility for conversation with men. Perhaps
in this culture, a conversation between two people of the
opposite sex, other than at a place of work, has indecent
or sexually explicit connotations.

If the criteria for granting asylum is different for men and
women which is secret, that is part of the framework that
hides the low intelligence of women to make everybody's
life a paradise

And if asylum is given to women for sexual activity
alone, that will generate a huge number of successful
female candidates, and we do have a huge number of
successful female candidates. Like if you have a test for
animals to squeak, the mice are going to be the toppers of
the class

A woman here does not ask for a man unless she wants to have sex here, as men and women are equal here. This place is wonderful for "normal" people(where women lie on their back and use mental health services in place of mental faculties), but unfit for habitation for "abnormal" people.

I moved to Kremlin against their rules.

They had to expel me from the refugee center in County West Sheath due to non-residence. This expulsion was delayed as I was seeing a doctor in Kremlin..

4-0008: Unusual kind of Stomach Infection and Cruelty of Pater Guards

I was staying in Kremlin after that, I got very sick and started vomiting. in the A and E, they measured my blood pressure and I saw my systolic for that to 250. The nurse hushed me, saying everything was normal. I was vomiting some blood in the very strange painful way I had previously done in London.

I was delirious and I kicked over a bottle of Coca-Cola from a man's groceries and bumped into everybody. then I just lay down on the floor and went to sleep in the waiting room.

At some point they gave me an injection to stop my vomiting, but I didn't remember it as I was hallucinating that I kept losing my handbag and shoes. Someone nice found them and brought them back to me.

They told me I was all healthy and I just had a stomach infection.

They told me to go home. I couldn't use my mobile because my fingers wouldn't work. I said I'd sleep it off in a chair till the morning. The guards threatened to beat me and kick me out. In the end, they just left it till morning and I used my mobile.

4-0009: Health Matters and Forced Roomshare with Psychotic

The doctor who put me on Bisoprolol asked for me to be moved from the rural district to Kremlin for ongoing medical care. At once RIA, the accommodation agency gave me a room at a south Kremlin center.

The room was shared with a maniac with no shower and I was weak and ill.

I left the place after two weeks of not having shower facilities. The manager Mark insisted I could shower in that room, which I couldn't. It's their way of giving unlimited reputation protection to the "mentally ill?" long-term residents.

I did not get sick until July 2018. A GP put me on Bisoprolol.

Later I didn't feel well and a GP (Ireland) put me on Bisoprolol. He left that surgery. Later, I still did not feel better when I went back to see a doctor.

She saw my blood pressure was high and my systolic was 200. She did not want me to understand that something was wrong. When she realized I knew, she said nothing needed to be done. I asked if she could increase my dose of Bisoprolol. She said I should come back after a week and she would do a blood test to see if I needed Bisoprolol.

I had been advised that a systolic of 200-250 is a medical emergency and knew it was wrong of her to come back in a week to do tests. High blood pressure patients like my dear friend the late Regent Exeter die suddenly and unexpectedly as a result of untreated high blood pressure. Regent's doctor let it happen to Regent. Some people feel this type of death is very common.

Well, in case of the stomach upset when my systolic as 250 the nurse lied, "Shhh! Shut up; everything is normal". They did not give blood pressure medicine and it went untreated. They LIED I had a stomach upset. It was a lot more than that.

I think I am an unwanted person for failing to "baby-produce" and not serving in women's organizations. The British newspapers had a scandal about GP's euthanizing Downs syndrome sufferers. If they ran into a crisis such as cardiac arrest, GP orders were given to not resuscitate them. DNR stands for "Do Not Resuscitate".

The newspaper said certain people including Downs cases, were allowed to die. I know some women who would say how can they know I am not mentally retarded. That's why I don't "liaise with" women.

I feel I am an unwanted person and doctors "know"
I should be allowed to die naturally. without the full
advantage of medical science available to those who
contribute to society. And like a cow is wanted for its milk
and meat, I am desired for women's services.

If I ran into a crisis, doctors would probably not resuscitate
me and there would be nothing in the news. If someone
shot me in the streets, the killer may not be brought to
justice, I speculate.

Anyway, I could have things that need to be treated right
now (today) which the doctor wants to leave untreated.
If I knew what they were, I would try and get treatment,
maybe from a different doctor.

But the months rolled by, I think the Bisoprolol kicked in
and my BP started improving although the improvement in
blood pressure and slowing the heart. Was slow and took
more than 12 months.

I ran out of cash and a Bulgarian homeless man told me
about Kremlin Homeless Services. Refugee Support like
MASI would not be willing to divulge such information.
They would rather I got dumped on the streets without
shelter.

Their support is for refugees and, quite understandably, for Africans. As helplessness is one of the main features of the female refugees, this is venerated. Such a delightfully normal person could not seek Kremlin Homeless Services. Fresh to the western world, they have not yet been inducted into local female glamor and are not able to seek it.

The only way a normal female refugee could get accommodation under my circumstances would be through the system itself when they see her lying helpless on the street. The other option is to prostitute to a male refugee; this method is the most common one used by women of all races.

Anyway, the refugee support agency would be hypocritical as I am not someone they would like to give helpful information to.

If I did have the Asian community helping me or had not been expelled by the Institute of Physics who is now busy flirting with the copulatory privates of women in Physics, I would not have taken a second look at the refugee help agency.

By flirting with the "copulatory privates of women in Physics" the physicists inducted thousands of women into Physics. "Maintenance" of those women takes priority over right and wrong. Promoting women is an uncontrollable process like having sex.

It also does not matter to the physicists if they hurt people, in the process of getting lots of women interested.

4-0010: LADY DOCTOR CALLS ME IRRESPONSIBLE RETARD AS SHE GETS GREAT SEX

The last few months of 2018 I was sleeping nights at the homeless Bru hostel.

They smoked heroin indoors in shared rooms. That did not help my breathing problems. It was, for the most part, a kind and friendly place. I did not keep well from the start. (A lot of homeless residents have more serious illnesses).

At Bru Homeless, I saw a lady doctor for my monthly prescription who realized I had come from the UK. I said I left my partner and came here. She started to treat me like an irresponsible mental patient and wanted to know if I had run from the partner without letting him know. She wanted to know if he is worried about me and if the police were looking for me.

That is crap, as I have a (legal) right to leave my partner and if I leave without telling him, that's the sort of person I am. Of course, that did not happen, but I felt insulted, so I did not answer.

She wanted to know, "Do you know what to do to get some more of this?"

She could not credit me with enough intelligence to know the word "prescription", nor did she feel I would know WHAT TO DO to get a repeat prescription.

The two of them decided I looked pretty run down and said they would try and get me a step up accommodation. But I realized women would try to be with me all the time in that accommodation and that it would be a psychiatric type of accommodation.

I realized a few months later what a good time that female doctor was having in bed, as her belly was swollen.

4-0011: St James Hospital

In fact, when I was admitted to St James hospital for 3 weeks before Christmas of 2018, for a breathing problem, I had sharp pains at random points of my body making me twitch. I also felt like my bed was moving and rotating, and knew it was all in my head. Surely it was my nerves, and they failed to treat me for nerve pain.

Instead, they made me see a psychiatrist. I was seen by a male psychiatrist for about five minutes, followed by a female one for an even shorter time. They went away after that.

The male psychiatrist said if I wanted favors from the government, to tell him, and he would get these favors for me. Now I have no idea if there is any truth in that statement, but anyone I have known would have a "funny" reaction to that. I said thank you if I can think of anything I will let you know.

Regarding the death wishes, I did say yes, but that I want to make a protest of various issues publicly before dying.

To the "mental health-friendly" lady in the office, the idea of protesting issues, is of course, ludicrous, like the fourth dimension. She is limited to food and sex. She herself is entirely comfortable with never being able to protest as all things are done for her. She is a heavy dependent who is protected from realizing it.

But we can't all be identical

After this, for a week I was detained but not sectioned. I was followed closely if I left the ward. I was not forced to take any drugs. After that they discharged me.

I had initially been isolated as they thought I had a lung infection. The nurses were nice and gave me plenty of oxygen when my levels dropped.

When they decided this was no infection, they took me off isolation, and did a heart scan before letting me go.

They gave me a prescription for 5 tablets of Haldol a day before asking me to leave. I asked the doctor who wrote it what it was for, and he said "for peace".

I did not ask him if he could prescribe something for "joy" and would that be LSD? I gave the prescription back and said I did not want it. I'd feel terrible chest discomfort if I swallowed things like that.

I asked what happened to the heart scan. The GP said it came out completely normal. I asked then, with no infection, why am I having all these breathing problems?

He answered, well, you have a touch of heart failure.

I asked, don't you want to give me treatment for it?

He said there was no need for treatment. We will wait for your legs to swell with water, then we will put you on water tablets.

I left and later tried to get the "perfectly normal" heart scan which they would not release. I sent a question and the doctor denied it. He said I had heart failure. The lady that carried the question to this GP tried to convince me that "heart failure" was some ambivalent and fluctuating quantity, with yes and no answers being simultaneously correct.

Of course, if doctors lie to me, I will be hurt. When they say you are normal, when you are not, you won't get a diagnosis followed by the fact you won't get treatment. The outcome can be as serious as death and as simple as keeping you ill and getting worse.

"The lady in the office" will understand if her own skin is hurt. Naturally, we as non-medical people won't understand a number of medical things. It is not the patients' responsibility to understand.

But in all matters, there has got to be a way for people

with a poorer comprehension to defer to people who are doing better than the other way around. I don't mean anyone should defer to me, but to have a conversation the rule has to be that the person knowing nothing cannot have a dominant opinion.

After which men will lie and lie for her and "beat the crap out of me" unless I respond pleasurably.

"Woman support", "paid support" and "paid and charitable listening".

Segregation is the answer. Take her home, go away, and don't speak to me again.

4-0012: Unpredictable as Weather Shes as Flighty as a Feather

At one point, when I saw a "homeless" GP, I saw this thing about one Dr. Kilbride who was alleged (on their computer) to be giving me ongoing care. This was UNTRUE because (1) I did not ever meet this person; (2)I was not forced to take any form of treatment AND did not receive any.

It turns out the above-named was the Department Head of Psychiatry at St James.

Anyhow, I wanted to say I don't have any complaint against the medical profession concerning psychiatry or mental health because they did not force it. Those things I have talked about have disappeared from their medical computer (or are no longer visible) since I was granted exemption from the Kremlin Regulation in October 2020 through a lawyer's help. The truth is, these ceased to exist at the beginning of 2020.

I think doctors are primarily used to dealing with adults whose reactions are the way mine used to be when I was five. A doctor is not at fault if he creates errors when (s)he takes charge of a five-year child while being protective of its body and life. (S)he has no obligation to maintain standards that are beyond the intelligence of a five-year-old child.

. Adult dealing with a doctor are hopelessly stupid, like a five-year-old child. The folks doctors deal with are to the doctor like the clay to the potter. The clay cannot tell the potter what to do. Apart from the ability to feel physical pain, the "clay" never suffers mental anguish. It stays content with nothing to complain about.

C stands for Clay, and C stands for Contented.

Clay would not remember the name of the doctor who saw them, and they would not ask. Clay would not notice or remember simple things- you are safe around Clay as you would be with a five-year-old child. Clay takes 60 seconds to spell a five-letter word. Clay does not question why someone they never met is on records as having seen them, and even dignity is a concept that "True Clay" lacks. Like a person born blind won't ever understand the views of sighted people.

If a doctor or medical community tells a lie to the public (which is to their advantage or for other reasons) nobody will mind/realize/question. People are 100% consumer; they are nothing but a combination of mouth, anus, and genitalia. People are forever seeking advantage. They want their female genitalia to grow nine feet tall and achieve marathons.

I have also explained that I had various mental conditions recorded on the medical computers, that varied like the weather. I asserted that members of the public have a romance in their heads as well as high self-esteem based on the mental health system. Females look nine-feet tall thanks to the existence of the mental health system, which is a gimmick provided by the medical community. Hence people have surrendered their reason when blindly obeying doctors, who are the God of the earth that makes women nine feet tall

They have lots left to the imagination regarding mental health. They will say maybe your mental condition changes as the weather and "doctor knows". Lies can fluctuate like the weather.

Mental illness (other than fabrications) has no cure. I think -not sure-they are looking into stem cell research and gene editing as cures for mental illness. Those flipping drugs- you will (hopefully) stop taking them if you never had a mental illness in the first place, but were bullied or prefer to think you are crazy. Some people are born with low intelligence, which also does not change.

I do not have a medical background. I dropped Biology and took an ancient language instead of Science in my school, leaving an exam in the science division. I took my school-leaving exam before you were born, more than 6,000 kilometers from your point.

I have explained that I was seen by a male psychiatrist for about 5 minutes, followed by a female psychiatrist for less time as an inpatient at St James Hospital. I was not forced to take treatment.

Now, I know the public doesn't like me saying that unconditional trust in the judgment of doctors. If you tell me you have no judgment, I don't trust you 100% but I will go ahead and believe at face value you have no judgment. In which case you should leave it up to the doctors.

I am not snubbing doctors. All I am trying to say is there are no humans on this planet who are infallible like a "God". And one does not need a medical degree or any type of college degree to have the mental faculty of judgment. Some folks have gradually become illiterate over the years, I think, through the censorship of the media.

So yes, I feel doctors are abusing me, but they are not abusing me through psychiatry. I am a sympathizer for those who are abused through psychiatry. But to win my sympathy a person would have to say (volunteer) that they are being abused, and how. I won't sympathize with third-party complaints about a person who sees nothing wrong with what is being done to them.

If a person could not understand what was being done to them, that abuse had to be purely physical. I have no medical background and won't be able to assess someone's physical damage. Anyhow, if people don't understand what is going on they normally won't suffer as a result, unless it is the emotional needs of a mentally-retarded person, which is out of my range.

I have nothing to do with all this, but keep hearing from women – just women- about this mental handicap and support and stuff like that. That's how I am learning how to use this vocabulary.

England is full of victorious complaints like that, where the remedy is like awarding pianos to swine, feeling, the mental handicaps are sacred, and they should not be deprived of all the good things that normal people have. It's not fair that people with the capacity to understand don't have the rights they need when insulted. Only people who can't understand they are insulted to have recourse to complaints.

So I was seen by doctors now and then and also to get my monthly prescription.

I was staying at the homeless shelters trying to get a medical certificate to stay there with a rolling bed. Otherwise, I was having to call every day to ask for a bed, and once in a while, this would not be available.

I did get some medical certificates but it wasn't possible

to get a rolling bed as RIA was supposed to provide my accommodation, not Kremlin City Council.

Then I came to Ireland and I'm talking about the Year 2019 around the year after I came.

My second bout of hospital admission with pneumonia was in March 2019.

4-0013: LADY BARRISTER CAR OVER MY FOOT LIES UNDER OATH TO GARDA NO PAYOUT FOR ME

Well, in the year 2019, in May, I had a car accident or a lady barrister from the Irish bar ran the wheel of her car over my foot where Smithfield LUAS crosses Bow Street in Dublin. I stayed in hospital for 3 weeks. I guess she may have used her powers, but the garda doctored my statement. That seemed more like a racial dislike than trying to sabotage my personal injury case. I know I am hated for not being with women all the time. I won't have money or companionship or any damn thing.

4-0014: Sugar Spice and Head Lice

I also got head lice. I was 61 years old and this was the second time. I had head lice at the age of 4, and have not since. I suppose it was from sleeping at Merchants Quay on the floors with other homeless men and women.

Anyhow, a female doctor gave me a sealed envelope to take in for a follow-up chest x-ray.

I "cheated" and opened the sealed envelope, only to find that the doctor's referral to X-rays was about my head lice and what type of sick and crazy person could get something like head lice at her age. I went to the X-ray without the lady doctor's note and gave a copy of the offensive letter to the practice manager.

4-0015: Female Doctor, Mental Worker on Same Level share Joke about Me

I was asked to ask the GP for a rolling bed when I had slept over at Merchants Quay. A lady GP, to whom I said I did not feel well, had a contemptuous conversation about me with the mental health worker in Merchants Quay, who was a non-offensive person who often kneeled when she served a man.

The point is, I have no facility to work as I am supposed to stay trapped in a woman's illiteracy prison. At that time there were additional factors such as no legal right to work and I felt a lot sicker. Getting accommodation is a question of paying and a GP may not have the power to get a homeless person accommodation.

It would be nice if the doctor could give me a diagnosis, although that's not going to get me accommodation. It is even more doubtful a mental worker can get me accommodation.

It would have been a waste of time if I hoped to get anything sorted out from a contemptuous conversation (or their findings from that conversation) between a lady doctor and a female mental worker.

4-0016: Your ECG is normal.
Stupid medical devices tell lies all the time

Coming back to August of 2019, I saw the cardiologist at Pater. I am a physicist who has been removed from Physics as an act of racial hygiene related to the copulatory privates of the women in Physics.

I know I'm very naughty and I know that this kind of behavior will probably make it worse for me with the doctor. I confess that I secretly taped my cardiologist.

It's a one-time thing and it didn't happen before and it's not likely to happen again. I have never attempted to take anyone unless I seriously suspected that there would be something interesting to take.

The Pater cardiologist said that I'm completely normal.

Then I showed him the ECG and asked him, is this normal. This was my ECG after the overdose when I had an agonizing experience. And there is no way it was normal. The cardiologist said, of course, it is normal. It's just fast.

So I pointed out the comments on the ECG and asked how

come when these comments say otherwise. He said yes
it is because these machines are silly and they tell lies all
the time.

The cardiologist could not assess patient literacy and what
someone would, or would not understand. . He thought I
would trust him if he said that medical machines lie all the
time, so trust me! He had a friendly and helpful manner
but was lying.

This is an example of a medical consultant telling a lie.
I am not going to be able to detect every lie a medical
consultant may tell.

As a patient, I fear what else they may be lying about. I
don't think anyone lies without a reason.

I think if a doctor lies in this matter, this should be taken
as a reason to believe I have an undiagnosed illness.
There are two possibilities. I am like the late Regent
an unwanted person, who should die naturally, without
medical intervention.

Lying that I am normal (when the truth is otherwise)
is needed to make sure I don't get that extra advantage
people did not have in the 19th century, and die naturally
like them. Look maybe a lot of people are getting that.

The other possibility is that there was some medical neglect in the past. This resulted in the present condition. I am not allowed to know this. So I am kept in the "normal" rut until - who knows - until it becomes serious - but at that time - who cares?

Also, if one medical consultant lies, why is it impossible that another one will?

4-0017: At Kerry Hospital in Tralee

I stayed 2-3 nights in a cardiology ward called Skellig at Kerry hospital. I was wheeled in and saw the sign "Coronary care unit" at the entrance. Besides, all the other patients in the ward were going for heart tests.

I fancied I had realized that one person in the ward was dying, which is confidential information.

He and his wife were walking sadly up and down. "There is nothing to be done and you can take him home," they said. "Whenever his heart slows down we can give drugs to speed it up."

I stayed there for two or three nights before leaving against their will.

They did some tests for me when I stayed there. They told me the results of each test came out completely normal..

As usual, they left my chest discomfort and symptoms unexplained, giving me a breezy picture.

I asked them why I am in a cardiology ward if I don't have any heart problems.

She said you're not in cardiology. This ward is a general one.

I said no, it's signposted as cardiology. She said not to trust the signs to trust her.

One lady doctor told me that I don't have any problems with my heart, but I must remember each day for the rest of my life until I die I should be taking a tablet of Bisoprolol.

I wanted to know why. She said it is to protect you.

When I was being discharged I asked for the diagnosis. They refused.

I said if you don't give me my diagnosis, I'll commit suicide. the consultant told me that I cannot be discharged now and he's going to bring the psychiatrist to see me.

I did not think anything good would come out of seeing the psychiatrist and one of the nurses, concerned about my well-being helped to escape Kerry hospital in the 20 minutes or so I had to wait for the psychiatrist.

Most nurses have always been very nice. In fact, a Nigerian nurse had tried to help me to get out of the hospital when the lady psychiatrist had placed me on restraint without sectioning.

People don't know, but the nurses knew it was unfair. I wanted my diagnosis. I was and am chronically ill, and they keep lying and lying.

The reason why I am alienated from people is they are thick as cabbages and go on talking about making me well through "doctor" and "mental health" comes before physical health and is devoid of logic.

When the shrink finally came they found that I was gone. The consultant made a police report to go after me. Unfortunately, I had given my temporary home address (at Railway Hostel) which I shouldn't do in the future.

So the police came to Railway Hostel. I sorted out the problem with the police in five minutes by calling the hospital. They left.

People at the Railway hostel, the staff such as Mr. John Crowley, became rude and abusive because the police had come on a psychiatric chase.

They started saying "this place is for happy people, this place is for holiday-makers, and we can't have you here.

You know, I took a lot of abuse from Railway staff, and

not really from the police.

4-0018: CALLING PSYCHIATRIST POWER WEAPON TO PREVENT TESTIMONY

On another occasion at Pater A and E, I said, "Give me my diagnosis, or I will kill myself. She told me to wait, she was bringing a psychiatrist. I contemplated leaving. I was quite weak and didn't want the indignity of being restrained by guards like I was strong like Mohammad Ali.

But she must have had a change of heart, probably realizing that it was not fair to me. She returned, saying, "Everything is okay. You are normal and may leave."

So you see, doctors (the medical community) do not want to give me my diagnosis until after i am dead. and then they will need to. in the meantime, restricted speaking only women organizations like a mentally-retarded prostitute. if lived another 20 years would still be alone living under woman-support agencies organizations.

"Migrant support can help you. They will tell you what to do."

Will they really?

Migrant support workers are illiterate women who can't speak English. They operate out of government-provided leaflets of a grade-five standard.

PART FIVE

Fictitious Book Interview

Mentoo Pantoo interviews the Author

First name : **Mentoo**

Family name: **Pantoo**

Other details of Interviewer: Product of the twenty-first century; byproduct of woman and man; An ambulatory teacup; A receptacle for a penis, A bottomless pit to pour information, Lies back and takes it from a man, sits back ad listens to a woman and for either "job" is paid, unless given an award for charitable contribution to society, A listening professional; paid listener; a mental health professional, Miracle machine that solves all problems on the planet for persons with female genitalia, Pot of Anti-suicide potion, One who is praised like a bride on her wedding night, having no blemish, someone exempt from harassment laws, A "talk-it-through", Someone with maximum protection by the greatest religion in the world never to criticize a woman; someone who stands between life and death, Pillow, paid comforter, Licensed comforter; charitable oracle; A vaginal node; A gifted authentic speaker of "Vaginese" who can be paid by the minute to speak this non-verbal tongue with vagina-holders

Her qualifications: "Primary school failed".

Mentoo Pantoo asks: Mohini! For more than a decade, various people have independently concluded that you are a pariah to the human race. Does this not prove that you have a mental illness?

Mohini replies: No, Pantoo. Mark my wordy response to this question and try to understand it.

Pantoo, when people reach adulthood, they stop growing any taller. Some adults are dwarfs, and others are giants. Likewise, human adults are endowed with unequal amounts of intelligence.

Whereas dogs are animals and they think less than humans. Dogs respond instinctively.

Human beings whose intelligence is lower, lack functions that a dog would not have. Unlike dogs, unintelligent humans can use speech and use their hands, but their spontaneous reactions come from instincts and urges, unhindered by the power of reason. People of lower intelligence are more animalistic.

In the UK (and to varying extents in other countries) there are thousands of agencies. People practice agency dependency in their daily life. To some extent, agency-dependency is a substitute for normal relationships and feelings. There are also no challenges as everything is given on a plate.

An agency has leaflets that contain thoughts in print that are needed to perform specific tasks, mostly ordinary, day-to-day ones needed by the mediocre person.

You may feel that "mediocre" is a rude, insulting word. "Am I mediocre?", you may ask. Because of the enjoyment provided by women in the bedroom, people that call a woman mediocre almost risk being "shot and killed". The penalty for criticizing a woman is far worse than criticizing a political dictator. So much racial hygiene to preserve mating joys with persons of inferior mental status.

Please understand, it is not my goal to criticize or insult a top pleasure, only to provide answers.

Apart from leaflets, an agency also contains agents (advisers) who are low-paid/ no-paid human beings. They read off, recite, or quote the leaflet's contents.

People visiting the agency use personal services. People depend on leaflet contents repeated like a parrot by the advice provider.

The agency system is slightly different from someone else running your life. It is more like someone takes you by the hand and uses your hand like a rag doll to move it, to perform your task.

You, therefore, lead a thoughtless existence and reap the rewards of thinking by mining the thoughts recorded in agency leaflets.

The agency system could be called a global virtual reality platform. !

"Global" because this system covers entire countries or is operational over a vast area. People "mounted" on this platform overachieve; they perform tasks they cannot perform and enjoy the advantages of the same.

Another advantage enjoyed by agency-dependent people is that their personalities appear to be (a)marvelously virtuous; (b) nice person(c) who gets instant approval from all people.

This creates a happy and fulfilled life for agency-dependents.

Why Pantoo, do I say agencies make agency-dependents look awesome?

Because the governments realized specific thoughts and ideas were needed to perform specific tasks. Each task, or similar group of tasks, has been assigned an agency, staffed by under-educated, low-paid, and "no-paid" people.

People do not need literacy skills nor do they need attributes like courage, everything is done for them.

The government leaflets contain only virtuous thoughts, at least what looks virtuous in the eyes of the state.

Dependents (service-users) using those agencies, then, cannot have any thoughts words (or deeds) that are not virtuous, nor do they have any thoughts antagonistic to the state. They are following leaflets like automatons.

These people are temperamentally content to feed and breed and nothing more. They have no interest in anything. They engage in little conversation that extends beyond their bodies.

An advisor reeling off sentences from printed matter which inspire courage, for example, experiences euphoria over her own kindness.

But really, the "kind" words are borrowed from a government-packaged leaflet.

The kindness she emits is a result of behavior training and sing-song repetition of leaflet materials. However, it looks like the kindness is her own. Service-users are impressed, and shower praise on the service-provider agent.

Continuous positive feedback and pre-planned social exchange boost the morale of feeble-minded people

The actions of people look extremely virtuous but monotonously identical.

As agency-dependent people use borrowed attributes, it is difficult to gauge their IQ or goodness. Assessing people's IQ or goodness is like judging a beauty contest where each person has covered their face with a brown paper bag.

Each person is a pleasant and perfumed legalistic "dark horse".

Coming back to your question Pantoo, you correctly observed that several people have commented (independently) that I am a pariah to the entire human race.

These folks do not know each other, but they are all agency-dependent.

These folks have nothing useful to say to me. My questions are not found in their agency leaflets, so I pose a situation where they are incompetent.

When these dependency-darlings feel discomfort arising

from fear, jealousy, or other, their tongues quickly tell lies to dispel the object of their fear or envy.

A variation of telling lies is to say they are feeling "concerned". They say that the object of their fear or envy can benefit from the mental health service.

Comfort is reserved just for them, not for the person on the other side of the fence. These people who say I am a pariah to the human race may not know each other but have something very special in common. I call that something "pussomancy".

Truth is like a bendy-bus that will turn around and go anywhere-up a mountain, down a tree, or to the bottom of the sea- anywhere your heart pleasures.

Low responsibility, coupled with a sky-high image is the name of the game.

Mentoo Pantoo asks: If people say you are a pariah to the entire human race? is that the truth?

Mohini replies: Based on the above-mentioned observations by so many people, I would qualify (somewhat but not entirely) as a pariah to the human race.

Mentoo Pantoo asks: So, do you believe you are a pariah to the human race?

Mohini replies: Speculatively yes. Pantoo.

Mentoo Pantoo asks: Why do they observe that you are a pariah..?

Mohini replies: No one has been kind enough to tell me what the reason is for the immense hatred.

Mentoo Pantoo asks: But surely immense hatred does not exist except in the minds of sick people. Why would anyone hate you? Hatred is illegal, and this is a safe just, and tolerant society. Let's call the GP

Mohini replies: 2+2=8; The earth is square. Not even one gray cell; your head is bare.

Mentoo Pantoo asks: Maybe you can do something about the hatred people feel for you? Why don't you just improve?

Mohini replies: People have not told me why they hate me; what can I do to improve it? Stand on my head or drop dead

Mentoo Pantoo says: Drop dead! Drop dead! Drop dead!

Drop dead! Drop dead! Drop dead! Drop dead! Drop
dead!

Part Six

Glossary of terms, Acronyms

Terms coined by Mohini from English for concepts in opposition to the current eugenics

Slides: About

Subchapter, slide name, no of pages, description

List of proper nouns found in this book

Proper nouns: about

Proper nouns found in this book: list

WORDS FREQUENTLY OCCURRING IN THIS BOOK AND THEIR FREQUENCY OF OCCURRENCE

Glossary of terms, Acronyms

Angiogram- a medical scan done of one's heart.

A and E -Accident and Emergency

Garda-an Irish cop.

Geolocation- location, geographic location

LBBB left bundle branck block, name of a heart defect, term showing on ECGs, medical term

GP-General Practitioner

AVM- assisted voluntary migration.

B and B-Bed and Breakfast

BNP brain natrio peptide, A blood test for the same,

a medical test to check of the death of a patient is guaranteed to die within the next few years

CEO- Chief Executive Officer

DOA- Dead on arrival

DNR- Do not resuscitate

ECG-Electro cardio graph-a scan of the heart to trace electrical waves

ISBN-International Standard Book Number.

IPPA-A term appearing as part of my roll number in immigration documents

This is in addition to the regular roll number that looks like that assigned to everybody else. An insider tells me this stands for International Protection Person of Attention. When immigration officers look me up on their record, they see my roll number, which is attached to my name. They cannot fail to learn I am a FLAGGED UP individual. This should mean I am special in some way, and the immigration believe (want) something special about me, which is EITHER A GOOD OR A BAD THING.

ICI-Imperial Chemical Industries, a multi-national chemical company that has been dissolved in 2007. Probably the parent company of Astrazeneca and Akso-Nobel

IDC Immigration Detention Centre, same as IRC

IDPL-Indian Drugs and Pharmaceuticals Ltd

IOP-Institute of Physics

IP-Internet protocol, but only used in abbreviated form is a (man made) string of numbers, eg 192.168.1.1 which defines where exactly you are located on planet Earth, or where an email came from.

IPO-International Protection Office

IRC-Immigration Removals Centre, same as IDC

LBBB-left bundle branch block, a heart condition or defect that shows up as such on an ECG, a medical term

Mencap- Name of a registered British charity, and a short form for "mental handicap". It is being used in the latter sense here. The author has coined "female mencap" referring to mental abilities a man might reasonably be expected to have, which a woman probably does not.

Neuroleptics-a class of commonly used psychiatric drugs that manufactures cripples, shortens life and can cause sudden death(Neuroleptic Malignant Syndrome). A cripple of course is a physically disabled person. This must be connected with how in Regent's story, Miss V, who had the intelligence of a child, commented that his GP was intentionally shortening his life to improve its quality.

OISC-Office of the Immigration Commissioner

PC-police constable

PCSO-Police Community Support Officer

Pembroker-a person who belongs to the Pembroke Pesthilenseroke-Corruption of 'Pembroke' but meaning nothing different

Psychiatric drugs

Flu-penthixol

Depakote (Sodium Valproate)

Haldol(Haloperidol)

Zyprexa(Olanzapine)

QT-Waves-name of a heart rhythm that when elongated to 400-500 milli-seconds can lead to death. It shows up on ECGs. People who take neuroleptic drugs often die of elongated QT waves. That may be the case, if they die of a heart attack

RAF -Royal Air Force

RBBB-right bundle branch block, a heart condition or defect that shows up as such on an ECG, a medical term

RIA-Reception and Integration Agency

sex slavery: slavery can mean what they did to people in medieval times, by putting them on chains and extracting forced labor. It also means what a person does psychologically, acting as a slave, only they are not in chains. They practice slavery voluntarily or have a slave personality.

As a slave forced slave or willing slave, people do all sorts of things for other people they themselves dislike. An example of slavery is when you have a relationship which you don't want, also known as bondage. Sex slavery is slavery in sexual matters

SVT-Supra Ventricular Tachycardia-a life-threatening heart rhythm that shows up on an ECG, similar to Atrial Fibrillation.

UKBA-United Kingdom Border Agency

Tardive diskinesia-A nervous disability induced by long-term intake of neuroleptic drugs, the person feels dizzy when they stand up and may not be able ever walk in a straight line.

UMIST-University of Manchester Institute of Science and Technology

WPC-Woman police constable

Terms coined by Mohini from English for concepts in
opposition to the current eugenics

Beggo-pleado-A name given to the behavior of begging and pleading, abject humility

Female mencap- An attribute in which a Shell-less Slug is strong

Pussomancy-Coined word, created along the lines of 'necromancy', and crystal-gazing, where spirits of the dead are consulted to predict the future or to divine answers to unsolved questions, or you examine the insides of a crystal ball for such answers.

In this case, pussomancy shall mean using a woman's facial and emotional reactions to predict things that cannot be seen by the eye, such as whether certain desired events will take place in the future, and whether a stranger is reliable, whether unknown parties committed a crime, whether they are guilty or whether someone suffers mental health problems

The idea behind this practice lies in the assumption that a woman is unable to articulate her opinions about others,(female mencap) whereas her feelings are a very sensitive oracle of the truth. By probing these, by interpreting these, one can divine all kinds of truths, same as crystal-gazing, or reading of tea-leaves.

Shell-less slug-An alternative way of describing a woman who uses "woman support", counseling and mental health services

Vaginese-Coined word-A special type of "natural" conversation occurring between two women, a conversation a woman cannot have with a man, the conversation is devoid of any worldly interests or content, concentrates on urges jealousies and feelings.

As there are only half a dozen feelings, Vaginese is a vocabulary-deficient lingo, no matter which human language the women speak. A primitive personality where the person is an island onto themselves with only body interests and not the world outside, concentrating on people, and feelings, and nothing of the world really matters.

If women speak Vaginese fluently, it means their brain is heavily-gendered. A mental health worker does not work. She is employed for being a native speaker of Vaginese.

Slides:

Subchapter, slide name, no of pages, description

1-0001 :Death certificate of Regent(1)

1-0043 :Newscutting(3), disciplinary report of Ramanath Gopalan(5) Gummy Bear Emails sample(10)Graveyard 3-0006 Email from PC Virdee Karnail and colleagues(7)

3-0020 My overdose of 16 January 2011, report(8)

3-0027: 2011-09-29 The Pesthilenseroke "stalked" me during my stay in their area, which started in mid-2010 after my father made a bogus missing person report through Indian police officer PC Virdee.

This "stalking" is narrated in **3-0006, 3-0007, 3-0009, 3-0010,3-0012,3-0020, 3-0022, 3-0027.** The intense stalking died down in March or mid-2011 and after this, men from there lurked outside the door using walkie talkies, hoping to start a chat in case i stepped out, as they lacked the legal right to have a contact with me.

I tried formal complaints and in September 29, 2011 Pesthilenseroke replied, which is the above 5 sheets of response

In this response, the Pesthilenseroke claimed they had to "stalk" me as my parents ordered it. I was psychotic not to understand I am a Hindu, said the Pesthilenseroke. My parents had told the Pesthilenseroke I was mentally unstable as I was not following the rules of their culture which said daughters must keep in touch with parents 24X7X365 and be obedient. My parents requested the Pesthilenseroke for my continued "medical treatment"and detainment to induce such a love.

List of proper nouns found in this book

Proper nouns: About

The following are a list of proper nouns that occur in this book. Only names of people, places (cities or towns) and institutions (bank, school hospital) are included in the order they (first) occur in this book

A proper noun in this book is either the real name or a fictitious name created by corrupting the original name. No indication is provided as to which of the names have been thus altered

Because most of the names of people have been replaced in this book by the real first letter of either their first name or their last name, people who have been referred to by name are being referred to by their real name.

The names of people that have been disclosed in this book belong to one or more of the following categories

They have requested to be written about;

I have a moral and legal right to make such information public;

In the interests of justice;

They are an official or employee acting in a public capacity, or their name is public;

They are someone who has no complaint, counter-complaint, or grievance The allegations are pure statements of fact with names, dates and events so that nobody on the planet can call it slander;

The allegations about the person are words of praise.

Proper nouns found in this book: list

Regent Exeter, The Willows, Shifnal, Marie Antoinette, Louis the XVIth, Austria, UK, British, Shropshire, Anne, Kevin, South Carolina, USA, America, Texas, Monopoly (board game), Canadian, India, Richard Lindsay, Father Brown, John Field, Westminster School, John Ray, Cambridge, Latin, Oxford, Ludlow, Fiji, Cambridge Polytechnic, Anglia Ruskin University, Cambridgeshire, Fulbourn, Queen Elizabeth, Nazi, Rosemary Kennedy, President JF Kennedy, Walter Freeman, Qatapa(Different from Abu Qatada), Pesthilenseroke Society, Non-EU, UKBA, Institute of Physics, University of Manchester, UMIST, Manchester, London, PC Karnail Virdee, English, German, Simon Smith, Solihull, Bridgenorth, Jobcentre, Robert Agar-Hutton, Pushmepullyous, Weight Watchers, Jehovahs Witnesses, St. Andrews church, WPC Carla Hammond, Russian (Mafia), Basingstoke, Mrs. Wortley, Viju, Birmingham, New Street Railway Station, Wolverhampton, Mark, Watford, Telford, Jewish, Leftelsex Arms, Waterloo, Oyster, David, Jonathan, High Street, Princess Royal Hospital, Gummy Bear series, Court, Google, Hackney, Bethnal Green Underground Station, Regent's Canal, St. Joseph's Hospice, Tonbridge Wells, Dundahera, Trisha, Trishna, Indian Drugs and Pharmaceuticals Limited, Anglo-Indian, ICI, Imperial Chemical Industries, Hampshire, Macmillans, Astrazeneca, Akzo Nobel, West Reading district, Atomic Weapons Establishment, Viju and

Steve Wortley, MP Mark Pritchard, Telford and Wrekin districts, Eastcote, Uxbridge, Arizona, Tucson(Arizona), Phoenix(Arizona), Tucson Hindu temple, South Indian, Dr. Ramanath Gopalan, Meena, University of Arizona, Kino Hospital, Pima County Superior Court, Dr. Scadron, Adobe, The Caterpillar(famous movie), Exit(Voluntary Suicide Agency), Mr. Ward, Communism, Calgary, Prince Charles, Nick Clegg, LibDems (a political party of the UK), Mr. K. Venkataramanan, Thambi, Hindu Tory MP Alok Sharma, Eaton House, Dr. Siddiqui, PCSO Anna Haggarty, Sikh, Yarlswood, Bedford, Brazilian, Thelma Correa, Heathrow, Portuguese, Mr. Passmore, Radha, Chechi, Berkshire, London Met police, Da Silva, Mike Stafford, Harley Street, Sabina Wortley Okejoy, Dr. Wafaa Jouhargy, Martin Morris, rectel.co.uk, Sobo hostel, Brighton, Allah, Professor Mohammad, Liverpool, Kremlin, Edinburgh, Tarzan, Laxmi, Rhinoskin, Busaras, County West Sheath, Taslough, Bru Aimsir Homeless Hostel, St. James Hospital, Smithfield LUAS, Bow Street, Merchant's Quay, Pater, Kerry Hospital, Tralee, Railway Hostel, Mr. John Crowley, Mohammad Ali

Words frequently occurring in this book and their frequency of occurrence

death-machines-1, death-hole-1, death-91, Death 5, DEATH 2, dies 2, died 42, die 48, DIE 1, died 42 **TOTAL 235**

immigration, **Immigration 78**

deporting3,deportees3, deportee2, deported 33 Deported 2 DEPORTED 1deportations 1 deportation 52, Deportation 7deportable1 deport1 TOTAL **106**

lawyers 41 Lawyers2 lawyer's 2 lawyer 53 Lawyer 4 TOTAL **102**

law 50 Law2 laws 8 Laws2 lawful 1 law-loving TOTAL **63**

detainment 3,detaining 3 detainees 3 detainee 1 Detainee 2 detained 22 detain3 TOTAL **37**

prison 6 prisons 3 prisoner 4 prisoners 2 imprisoned 2 TOTAL **17**

Incarcerating 1

sectioning 4 sectioned 11 TOTAL **15**

committed 3,Committed 1, committal 11 TOTAL **15**

court 24 courts 1 TOTAL **25**

judges 1judge 17 TOTAL **18**

caseworker 2, caseworkers 1 Caseworker's 1 Caseworkers

1 TOTAL 5

private 22 Private 2 privately 1 TOTAL 25

privates 6 genitalia 15 penis(es) 13 TOTAL 34

trans**sexual**1, sexually-gifted 2,sexually 3 sexual 17 sex-trained 13 sex-specific 1 sex-brained 1 sex 63 same-sex 4 homosexual 3 Sexual 3 Sex7 SEX-TRAINED1 SEX 1 TOTAL=120

illness 41 illnesses 1 TOTAL 42

drugs 23 Drugs 3 drugging 2 drug-resistant 3 drugged 2 TOTAL 33

psychiatry15 Psychiatry1psychiatrist 36 Psychiatrist 2 TOTAL psychiatrists 19 Psychiatric 6 non-psychiatric 1 PSYCHIATRICALLY 1 psychiatric 68 TOTAL 149

grave(s) graveyard(s) 29

gravely 15

disabled 26

UKBA 52

hospital(s) hospitalized **62**

Happy Reading!

Don't miss out!

You can sign up at the link below

https://books2read.com/r/B-A-TUNM-IXDVB

Or send an email to papertigers@papertigers.me.uk

to receive emails whenever Mohini Hersom publishes a new book. There's no charge and no obligation.

Connecting independent readers to independent writers.

About the Author

Mohini Hersom wants her book to be read by millions. My other creations will soon be uploaded to D2D. I also have another book in the making

Read more at http://www.papertigers.me.uk

Lightning Source UK Ltd.
Milton Keynes UK
UKHW040640070322
399685UK00001B/80